Film and Urban Space

Film and Urban Space
Critical Possibilities

Geraldine Pratt and Rose Marie San Juan

EDINBURGH
University Press

To all our local cinemas, in Vancouver and elsewhere

© Geraldine Pratt and Rose Marie San Juan, 2014

Edinburgh University Press Ltd
The Tun – Holyrood Road
12 (2f) Jackson's Entry
Edinburgh EH8 8PJ
www.euppublishing.com

Typeset in Monotype Ehrhardt by
Servis Filmsetting Ltd, Stockport, Cheshire,
and printed and bound in Great Britain by
CPI Group (UK) Ltd, Croydon CR0 4YY

A CIP record for this book is available from the British Library

ISBN 978 0 7486 2383 9 (hardback)
ISBN 978 0 7486 2384 6 (paperback)
ISBN 978 0 7486 3020 2 (webready PDF)
ISBN 978 0 7486 7814 3 (epub)

The right of Geraldine Pratt and Rose Marie San Juan to
be identified as authors of this work has been asserted in
accordance with the Copyright, Designs and Patents Act
1988 and the Copyright and Related Rights Regulations 2003
(SI No. 2498).

Contents

Figures

Acknowledgements

As a co-authored endeavour, this book has been shaped through many conversations and the sharing and testing of ideas. Our own conversations were enriched by others, those with our students, colleagues and friends. We thank Rosemary Collard, Mechthild Fend, Jessica Hallenbeck, Chris Harker, Mara Ferreri, Maria Loh, Ernest Mathijs, Laura Marks, Laura Mulvey, Nazanin Naraghi, Lynda Nead, Marcus Power and Frederick Schwartz, for conversations and their generosity with exploratory ideas and leads. Thanks to members of the geography department at Durham University for thoughtful comments on the Introduction and Chapter 3. A number of busy people agreed to speak with us about their experiences making and/or distributing films and we are especially grateful to Anna Godas, Ann Livingston, Philip Owen, Nettie Wild and Inass Yassin. We also thank Nettie Wild, Inass Yassin and Dennis Doros for careful review of portions of the text. Artificial Eye, Assemble Studio, Elaine Briere, Cinema Guild, Celluloid Dreams, Gallery Koyanagi, Elizabeth Lee, Milestone Film & Video, the Universidad del Cine in Buenos Aires and Inass Yassin generously gave us permission to reproduce stills of films and photographs. We very much appreciate the help of Juliane Collard and Mara Ferreri in preparing the manuscript.

Introduction

In November 2000 Lars von Trier challenged his teacher Joergen Leth to remake his offbeat short film, *The Perfect Human* (1967). He declared the original to be a perfect film, one that he had viewed repeatedly. And yet he proposed to Leth to remake his film keeping to certain conditions. Leth's struggles to remake the film following von Trier's demands, as well as the five new films that he completed, form the structure of the 2002 documentary, *The Five Obstructions*.[1] The documentary also includes discussions between von Trier and Leth that reveal a process of film-making in which confrontation with limits – and especially failure – open rather than close possibility and in which experimentation with unpredictable results becomes a creative way to produce new thinking. As the process unfolds, it becomes clear that one obstruction begets another, and that instead of simply being imposed by von Trier, obstructions arise from the way that Leth takes up and responds to the challenges that have come before.

Lars von Trier, the controversial author of the manifesto of Dogme 95 and its strict rules of film-making, offers in this film playful yet serious insight into the critical potential of film and film-making. Even as he imposes his rules, he expects them to become the site of experimentation and embattlement. Literally so: when he meets up with Leth after the completion of the first remaking of the film, he evinces surprise that Leth does not look physically battered. It may seem like von Trier is merely teasing his teacher, but the idea of a fractious relationship between rules and practice is crucial, not only in this film but also to the entire history of critical thinking on film. Our book is about this history, and we grapple throughout with the debates on criticality and film, including those proposed by film itself. We live in an age when what counts as political is hotly debated and the same could be said for what constitutes criticality. The political possibilities of film have often been articulated through manifestos and the inevitable failures to live up to their strictures. More recently, an ethical approach, both to film-making and to film viewing, has raised not only new demands but also new problems about these demands. It is our intention to bring out this history of debate and show that it emerges through a restless articulation of rules and practices of struggle within and against them. Some rules have changed while others persist, but what remains is a creative engagement with the issues at stake.

What do we mean by critical possibilities? Conceptions of criticality have been associated with the turmoil of modernisation and social change since the beginning of the twentieth century.[2] From its inception, film has had a central role in the notion that experimentation in the arts could contribute in fundamental ways to revolutionary change. As a new medium of reproduction, film was thought to have the potential to disassociate itself from established authority and through its very mobility become political.[3] While traditional forms of art continued to be conceived in terms of the authenticity of the original, film, like photography, was unhinged from the source of its authority because it could be reproduced and circulated. At the same time, the seductive and escapist aspects of film troubled its political potential right from the start. Even so, film as a space of dreams became a useful foil for the development of a critical stance in which film would serve to wake up viewers, not simply from a dream world but from a 'real' world obscured through the forces of modernisation.[4] In holding this potential, film was not different from other forms of work and technology. Aligned to new modes of movement and transition, film with its capability to move the image would now claim to produce a new kind of urban public space. Towards this end, intellectual, artistic and manual forms of labour were to be conjoined and play equal but different roles in bringing about social change.[5] In that sense, the role of philosophy, conceived as critical theory, was no longer simply to understand the world but to change it. The documentary, the preferred mode of political film, was also intended to do more than represent this new urban world of social upheaval, speed, movement and transition.[6] Above all it was to bring the viewer into a different and critical relationship to it.

The claim has been made that *The Five Obstructions* 'says more about the ethics of movie-making than any film yet made'.[7] The turn to the ethical represents a change in the debates about what is deemed to be political.[8] In this film, the ethical responsibility of the film-maker emerges when von Trier criticises Leth for always taking a distanced position as a film-maker. The film also questions the possibility of the medium itself in relation to established norms of film-making. In effect, the viewer is challenged to think about what might be an ethical approach to film-making. For many, von Trier's film is not political in that it has no prescribed meaning and does not insist on what the viewer is to believe. This is quite different from the recent type of political documentary that argues for a particular position and seeks to have a public effect.[9] A case of the latter would be Michael Moore's documentary films, which adopt an overtly oppositional stance and seek to 'wake up' viewers by presenting evidence for its argument. Yet Moore's strategies of film-making have been critiqued, especially for disregarding the power of the medium itself to entrap and expose people and using it to its own advantage.[10] There might be no question that Moore has political goals, but his apparent lack of concern with the ethics of film-making has brought into question the goals themselves.

In our notion of critical possibilities, we are drawing from traditions of critical thinking that are implicated in both ethics and politics but are not synonymous with either. We accept that change happens in more than one way and that ways forward are uncertain and unpredictable. Our understanding of criticality is that it involves wrestling with our assumptions, questioning the norms, and generating conversations, knowing that we cannot predetermine the effects. This is neither an individual terrain, as sometimes ethics is interpreted to be, nor the formation of an interest group, but rather involves creating communities of conversation and debate that are shifting and have porous boundaries. The goal is to stimulate shared discussions among dissimilar others. It also involves questioning one's own assumptions, complicities and attachments. After all, the liberal subject thrives on distress over the injustices of the world, and so empathy is no sure-fire sign of criticality.[11] Our engagement with Lars von Trier's film is in effect a provocation to start a new discussion within an already charged terrain. Try typing into Google Search the phrase, 'is lars von trier' and, as the sentence is completed for you, a raft of questionable possibilities present themselves (e.g. a misogynist; a racist). Rather than a doctrinaire embrace of von Trier's work or method, we enter into his process of serious play and endorse his commitment to questioning conventions of all kinds.

What we bring to our discussion of the critical possibilities of film is the relationship to urban space. Whether the claim is about the importance of materiality or the production of cinematic time, the city has been integral to these arguments. Early experimentation with film technology was frequently associated with the emergence of new kinds of urban space. And indeed, these experimental films addressed dynamic change in the city as they sought to bringing physical movement into view.[12] This early conjoinment of the two forged a connection that would have long-lasting consequences. When the eminent film theorist Siegfried Kracauer points to the materiality of the screen he is thinking about the street.[13] Notions of movement, speed, continuities and discontinuities would belong to neither one nor the other but to both.[14] When film-makers claim to have been provoked to make politicised film by seeing other films, for instance the 1948 Italian neorealist film *The Bicycle Thieves*, they invariably invoke the ways film and urban space produce not only something 'real' but also a compelling exchange with viewers.[15]

In stressing the significance of the urban for theorising film's critical potential, we are contributing to a substantial and wide-ranging literature on cities and cinemas. Over twenty years ago, Karen Lury and Doreen Massey identified the focus on space, place and film as an emerging 'subfield of enquiry'.[16] Films are studied to glean insight into 'structures of feeling' and urban anxieties, social conditions and the marketing and branding of cities.[17] The utility of archived film for a critical 'urban archaeology' that can uncover repressed histories and alternative futures is widely recognised and there is an abundance of research on the ways in which cities have been restructured through the cinematic, whether through themed Disneyification or narrativisation of urban space, or the remaking of cities in the service of the film industry.[18] There is an interest in the way in which films represent particular urban spaces, for example, the distinctiveness of filmic representations of Los Angeles and New York, and the capacity for film to represent particular moments of urbanisation such as the increasing securitisation and polarisation of urban space.[19] The literature is replete with edited collections, the introductions of which lay out the breadth of possible engagements between cities and cinematic experiences, followed by often fascinating case studies across a spectrum of topics.

Emerging out of and within this community of interest, our book is more specific and narrower in scope: we focus on the critical possibilities of cinema believed to emerge precisely through its entanglements with urban space. While the relationship between film and urban space has been the focus of much attention, its importance to political and ethical claims about film remains less examined.[20] We are proposing to show that arguments for the political efficacy of film are intricately connected to the relation between film and urban space, and that by considering the specificities of these arguments, the relationship itself will emerge as much more reflexive and complicated than it has hitherto been regarded. In particular, we argue that the debates themselves have sought to construct a more active relationship between film and urban space as a means to produce something between the two. What ultimately is regarded as politically effective is this inter-space, a space always open to the challenges of actual urban space and yet itself challenged by the disembodied possibilities made visible by the technology of film. Through these debates, many seemingly familiar yet surprisingly unexplored, we attempt to retrieve a much more specific reading of what constitutes the relationship between urban space and film.

In a number of the early edited volumes on city and cinema, the editors are explicit about the catholic nature of their collection and their reluctance to legislate a perspective: 'the aim of this volume is to provide for the *exploration* of the cinematic city without imposing, a priori, any single interpretation';[21] 'this volume is not an attempt to stage any theoretical coherence or continuity for this embryonic research area'.[22] Nonetheless there has emerged within this literature some strong criticisms of and arguments for particular approaches, which have serious implications for thinking about the effectivity of film. Foremost is the understanding that the urban or cities are not most usefully conceived as mere context, content, setting or narrative support.[23] The (and our) interest is not so much in how this or that city is represented in film but in the more closely entwined workings of cinematic and urban space, within both films and the material spaces of concrete cities. Two things are being said here. First, space and urban places have a liveliness and agency that needs to be reckoned with in accounts of film and cities. The geographer, Doreen Massey, was explicit about this in her conversation with media theorist, Karen Lury, in a 1999 special issue of *Screen* on Space/Place/City. Cities in her view intensify the inherent properties of spatiality, which she understands to entail continually open processes of juxtaposition and encounter across difference.[24] The liveliness and continual openness of space is key to its political potential: space's 'availability to politics is that it is always being made'.[25] Film has some of the same characteristics: for instance, mobility and the capacity to create unexpected juxtapositions, and both film and the appearance of the urban within film can work on and with geographical imaginations in new and critical ways. Second, to say that we are interested in more than how cities are depicted or represented in film as context or narrative support is also to gesture to the materiality of cities and film (along with its spaces of distribution and viewership).[26] In Yomi Braester's view, even when the concrete materiality of the city and the cinema have been considered within film studies, it is often too narrowly conceived. To its detriment, the epistemology of cinema has been focused too exclusively 'on speculating about the moment of sitting in the film theatre as a singular event'.[27] This narrow geographical (and temporal) scope likewise limits assessments of the political potential of cinema, because cinematic effects tend to be restricted to considerations of individual subjectivity, consciousness and filmic form. Through a close reading of urban planning and development and cinema in China from 1949 onwards, Braester argues that

> it is not the city that gives rise to movies; the cinema is not even merely the continu-
> ation of the city by other means . . . it is rather films – in direct interaction with
> political decisions and architectural blueprints – that forge an urban contract and
> create the material city and its ideological constructs.[28]

The spatialities of film and urban processes are in other words entirely interdependent and far-reaching in their effects. And although Braester is more concerned with the ways that cinema has secured and consolidated a shared vision or contract about ideal urban form in China, he allows that some films carved out a space for criticism as well.

There are three further observations that we take from the literature on cities and cinema. In her conversation with Lury, Massey bristles at talk of 'the city' and 'the urban sensibility' and a propensity to reify and decontextualise the city. One aspect of her influential understanding of places as open sites of connection and juxtaposition is that many worlds – literally people, ideas and goods from around the globe – come and go, collide, pass through and sometimes settle in them. A feature of all places, this happens with more intensity in cities. All places, including and most especially cities, are unbounded and necessarily in the middle of and shaped by distinctive histories of colonialism, imperialism and globalisation. And because of the distinctive sedimentations of crossings, collisions and histories of settlement, no two cities are exactly the same – even in this era of globalisation. Likewise, the meaning and critical potential of film emerges – and can emerge differently – within particular contexts. In what follows we attempt a delicate balancing act of developing general arguments about the criticality that can emerge through the articulation of urban and cinematic space while remaining attentive to the fact that the films and spaces of exhibition that we analyse are located in distinctive cities in particular historical, national and geopolitical contexts.

Theorists working at the intersection of cinema and cities have been equally critical of the propensity to posit an abstracted counter-public sphere and, possibly as a consequence, to be too grandiose in claims about the critical potential of film. Writing about film criticism of the 1970s and 1980s, James Hay writes: 'film criticism and deconstructive films assumed a counter-public sphere from which to intervene in social relations without addressing the locational politics of such a sphere';[29] and Braester reminds film theorists who celebrate the body and affect as sites of alternative signification that self-expression and resistance often stabilise and solidify the status quo. David Clarke historicises film's critical potential:

> the muffled echoes of the explosive potential that Benjamin (1968a, 236) once
> detected in 'the dynamite of the tenth of a second' are, by now, barely audible – so

that today, when 'we calmly and adventurously go traveling' through the world left
in the wake of cinema, we rarely embark on more than a trip down memory lane.[30]

Our book is a genealogy of how the liveliness of cities has entered into
thinking about film's potential and into the actual production of films that
attempt to disrupt normalised thinking, and how films have sometimes
generated and shaped critical debate; we have no illusions that counterpublics had sprung up around many of the films that we discuss (although
we do discuss one such case in detail in Chapter 4). But we are committed
to a sustained, focused discussion of how the criticality of film is thought
and made to work through urban space. We strain to hear its explosive
potential, convinced of the widespread influence of film on popular consciousness and determined to open up a discussion of how this influential
medium can be used more critically. To quote James Donald (citing
Walter Benjamin): 'But also, maybe, it is in cinematic cities that we hear
the quiet yet insistent rhythm of the wings of desire.'[31]

Many statements in the literature on city and cinema declare the end of
cinema, as a place and event. The widespread dissemination of video, the
Internet, the direct mediatisation of the surfaces of urban infrastructure
can make the cinema appear as an anachronistic urban form. Maybe so,
in part, but, as Braester and Tweedie suggest, the cinematic remains in
post-cinematic debates and forms.[32] And declarations of its death are, in
any case, premature. We will argue that the history of cinema has within it
a history of critical debate about film that has not received enough attention and that continues to be relevant today. Moreover, as one of those
debates is the relation between the screen and the world, we seek to retain
the importance of the cinema space itself as a public, albeit faulty and
incomplete, space. Perhaps now, when privatisation of interests seem to
be at their most rampant, the urban spaces in which we encounter others
who do not necessarily think as we do are especially important and in need
of nurturing.

We now turn to four critical debates that have forged the inextricable
connection between film and urban space; these are the debates that shape
the structure of the book. According to Gilles Deleuze, thinking with film
is productive because it enables one to think the unthinkable, a proposition that made his film books initially less than appealing to film scholars.
For Deleuze it is film's production of time apart from the traditions of
narrative and bodily movement that gives film its edge as a thinking tool
and enables one to think beyond what is already known and recognisable.
But Deleuze never separates time from space or time from memory, so we
keep to his proposition but bring the thinking back to the relation between

film and urban space. Given that this book follows Deleuze's proposition that film is good to think with we introduce these debates by continuing to think with *The Five Obstructions*.

Four Critical Debates

One of the most persistent debates of the political efficacy of film is about the importance of shooting on location.[33] While it is by now unremarkable to shoot a film on location, such locations are often a regulated space possibly not that different from a film set. The political arguments about shooting on location are not about these policed spaces – quite the opposite. They are about what is possible in a transient and unpredictable space. One of the critical potentials of location – both its problem and solution – is that it allows us to see things we do not normally see due to our cultural and social conditioning. It is therefore not a matter of simply shooting on location but of how you do it. In *The Five Obstructions* von Trier compels Leth to confront the ethics of shooting on location when, for the second remake, he asks Leth to film in the location he considers to be the most miserable place on earth – but not to show it. Leth elects to shoot his film on Falkland Road in Kamathipura, Bombay's oldest and poorest 'red light district' and to veil the location through a transparent screen. It is in this location that the scene of the 'perfect human' eating is restaged, revealing how the contextualisation alters the potential of the narrative entirely (Figures I.1 and I.2).

Figure I.1 The human eating; *The Perfect Human*, 1967. (Courtesy of Vibeke Winding.)

Figure I.2 Leth eating on location in Bombay; *The Five Obstructions*, 2002. (Courtesy of Zentropa Real.)

Figure I.3 Leth, in taxi, encounters a woman with a child in Bombay; *The Five Obstructions*, 2002. (Courtesy of Zentropa Real.)

Von Trier is extremely displeased with this directorial solution: to film Falkland Road directly is not necessarily to get close to or be affected by the location and the spectatorial distance is only increased by the aestheticisation produced by the transparent screen. Von Trier takes revenge in part by including in *The Five Obstructions* a scene from film footage taken as Leth makes his way in a taxi to Falkland Road. As the taxi is stopped in traffic a woman holding a child appears at the window and confronts Leth, asking for money (Figure I.3). Throughout the scene Leth is entirely disarmed as he fumbles unsuccessfully to open the window, asks

Figure I.4 The human body; *The Perfect Human*, 1967. (Courtesy of Vibeke Winding.)

plaintively for money from an assistant off screen, and even predicts von Trier's delight in his discomfort. It is in this unexpected moment that the task of the remake is actually achieved, namely to film 'dramas from real life' that disrupt Leth's distancing composure. After all, the potential of location is not to objectify those in urban space but to destabilise the viewer.

A second persistent debate is about the time that cinema produces and whether the cinema produces a productive relationship between the time within the film and the time of watching the film. In the first set of obstructions, Leth is required to remake his film using edits of no more than twelve frames long, which is to say half the number of frames required to achieve what is called 'real time', the standard term for a film's ability to appear to keep to real life.[34] It would seem that von Trier's intention is to disturb the bodily time of the original film. *The Perfect Human* is in fact an investigation of the human through the body. Filmed in a featureless white room, in *The Perfect Human* nothing obstructs our observation of two elegant specimens: their body parts, their movements, their bodily hygiene, their capacity and need for food and sex, the feel of their skin, the reverberation of sound on the skin (Figure I.4). In keeping with a running theme within *The Five Obstructions* – through confronting rules new creative possibilities emerge – to von Trier's evident frustration, the remake and its use of twelve-frame edits only seems to extend its bodily time. The initial film already works through the repetition of phrases and shots, suggesting obsessive repeated looking. In the remake, the very system of cuts keeps slicing in what seems like an insistent repetition, making it more like itself than the original. For von Trier this is a disappointment and a surprise.

The cut in the remake seems to work differently for urban space. While the experiment moves within and even exaggerates bodily time, another kind of time emerges in the city. Filmed on location in Cuba (as stipulated by von Trier), Havana is represented through a few shots of the old ruinous colonial city, punctuated by iconic images of the revolution, such as Alex Korda's celebrated photograph of Che Guevara. Due to the twelve-frame shots the views of the city, like those of the revolution, appear as still photographs that have been cut into a sequence. This is a city frozen in the past, a city in which the memory of the revolution overwhelms any sense of the present. While the philosopher of film, Gilles Deleuze, has proposed that the disjuncture of film time and bodily movement makes possible a politically significant disruption of how we perceive time and space, in this instance we seem to return to a nostalgic and normalised notion of urban space.[35] This is not to say that nostalgia offers no grounds for critical thought, and the new film made by Leth creates different opportunities for reflecting on memory, place and human perfection. The perfect human no longer moves within abstracted space; ideals of perfection are now socialised and open to contexualised reflection.

Memory has been a persistent focus of debate, especially how the conjunction of film and urban space has produced particular kinds of memory; this is a third focus of our attention. Film itself has become an archive of urban space. Whether documentary or fiction, when shot on location film inadvertently or intentionally records a particular place and time. This sometimes becomes the only record of urban spaces swept away through processes of urbanisation. But the politics and the purpose of the archive remains indeterminate until the opportunity arises for it to be activated, and it can become an object for nostalgia or critique. Leth never could have anticipated that his reputation-defining film *The Perfect Human* would become the archive for undoing his sense of self as auteur film-maker.

One of the principles of the archive is that it needs to be reproduced, for instance through photocopying or photographs, in order to activate it and bring forth different potentials.[36] In *The Five Obstructions*, as the archive is reproduced and one film follows the other, von Trier's hope is that Leth's role as the film-maker will be undone. It is only with the fourth film, with the instruction that he cannot film anything new and must create an animation, that Leth must self-consciously use the by now extended archive (the original film and the three previous remakes) rather than conceiving his task as making a new autonomous film. Nonetheless the animation is another startling success; by putting his archival material in a new context Leth in effect creates a new place to contain its unsettling potential.

Disappointed with Leth's apparent successes and evasions, in the fifth and final remake, von Trier takes control. Using the film stock of *The Five Obstructions* – in other words an archive of the making of the remakes rather than Leth's actual remakes, von Trier compels Leth to read a script of his own devising. The textual script moves back and forth, with Leth first claiming that it is Lars who should have learned, then acknowledging that he himself has learned, and finally enfolding the two: 'As we all know it is the attacker who really exposes himself . . . You [von Trier] fell flat. This is how the perfect human falls.' (The voice-over accompanies an image of a seemingly vulnerable Leth rehearsing a scene from the original film that involves awkwardly falling to the floor – in this case in a hotel room in Bombay (Figure I.5). The enfolding of von Trier's text with Leth's voice and the process of remaking the archive has produced a memory that is shared and embodied. The memory is never in the archive, for it has to be produced and become embodied through any number of contingencies. Towards this end, the conjoinment of urban space and film has served time and again to challenge traditional ideas of the archive as the repository of memory. Indeed, this crucial relationship has brought visibility to the archive as a site of the breakdown of memory as well as the production of memory in the present. Even if this is not a preoccupation of von Trier's film we can find this notion of memory within it. Debate

Figure I.5 Leth falls to the floor in a Bombay hotel room; *The Five Obstructions*, 2002. (Courtesy of Zentropa Real.)

about memory, which itself has been so dependent on space, becomes even more challenging when thought at the interface of filmic and urban space and we will engage these debates.

Our last site of debate is less easily considered through the film alone. Arguments for the political efficacy of film have always held onto the idea that film must move off the screen into the world. In fact some of the most provocative debates are about the cinema itself as a public urban space. Recently the move of film to other spaces, such as the private space of the home, the art gallery, the film festival, the space of community organisation, has been of particular interest. Is it relevant that we first saw *The Five Obstructions* at a film festival, where one is possibly primed for serious engagement with film, in our case even more so because we were simultaneously teaching a course on the subject? New modes of distribution have brought fresh political potential to film, but have also raised questions about fragmentation and identitarian politics and reappropriation through the market. While film now reaches a wide range of spaces, we want to consider the critical implications of the kinds of space in which films are shown, viewed and actively shared. The physical site of the cinema has been regarded as somewhat anachronistic, with other spaces seeming to offer more political potential. Yet the cinema has also been represented as the space of community, the space where in the past community was forged. Different traditions of cinema have shown the space to be experienced as a dynamic space of exchange, for instance in Bollywood film.[37] We want to reconsider the ongoing potential of the cinema to gather a public of dissimilar interests for discussion and debate.

Just as in *The Five Obstructions* where certain issues of an ethical cinema emerge and reemerge, we are going to trace and discuss debates that have been recurrent in the history of film. These often have been considered in terms of rules and manifestos. But as Lars von Trier's film reveals, this history of thinking about the political efficacy of rules is as much about engaging and struggling with the rules as about the rules themselves. Dogme 95, of which von Trier is co-founder, is one of the most recent examples of a rigorous manifesto, including several demands that have been made in almost all previous film manifestos, such as shooting on location and stipulating that sound must be produced as part of the image (that is, without extraneous sound and music), along with some unusual new demands such as the requirement that the film be in colour and that the director not be credited. The rules were first announced in Paris in March 1995. The founders had left the movement by 2005, but these rules were broken from the very first Dogme film. In its engagement with the rules, *The Five Obstructions* proffers a case that provides us a way into the thematic debates that structure this book. Our use of the film models our insistence that the debates about the efficacy of film take place not just in text, but also in film and its practices. Theory is found in film as well as texts.

Chapters and Films

Our attentiveness to the practices around these critical debates offers a challenge to some of the binaries and assumptions that keep resurfacing in film theory and writing about film and the city. We consider the films that we engage in this book to be particularly rich sites to think about these practices and to raise new issues that one might take forward. Another consideration in the choice of films has been to represent different historical moments in different geopolitical contexts in order to enable new and unexpected insights. This is not to say that we are disinterested in working with films that are part of the canon but that we intend to open them up in a new way, in part by putting them in conversation with an eclectic selection of films.

In Chapter 1, which deals with the persistent arguments about shooting on location, we start with Dziga Vertov's 1929 *Man with a Movie Camera* as an unusual 'city film' that has experimentation within urban space as its primary goal. The second film discussed is Roberto Rossellini's 1945 *Rome, Open City*, which has become mythic for the urgency and danger of its location shooting during a time of military occupation, as one of the primary examples of neo-realism's engagement with the political potentials of film. Both films work with the long-standing concept of the street as the desirable site for shooting on location. The 1996 film *Moebius*, produced in Argentina's film school Universidad del Cine, upturns this traditional demand of the political film by proposing the very disappearance of location. It is through the disappearance of the ubiquitous street that this film extends the political potential of what it might mean to capture urban space itself.

Chapter 2 addresses the complex issue of urban time and cinematic time. Vittorio De Sica's 1948 *The Bicycle Thieves* has been discussed as the first film to unhinge the traditional narrative structure to become a journey with new possibilities for cinematic time. A recurrent model for the 'alternative' film, it still has much to say about the ways that embodied time is not simply a local version of historical and political time, but actually works to both activate and challenge larger concepts of time. Time is literally inscribed in our second film, Agnes Varda's 1961 *Cleo from 5 to 7*. The experimentation of 'real time' sets this film apart from the disruptions of other French New Wave films, yet it produces a sense of time that is perhaps more attuned to changing time and to how film and urban space are conjoined in how we come to perceive it. The urgency of urban time is enacted as a number of women negotiate the spaces of Tehran within Jafar Panahi's 2000 *The Circle*. The camera and urban space are both conjoined and at odds with each other, prompting the viewer to consider the continuities and discontinuities of time produced in the process.

Chapter 3 deals with the explosive relationship between archives, memory and urban space. We start with Thom Andersen's *Los Angeles Plays Itself*, an unusual 2003 documentary that is an archive of Los Angeles in film and one that has been consciously put together to problematise the history of urban development and the politics and potential of Hollywood and non-Hollywood film archives. Exemplary of the productivity of the archive, Andersen's film brought to wide public attention Kent Mackenzie's 1961 docudrama, *The Exiles*, as one of the first and only films of Native American urban experience; we focus on this as well. Directed by one of the 'urban generation' of contemporary Chinese film-makers, Jai Zhangke's 2008 *24 City* also takes up the theme of filmic memory of the destruction and reconstruction of urban space, in this case filtered through a troubled nostalgia for a socialist past and a critique of China's transition to a post-socialist globalised economy. A hybrid of direct and constructed testimony and memory, we work with this film in relation to contemporary debates about the politics of nostalgia. Memory in relation to the ethics of viewing is foregrounded in Michael Haneke's much discussed 2005 *Caché*. Drawing on the breakdown of memory from trauma theory but eschewing the traumatised subject, the film puts the viewer on the spot, compelled to engage with unrecognisable images and confronted with the ways filmic technologies produce the uncertainties of memory.

In Chapter 4 we move from the screen to spaces of exhibition and distribution to consider a long history of thinking about the space of the cinema as a public sphere that gathers together a diverse audience of strangers in an oddly intimate public-private space. Though the political potential of the immersive experience of the modern cinema is contested and many assume, in any case, that the modern cinema is now a limited form of exhibition and viewing relative to distribution through the Internet, legal and pirated DVDs, and other forms, we hold onto and explore the cinema as an evolving public space that affects both how films move into the public sphere and the life of the city. For a close examination of this, we turn to the work of the documentary film-maker Nettie Wild to examine how the space of the cinema was integral to making her 2002 film *Fix:*

The Story of an Addicted City a key ingredient in a profound urban debate about drug addiction policy and the health and wellbeing of some of the most marginalised residents of the city. We focus as much on her process of distribution and circulation as on the film itself, and in particular on the importance of the space of the cinema as a space of vigorous public debate. We consider as well other forms of contemporary cinemas, such as pop-ups and cine-clubs. Rather than the death of cinema, we are interested in its permeations and new hybrid forms and its possibilities in relation to new publics.

Locating our Approach

We came to this project through a shared interest in urban space and the pleasures of going to films in Vancouver. This led to an unusual collaboration co-teaching a seminar located in and between two seemingly very different university departments: History of Art and Geography. The conjoining of students and issues that are normally located in different disciplinary contexts brought to the course an ambition and appetite for experimentation. We immersed the course in the city, not only building into the course attendance at the Vancouver Film Festival but also scheduling actual seminar sessions in different locations, such as an art gallery and a film production facility. In part we imagine our book being read in this mixed context, one in which interdisciplinary academic opportunities open up to a variety of urban spaces with interested readers whose concerns with cinema and urban space are of different kinds. Each chapter traces one line of argument for the criticality of film and can thus be read independently from the rest. The discussion of the films, while located within particular strands of the argument, also move around and could and should be discussed in relation to arguments presented in other chapters. Vertov's *Man with a Movie Camera*, the film with which we started our course at the University of British Columbia all those years ago, became very unruly and tended to enter almost every chapter one way or another. The open-ended aspect of our argument is one we hope will be continued and extended through the viewing and discussions not only of the films we discuss but also of all kinds of films.

Finally Vancouver, as urban space and cinema city, is what has given shape to this book. Vancouver may not be unusual in holding strong links to the production and experience of film, but in this city film literally pulses through urban life. For many living there, the autumn is marked by the Vancouver International Film Festival. Started in 1982, it is one of the largest film festivals anywhere and yet it is oriented to broad audiences rather than to the film industry. It is also distinctive in that it screens the largest selection of East Asian films outside of East Asia, and is committed to making accessible a comprehensive selection of Canadian and non-fiction films. Vancouver is also a preferred site of the film industry, due to financial considerations, proximity to Los Angeles and the utility of the city for location shooting, so much that it has become the third largest production centre for film and television in the world, and is commonly known as 'Hollywood North'. Film-making has become an everyday experience in Vancouver as film crews are ubiquitous and familiar sites are temporarily remade into something unexpected. More often than not, the city does not represent itself, rather it becomes a substitute for any number of cities; we have been struck by the extent to which our students are both intrigued and deeply disturbed by these distortions. There is also a tradition of Vancouver documentaries that have been seminal to politics and life in the city. A case in point is Veronica Mannix's 1999 *Through a Blue Lens*, which documents the social conditions of drug addiction in Vancouver's Downtown Eastside. It is an unusual collaboration between the film-maker, the Vancouver police and street people; the film not only incorporates footage taken by the police officers themselves (the blue lens) but it forged new relations through its very making. The relation between Vancouver and film extends to the provocative production of urban images by the Vancouver School of photoconceptualism. Introducing the grand cinematic scope to Vancouver as itself (rather than as substitute) and its social predicaments, the work of Jeff Wall and Stan Douglas, as key artists within this tradition, has generated considerable debate about its political efficacy.[38] The much regretted closing of the city's largest and most comprehensive and alternative video rental business in 2012 has resulted in a new archive of film in the city. Recognised as an important public resource, the collection has been purchased by and relocated within the city's two major public universities. Finally, Vancouver is dotted with many neighbourhood cinemas, some of which have continued to show a diversity of films and persisted against the odds, each supported by its loyal audiences. And it is to our favorite small cinemas – the Park, the Ridge, the Fifth Avenue, Pacific Cinematheque, the Vancity Theatre, and especially the recently defunct Hollywood – that we dedicate our book.[39]

CHAPTER 1

The View from the Street:
the Politics of Shooting on Location

The cinema seems to come into its own when it clings to the surface of things
Siegfried Kracauer[1]

A location is a real place

Location Scouting and Management Handbook[2]

Few debates about the critical possibilities of film have been more persistent than the argument about the importance of filming on location. The claim is that film, by simply capturing a 'real' place rather than using a constructed set, can significantly affect how the film is perceived. Urban space was crucial to the initial formation of this argument, especially because early film experimentation was frequently carried out within the modern city and its new forms of dynamic movement. By the 1920s the city film had become not only recognisable as a genre but also the basis for the argument about the importance of filming on location.[3] There was, however, little consensus about what the 'real' within urban space might be, let alone what would be its effects. Two overall directions can be distinguished in this argument, one of which is the insistence on the value of capturing something of the real for itself. The justifications vary: the camera's ability to capture a specific place at a particular moment in time, the bringing into visibility of the materiality of things before they have been inscribed with particular meaning, or the revealing of aspects of the world too far or too close to be seen by the human eye.[4] By focusing on the thing captured by the camera, this direction of the argument about location shooting has tended to produce a decisive division between the 'real' and its opposite. Thus it has tended to feed ideas of 'real' versus 'false' and even authentic versus fake. But it also has nourished the increasingly important idea of film as an archive of urban space forged by the camera, which can purposefully or inadvertently capture something that is bound to change or disappear.

The second direction of the argument is less about the thing captured by the camera and more about the possibilities opened up through the process of shooting on location itself. The major exponent of this concept is the early twentieth century cultural and film theorist Siegfried Kracauer, whose influential writings proposed that film and urban space, through their conjunction, can reveal something that is not pre-planned or already assimilated into the conception of the film.[5] It is the street, with its diversity, unpredictability and transience that moves the argument about shooting on location from the physicality of urban space to the uncertainties of modern urban life. The idea that filming on location can capture something unexpected has led to theories of the real as process rather than as substance. Gilles Deleuze, for instance, argued for the potential of film to hold within it unexpected moments that could signal the possibility of another film, barely nascent but one that might become more visible over time.[6] Deleuze's concept for the film within the film is the basis for his proposition that the actual and the virtual are not separate but are always enfolded upon each other.

The breach between the real as matter and the real as process continues, keeping the relation between the real and the fictive at the centre of the argument for filming on location. Of course the divide between the real and the fictive has recently undergone considerable rethinking, both in film theory and film production. Today, film, even if shot in a camera, is edited digitally and in this phase of post-production film's relation to the so-called real changes. With the use of computer-generated image software, film has become a seamless mixture of film stock taken in the external world and animated images produced within the computer. Even so, studies of film and the city have continued to argue that film draws attention to the differences between the real and the fictive by representing abstractions of space on the one hand and the distinctiveness of place on the other.[7] The distinction between the real and the fictive may no longer be as stable as when Siegfried Kracauer argued for the importance of physical reality in film, but the question of film's relation to the actual world continues to exert its grip. The focus on authenticity, whether in film or in film studies, seems to undermine the argument for filming on location precisely by drawing a binary opposition that shuts down discussion. Yet, it is an indication of the worry that surrounds the blurring of all distinctions. The recent scholarly turn to Kracauer's writing on film demonstrates the importance that his arguments about physical reality retain now, especially as these arguments are not simply about the real as a thing already in the world, but as something in the world that film, through its apparatus, alters and enables to be seen anew.

In the early documentary, which is where claims about the critical potential of film were initially located, the idea of shooting on location was not presumed to entail a transparent camera and an autonomous urban space. On the contrary, the cinema apparatus was presumed to be crucial as a means to capture the world in a 'raw' state. In some traditions of the political documentary, dramatisation through narrative was considered to be important, while many Russian and German advocates of the documentary were concerned with the contradictions and paradoxes of trying to capture the 'real'.[8] Soviet film-maker Dziga Vertov argued that the documentary could present 'life caught unawares' but he also explored how the camera and other aspects of the film apparatus affected urban space as it brought the world into view more accurately than the human eye. Vertov's *Man with a Movie Camera*, the first film to be discussed in this chapter, is a key example of the city documentary that examines speed, transition and fragmentation as both a condition of urban space, and as an opening offered by the cinema to the viewer to understand the world and become a politically engaged participant.

The strategies of shooting on location associated with the documentary were adapted to other kinds of films with critical or political ambition, entailing a different confrontation with questions of the 'real'. In the 1940s, film-makers attempted to address the post-war physical and social conditions of cities and drew on traditions of newsreels and documentaries to produce provocative mixtures between fiction and documentary film. Roberto Rossellini's 1945 *Rome, Open City*, the second film discussed in this chapter, became the symbolic centre of this new kind of politicised film, in which the ruinous streets of post-war Rome served to produce a set of distinctions between the fictional narrative and the real conditions of the street. Rossellini's film is anything but pure, either about shooting on location or about politics. Before the war Rossellini had worked in the film industry supported by the fascist government, and drew on practices of shooting on location advocated by fascist films, not only in the production of documentaries but also narrative films; yet through new ways of intermixing the fictive and the real, *Rome, Open City* challenged ideas of authenticity that tended to be inscribed in pre-war Italian fascist film.

It is informative to consider the effects of filming on location in the context of the emergence of the film industry to see how it could become detached from its critical agendas. The 1953 Paramount Pictures comedy *Roman Holiday* directed by William Wyler is regarded as the first Hollywood film to assert the claim of location shooting to its audiences. The declaration in the opening titles 'This film was photographed and recorded in its entirety in Rome, Italy' could be compared to the political manifesto in the opening titles of Vertov's 1928 *Man with a Movie Camera*.

Figure 1.1 A Roman fountain and street; *Roman Holiday*, Paramount Studios, 1953.

Yet what are the implications of this claim in the case of *Roman Holiday*? For the latter shooting on location is usually attributed to the director who agreed to work on the film on the condition that it was shot in Rome rather than in Hollywood, apparently in order to give him some autonomy from the studio. Within the traditional narrative of a princess who spends a day wandering in the city, the film offers scenes on the streets that capture, through long shots, dynamic urban life beyond the limits of the fictive narrative (Figure 1.1). In the location shooting for this film, urban space was not as controlled as it would become in the future, and it achieves moments of spontaneity that evoke Kracauer's celebrated argument about the productive meeting of the camera and the street. Many of the film's reviews comment on how the street scenes convey a lack of limits and an unpredictability that resembles the aggressively anti-narrative contemporary films of the French New Wave.[9]

Yet the effects of shooting on location cannot be separated from the editing of the film, which in *Roman Holiday* transforms the spontaneity and diversity of the street into a more coherent conception of the city. Film sequences shot in different parts of the city are edited together to forge a Rome that is in effect a touristic setting; at one moment the princess is in the artistic Via Margutta and in the next she encounters the Trevi Fountain, only to turn the corner and find herself in front of the Spanish steps. The city's topography is rearranged and becomes a continuous sequence of celebrated monuments that reduce the complexities of urban space into a singular identity. This does not detract from the film forging an archival storage of Rome in the early 1950s.[10] The street footage records the city at a particular moment of rapid transformation, revealing the post-war expansion of modes of transport and circulation. While in relation to today the city seems less congested and more dynamic, it also shows the encroachment of traffic routes in areas of ancient remains, which due to archaeological excavation and preservation would be removed by the 1980s.

The instrumentalisation of the city in *Roman Holiday* in order to serve the aims of the film is indicative of how shooting on location would come to affect urban space itself. There has been much discussion about the consequences of the now long history of transforming places into sites for location shooting.[11] As the handbook for location scouts states, the location is more often than not real in one way and a substitute in another way.[12] The Hollywood film industry produces films on many locations outside of Los Angeles, usually for financial reasons, and regularly disguises places to serve the representational needs of the film. Even films that hold critical ambitions and argue against the colonisation of particular places have themselves been critiqued for doing just that.[13] Recently, shooting on location has increasingly served to displace rather than open up particular urban spaces. Vancouver, for instance, is a city where the American film industry is very active and where many films are shot, usually disguised as any number of American cities. Of course this kind of substitution can produce its own effects, as it risks viewers recognising the disguise and becoming interested in the film's artifice. In the case of Toronto, however, it has been argued that even this kind of disruption is no longer possible, as the financial incentives to attract film-making to the city have resulted in 'the global placelessness of Toronto's downtown core'.[14]

With the recent politicisation of world cinema, the claims for shooting on location have turned back to the filmic strategies of early documentaries, combining close attention to the materiality of the world with the ways that film technologies have intervened in that materiality. Other strategies have emerged to address the legacies of modernity and its troubled relation to urban space. The experimental Argentinian student film *Moebius*, the third film discussed here, addresses the issue of place by thematising its very disappearance. The complex relation between actual and virtual setting has now become a way to reconceive the historical relation between the real and the fictive, introducing more psychological and affective notions of space. This is also the approach of the Danish group Dogme 95, which continues to draw on a manifesto for an ethics of film, one which separates it from the film industries that have come to dominate the production and experience of cinema.[15] In the Dogme 95 manifesto, the first of the ten rules to which any Dogme film must conform is 'Shooting must be done on location'. It is arguable, however, whether what is at stake is location filming in itself rather than the explicit negotiation of the real and the fictive within the complex historical relations between film and urban space.

Kracauer and the Street

> The medium's affinity for the flow of life may explain the attraction which the street has exerted on the screen . . . A street serving as background to some quarrel or love affair may rush to the fore and produce an intoxicating effect.
>
> Kracauer, *The Theory of Film*[16]

All the films examined in this chapter focus on the street, the privileged site for location shooting in arguments that conceive of the real as process rather than as substance. Siegfried Kracauer's influential writings on film offer perhaps the most cogent discussion on the importance of the relation between film and street.[17] According to Kracauer, the street is a crucial site in which to consider the random and alienating aspects of modern life; film, given its materiality, is regarded as specially suitable for capturing the transience of the street, while the camera is the perfect street observer, Kracauer's so called *flaneur*.[18] The street holds within it the potential for the unexpected. It might appear in a film in order to advance the narrative, but it can suddenly affect us and become 'a fragmentary moment of visible reality, surrounded, as it were, by a fringe of indeterminate visible meaning'.[19] The 'real' is raw matter before it has been transformed into meaning and fitted into narrative form. This argument about the potential of 'the real' in film is located within a larger critique of modernity's moves towards abstraction and alienation. For Kracauer the 'real' in film provides an antidote to Hollywood as a 'dream factory', offering a state of awakening crucial to critical forms of seeing and knowing.[20] He returns time and again to the interplay in film between dreaming and awakening.[21]

According to Kracauer the modern condition is characterised by a weakening in consciousness about the material world and everyday life. He offers two main reasons. The first is the decline of common beliefs and established traditions that bind people into a whole, and the second is the abstraction brought about through the forms of conceptualising and seeing of science and technology.[22] This process of fragmentation and abstraction that defines modern life is within film itself, which after all is one of the new technologies. But the difference is that science and technology, while referring to physical phenomena, usually move us away from the complexity of the material and make unfamiliar areas of the everyday world that further increase a sense of fragmentation. Film, according to Kracauer, enables one to see the material world and retrieve it from a state of non-existence. Given that 'individual consciousness must be thought of as an aggregate of splinters of beliefs and sundry activities', and that reality can only be experienced in fragmented ways, film is especially effective because it offers fleeting glimpses of the 'real'.[23] In this respect film is more powerful than the more traditional arts, for instance theatre or painting, which, according to Kracauer, aim to bring a view of reality but only by producing a coherent entity that ultimately has to extricate from itself anything of the material with which it started. Thus, for Kracauer, the usual differentiation between art film and entertainment film is not relevant since both, for different reasons, can activate the medium's inherent potential to present glimpses of the world as raw material. In effect, he declares himself to follow 'Fellini's dictum that a "good picture" should not aim at the autonomy of a work of art but "have mistakes in it, like life, like people"'.[24]

Kracauer, then, does not argue that film's ability to reveal the material world is predicated on the separation of the real from the fictive. On the contrary, he proposes a constant enfolding of the two, and a process through which the real emerges in unexpected ways. Film presents the real in incoherent bits and pieces of material life, and it is due to a fragmented consciousness that we can access these pieces.[25] The street, with its constantly changing forms, is not only in itself a site for fragmentation but within film becomes the potential site for what fragmentation can reveal. Fragments within film depend on chance, and carry something that is not digested into the narrative coherence of the film and that might or might not emerge.

But Kracauer's argument is not over, for ultimately he argues that reality is that which we fear and avoid, but must confront in order to incorporate it into memory and remove it from the status of a taboo.[26] He evokes the myth of the Medusa, in which Perseus, in order to kill the monstrous Medusa whose appearance turned people who looked at her to stone, had to use her reflection on the shield given to him by Athena. The cinema screen becomes the shield of Perseus for it is the means to access that which cannot be confronted through experience and must be dealt with through a kind of reflected reality.[27] The screen then can incorporate into memory things too dreadful to be seen in reality, thus redeeming 'horror from its invisibilities behind the veils of panic and imagination'.[28] But there remains the problem of whether seeing the material world makes one believe (as with science) or makes one question and thus aware of the implications of what one is seeing. It is our received notions of the physical world that Kracauer wants to question, and he suggests that film has the potential to enable us to see critically.

Man with a Movie Camera (1929)

Dziga Vertov's *Man with a Movie Camera*, released in 1929, is a provocative example of how shooting on location might operate to produce a critical relation between cinema and urban space.[29] The experimental aspirations of the film are announced from the start, with the titles of the film becoming a kind of manifesto for the group known as the *Kinoki* or *Cine-Eyes*.[30] In the titles, the film is defined in part by what it is not: a silent film that uses inter-titles, based on a script, employs actors and filmed in a studio. In other words, this is not a film that pursues artifice but one that seeks to examine the actual world. The titles insist that the primary aim is to create an international language that is entirely different from the language of theatre or literature. In 1929, responses to the film acknowledge its experimental goals to be about separating cinema from more traditional artistic forms that are dependent on a narrative, frequently from a literary source.[31] Instead of keeping to a unity of time and space, the film works as an assemblage of material things that produce movement and change, and seek to both reveal and intervene in a moment of contemporaneity.[32]

The explicitly political aims of Vertov's film have been much discussed.[33] He is aligned within Russian politics in the wake of the Bolshevik Revolution and the ongoing economic crisis of Soviet Russia at the start of Stalin's rule, but his position is said to waver between loyalty to Stalin's policies and critique of the emerging orthodoxies.[34] He is also frequently situated within a conflictual Russian avant-garde that advocated experimentation, and that sought to challenge the effects of narrative melodrama with documentaries that focused on everyday life.[35] Vertov certainly shared a leftist prevailing interest in the process of work rather than in the end result, and thus shared Constructivist goals of revealing production itself.[36] In the film, the work of cinema is revealed in every possible way, including how the camera both captures the material and the ephemeral within the city, and also actively intervenes in urban space and like other forms of technology reshapes experiences of modern life. In other words, film, itself part of new modes of progress and modernisation, records the materiality of things, both the animate and the inanimate, and ultimately produces a new reality.

For Vertov, shooting on location is not simply about capturing 'the real' but about revealing that which tends to remain hidden within urban space. For this process to emerge there has to be, according to the film, a very close and considered relation between cinema, city and viewer. It is usually claimed that *Man with a Movie Camera* has as its goal to record the city untouched by the technology of the camera, an idea suggested by Vertov's writings.[37] In the 1924 'From the cine-eyes field manual', Vertov sets out his instructions for shooting on location and how it should keep to the strict goals of the documentary.[38] While the first point, the idea of catching 'life unawares', is indeed the one that has received the most attention, Vertov's advice (as well as his film) suggests a more complex process. He proposes diverse ways in which the camera should engage with the street, and seems particularly interested in encounters in which the camera's presence is revealed. Hence he discusses the speed and assertiveness with which the camera must be used to negotiate such encounters.[39]

The film itself, while demonstrating the many locations of the camera within urban space, also shows that these locations almost always bring the camera out into the open. There are many unexpected encounters between camera and people. Some, like the street boys suddenly awakened from their sleep (Figure 1.2), or the woman who notices that she is being filmed while in the divorce office, are about being surprised by the camera and reacting to it overtly. Others, such as the cameraman in pursuit of a

Figure 1.2 A young man on the street looks at the camera;
Man with a Movie Camera, 1929.

Figure 1.3 A cameraman filming people in a horse carriage;
Man with a Movie Camera, 1929.

group of people riding in a horse-drawn carriage, are about the camera exerting its power, and oscillates between a playful game and outright harassment (Figure 1.3). In these instances the camera records unexpected and ephemeral moments on the street, but rather than catching them accidentally on film, they are prompted by the presence of the camera itself.

There are many scenes in which people are shown to be unaware of the camera, but these tend to offer the possibility of reflecting on the activity of viewing itself. Different groups of people appear to look attentively, yet the connection between viewing and what is viewed is frequently unhinged. In the case of an audience of children, which reappears at different times in the film, the effects of viewing on the face become the focus of our close observation (Figure 1.4). The children's expressions of wonder point to ways of seeing that seem to keep criticality at bay. Even so, it is also during the scenes in which the children are shown mesmerised by what they see that the film suddenly stops, and the moving image turns into the photograph. Various children are shown as the still image that makes up the film strip (Figure 1.5); when the film strip is reactivated, what had become the observation of the materiality of film itself, now is turned into the wonders of the animation of the moving image. The revelation of the still image brought into motion is thus about the pleasures of being caught in the magic of visual effects, and indeed when the scenes of the children watching are repeated later in the film it is to reveal that

Figure 1.4 Children watching a magician; *Man with a Movie Camera*, 1929.

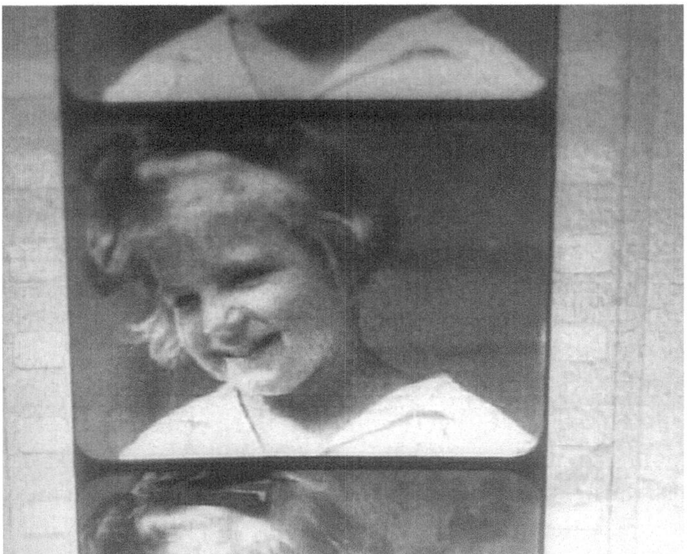

Figure 1.5 A film strip; *Man with a Movie Camera*, 1929.

they have been watching a performance by a magician. Yet we are shown how film itself produces these effects through its ability not only to reproduce time but to actually manipulate it. The viewer is thus encouraged to reflect on the importance of looking critically at film's engagement with

Figure 1.6 The cinema; *Man with a Movie Camera*, 1929.

space, which is not to say that the captivating aspects of this engagement are omitted. Ultimately, the film connects processes of seeing and being seen in the film with those that take place outside the film, namely in the audience, and nowhere is this more evident than when the audience is able to watch itself watching the film.

As if to assert its self-reflexive approach, the film starts with the physical site of the cinema and the arrival of the audience (Figure 1.6). Within the preparations that take place in the space of the cinema, the film itself is shown as an object amongst many others. It appears in the form of a stack of film tins, labelled 'Man with a movie camera' from which someone pulls out the first reel. Thus the circulation of the film, a process that involves actual urban space, actual people and actual urban time, is now made part of the film itself. The space of the cinema, which is no less of interest than the process of making the film, forges an overt link between film and city. Indeed, one might argue that the scenes of the cinema serve as a frame through which to see the film, a frame that declares the film's identity as a documentary for which location shooting extends to its own practices. In effect the film records 'real life' in urban space and 'real life' in urban space now includes exchanges with new technologies: the camera on the street, and the cinema in urban space.[40]

Man with a Movie Camera was conceived as a documentary, yet is not detached from the viewer's place within it and provides no particular predetermined interpretation. The film is not dependent on narrative development and thus its structure and meaning has been the focus of much disagreement.[41] If there is a narrative path it is about a process of assemblage through which cinema and urban space are shown to be inter-twined and to hold critical potential. The idea of gathering material from the actual world, bringing these materials together in a new conjunction and dispersing them outwards works at every level and at every stage of the film. As Gilles Deleuze notes, 'Montage was already there everywhere'.[42] The idea of the film as an assemblage precedes filming, and emerges in the choice of material. As is well known, the film uses footage from various cities in Russia, which are then brought together into an assemblage of one city.[43] For instance Moscow's Bolshoi Theatre, which is famously split apart in the film, is conjoined with scenes of trams shot in Odessa.[44] The filming itself conjoins all kinds of urban spaces: interiors and exteriors, above and below ground, in the dark and in the daylight, of leisure and of work. The process of editing the footage is where one expects assemblage, and is thus where debate about the film's unorthodox approach to montage has been located.[45] The editor, Elizaveta Svilova, is shown working in her studio (Figure 1.7), splicing and reconnecting film strips from many kinds of film stock, itself kept in many boxes each labelled in relation to place and time. Finally there is the assemblage produced by the film's audience, which is shown watching the film and comparing it to life in the world.

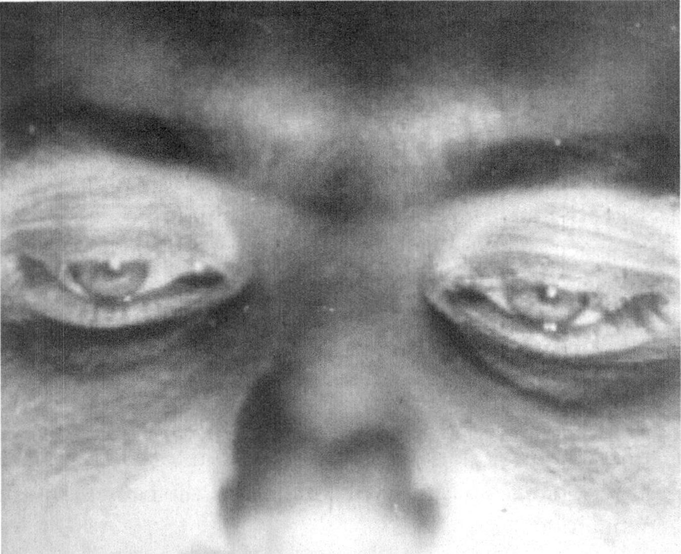

Figure 1.7 Elizaveta Svilova editing; *Man with a Movie Camera*, 1929.

The relation between shooting on location and the production of a critically aware film viewer is what initially sets *Man with a Movie Camera* apart from the city films to which it is often compared.[46] The film does follow the concept of the arc of a day in the city from dawn till night, but even this established format for city films becomes part of the potential for criticality offered by the film. In this film the transition from dark to light is conveyed through the technology of film as much as through the timeliness of the city. The process of showing the film, of transmitting it through the projector, is shown to be one of passing it through light, much as the visibility of urban space is shown to depend on the dawning of the day. This close attention to how light brings about urban visibility is reiterated as the film presents a virtual laboratory of the interrelation of camera and light. There is an inherent sense of the camera's power to capture things hidden from view, and this visibility is in contrast to the darkness within which the film starts. In his 1929 review of the film, Kracauer points out how the predawn hours imply a secret sphere in which the dead and the living are reversed, a relationship that keeps transforming the city from invisibility to visibility and back again.[47] The idea of an awakening, which is a theme that initiates the film's exploration of the city, applies not only to the city and to the ability of the camera to bring things into visibility, but also to the viewer who is pressed to think about the contrast between dreaming and being woken up, and how film can lead in two such different directions.

If Vertov's film argues for the inextricable links between urban space and cinema, it also argues for the advantages of linking the human eye to the camera. While shooting on location is conceived as the reciprocal relation between urban space and the camera, its ability to be politically effective is what still remains to be achieved for the future, and this cannot be done by the human eye alone. In the film, the human eye appears at different stages (Figure 1.8), fitted within the full expanse of the film frame. While the eye is shown on its own, apart from the rest of the body, it is also not disembodied, as it occupies its bodily organic context and is framed within lids, eyelashes and brows as much as it is framed within the film frame. Invariably the eye is intercut with the implied direction of its look, urban space traversed across large distances and extended in multiple directions. These spaces have been traversed before, by the camera that shot the sequences the eye is now able to see. The camera is itself shown being taken to all parts of the city by the cameraman and shooting film on all kinds of locations. The cameraman that appears in the film is Mikael Kauffman, who is also given credit for doing all the filming. This paradox is crucial to the premise of the film, which is that the movements of the

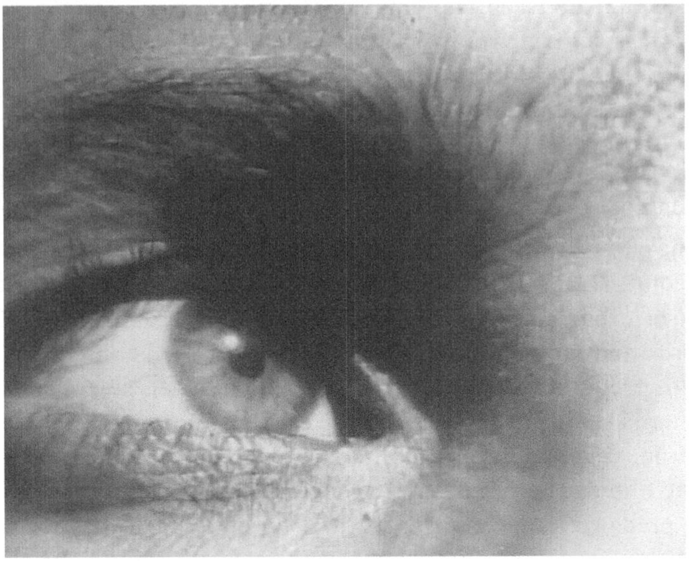

Figure 1.8 The human eye looking; *Man with a Movie Camera*, 1929.

eye and the movements of the camera have become continuous circuits. In the scene in which the cameraman is in pursuit of the people in the horse carriage, we are shown Kauffman operating the camera and we are shown footage that seems to emerge from what we saw him shooting. Who was working the camera when the cameraman is on screen remains unexplained, but there can be no question about the claim for the continuity between camera and eye.[48]

This relation between eye and camera is made tangible in the film's most celebrated image of the eye, what Vertov called the 'keno-eye' or 'cine-eye' (Figure 1.9).[49] In this assemblage, the human eye is said to have superseded its own physical limitations. Yet the Kino-Eye is not the human eye framed by a camera lens, as if the latter supported and extended the former. Rather it is a confrontation between camera and eye, a face-to-face encounter. This is suggested by the way the camera lens is shown as if seen from the back, pointing towards the human eye and thus with the lettering on the lens reversed. It is as if the human eye and the camera lens are confronting each other and moving towards each other. The camera lens, which probably was filmed in a mirror as the cameraman working the camera is sometimes reflected on the lens, is represented as a system of frames that literally are intertwined with the biological frames – the eyelid and eyelashes – of the eye. With each reappearance of the Kino-Eye, there are discernible changes and readjustments, and the encounter increasingly

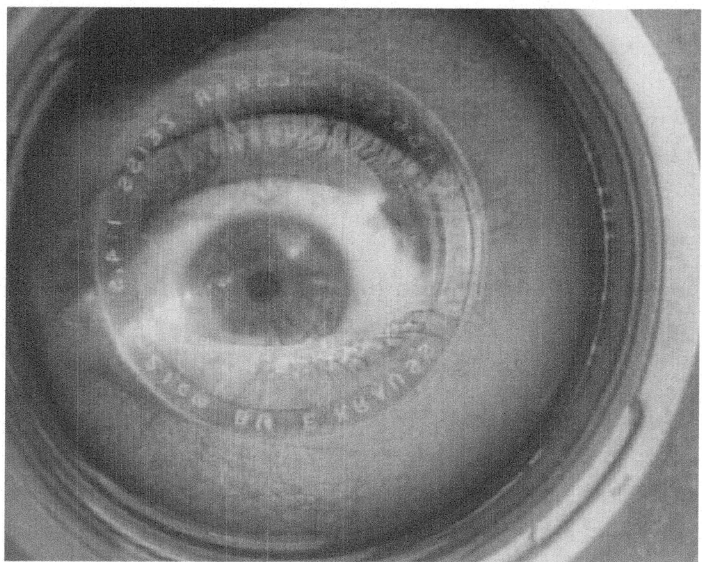

Figure 1.9 The Kino-Eye, *Man with a Movie Camera*, 1929.

brings the two closer. The adjustments require the incorporation of light, which is not only the crucial component in the functioning of both eye and camera but also enables the production of dynamic urban space so crucial to the Kino-Eye's inclusion of a social community within its assemblage.

The eye is startling, no mere imperfect organ as it is usually claimed,[50] but an eye that is shocked to see and is all the more shocking for making us worry about what it sees. Initially it seems as if the assemblage has entrapped the eye into seeing too much. But as the film gathers speed, and the movement across space becomes increasingly unobstructed, the Kino-Eye projects further forward, and its surface starts to emit a smoky yet transparent substance. This is the light through which the camera encounters actual urban space and urban space encounters the camera. This light passes through the combined frames of eye and camera, and begins to move out, presumably beyond the reach of the human eye. Deleuze proposes that unlike French films of the 1920s that focus on water and other forms of liquid to convey the extension of sight, in Vertov's case, sight moves even beyond fluidity to gaseous fumes in which there is finally free movement of each molecule.

With the increased speed of movement, exchange and dispersion, what happens to the material matter of the street recorded through the camera? Does the incentive to move the still image at all costs undermine the traces of the material world that the image carries? While Vertov's film constantly offers the unexpected encounters on the street assured by shooting on location, the pursuit of movement through editing seems to favour the desire to see everything over the confrontation with the unexpected and ephemeral. Yet the enfolding of actual urban footage within strategies of assemblage enabled by film editing is entirely strategic. Unlike many other city films, *Man with a Movie Camera* does not conceive of location shooting as a means to adhere to accurate topographical and geographical formations. On the contrary, Vertov's techniques of montage worked not only to produce movement and transformation, but also to produce an image of the city that has utopian aspirations. As already noted, location shooting was carried out in various Soviet cities over the course of five years.[51] Out of this diverse film stock, a new city was formed through editing, one that can only exist within the film itself but one that is based on what is potential within actual urban space. Thus once again assemblage produces new possibilities by bringing together actual things that are otherwise dispersed. For this virtual city to emerge, location shooting must capture different cities and have encounters with multiple communities: poor people living on the street, people engaged in harsh labour and the leisurely bourgeoisie. It must take into account new technologies and old rituals, urban spectacle and private spaces. Instead of drawing on location shooting to show the actual situation of particular urban spaces, the film is constructing a virtual space, one that seeks a vision of future possibilities but one that finds these possibilities by considering the current situation and extending it forward. Thus the actual activates the virtual and vice versa. The claims of location shooting as a strategy to enable the cinema viewer to see and think critically turns out to be more ambitious still, for *Man with a Movie Camera* provides nothing less than a model for the future. This model, however, being virtual rather than fictive, is unstable for its documentary evidence is part of the present (and thus of the past) always moving towards the future.

Rome, Open City (1945)

The location filming for Roberto Rossellini's *Rome, Open City*, which has long been granted a privileged place in film's political claims, works in very different ways.[52] In this instance, location becomes a means of drawing differences between film frames, and the ensuing breaks become the points where vision is most acute. While the film was made shortly after the 'liberation' of Rome by the allied forces in 1945, it has been associated with arduous and dangerous filming conditions, even resembling the urban situation during the occupation by the Nazis.[53] Usually considered to be the first film to develop the filmic strategies that would come to define Italian Neorealism,[54] *Rome, Open City* was burdened with the task of representing an entirely new and radical form of film-making.[55] In the unwritten manifesto of neorealism shooting on location was a primary requirement, and for many years the story persisted that Rossellini's film was shot on location because the studios of Cinecittà were being used to house refugees.[56] The film facilities of Cinecittà were associated with the development of the film industry during the years of fascist rule, and thus this claim for location shooting both separated *Rome, Open City* from the fascist past and conjoined it with new political agendas. In fact, shooting on location was not a new strategy of neorealism but was developed in pre-war films, and as early as 1933 was advocated in fascist film theory.[57] Recent interest in the close connections between pre- and post-war film-making has resulted in the reassessment of this film's politics.[58]

Yet, in *Rome, Open City* filming on location served as a kind of witnessing to what had transpired during the years of fascist rule. Made immediately after the war, the film reveals Rome's urban surface marked by years of conflict and destruction, and in this respect serves as a kind of documentary.[59] Moreover, this link to the immediate past made the film highly charged, especially given the political vacuum left in Italy after liberation. While it is now agreed that *Rome, Open City* combined location shooting with filming carried out in four purpose-made sets,[60] the importance of location as the primary indicator of both filmic innovation and political change remains. The film continues to carry within it the promise of the future, a future that by now can only be regarded through the disillusionment of Italian post-war politics.

It is precisely this intersection of charged politics and film strategies that has made *Rome, Open City* the focus of debate about the critical possibilities of film itself.[61] Siegfried Kracauer held it as a key example of a new kind of post-war film that was fiction but worked as a kind of documentary.[62] In the context of considering the idea of the found story versus the narrative, Kracauer argues that 'a found story is part of raw material in which it lies dormant' and which 'emerges and disappears in the flow of life'.[63] He proposed that *Rome, Open City*, while episodic, was developed not from the prepared script but from location shooting and the immediacy of the raw matter found in particular locales. The units of the film may form part of a sequence, he argues, but there is also a more open-ended narrative, in which cinematic components cannot be contained by uncinematic narrative structures and which invariably returns to what Kracauer called 'the flow of life'.[64]

More recently the film has been critiqued for its all too traditional

narrative structure.[65] While Rossellini's *Paisa*, which immediately followed *Rome, Open City* and also deals with the war years, is held as an
example of the undoing of the narrative, the latter has been critiqued for
simplifying the complexities and ambiguities of the time of occupation.[66]
Its narrative, as has been noted by many critics, is decidedly heroic, representing the collective effort of Romans to fight the German invaders in
the city and by implication the forces of fascism, especially through the
courageous activities of members of the resistance. But if the narrative
insists on a clear divide between those for (Germans) and against (Italians)
fascism, the film raises uncertainties through the dispersion of urban space
itself. It is in urban space, starting with the political idea of open city, that
social tensions and conflicts emerge within local communities, revealing
the class, gender and generational divides that would rupture any idea of a
coherent community of resistance.

While *Rome, Open City* has the appearance of a documentary or newsreel, it does not propose a direct relation between screen and viewer. For
Kracauer, the documentary's claim to being truthful, in effect to witness
through filming on location, is important to the way the film compels its
viewers to take these visual components seriously and commit them to
memory as real life events, and thus transform the uncertainties of the
witness into a conscious observer.[67] In the 1950s the film theorist André
Bazin, who was concerned that *Rome, Open City* depended too much on
an extraordinary political moment for its charged narrative, argued that
neorealism worked best when it weakened narrative structures precisely
because it then offered, through location filming on the street, a new
kind of challenge to the viewer. The challenge was not to confront the
dire social conditions of poverty and need, in effect what had become the
standard interpretation of neorealism, but to engage with what remained
undetermined and undeciphered in a film that nonetheless had a fictive
narrative structure.[68]

This is the direction that Gilles Deleuze followed in his interpretation of
post-war Italian film. He argued that these films posed new challenges by
presenting to the viewer – through location shooting – concrete evidence
of the recent destruction of urban space (Figure 1.10). The ubiquitous
sites of destruction in European cities with their proliferation of ruined
buildings produced within film what Deleuze called 'any space whatever',
urban spaces at once deserted and inhabited, cities in the constant course
of demolition or reconstruction, and for this very reason spaces that
opened up new circuits of thinking.[69] Deleuze was thinking of filmic space
rather than actual urban space, and noticed that the characters in post-war
film have a tendency to become disoriented, tired, distracted, and that in

Figure 1.10 Urban ruins; *Rome, Open City*, 1945.

those moments optical and sound components become heightened and disrupt the traditional narrative. These moments of disruption of the flow are the moments when time moves out of the normalising effects of the narrative, effects that Deleuze associates with bodily movement, and when time itself and for itself emerges and questions the dominant notions of sequence and order.

But how is this critical form of vision produced through location filming? It is perhaps important to return to the notion of open city that informs the way urban space is represented in the film. In 1943, not long after Mussolini was removed from Rome, the city was declared an open city, which is to say a demilitarised zone. The declaration was an effort to keep the city from attacks by military forces and from bombing. Open city then refers to a city divested of its usual political and military protection, but with new opportunities for circulation. The change of status served as an invitation to enter; not only did excluded groups of the resistance enter the city, but also within a few months Germans occupied it. Not long after, allied forces started bombing it. A city defined in terms of new routes of circulation was thus short-lived, but the question of access and movement within urban space remained crucial not only to the city itself during the last years of the war but also to the ways *Rome, Open City* represents the state of social and spatial porosity.

Initially, it is proximity to the street and knowledge of its workings that

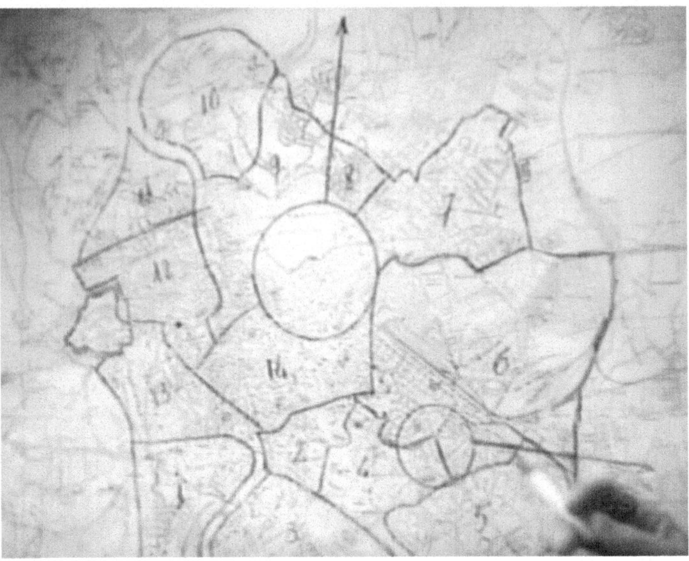

Figure 1.11 Surveillance map of Rome; *Rome, Open City*, 1945.

seems to divide those that belong from those that do not belong, the inhabitants from the invaders. Thus the official in charge of the German forces is introduced as he explains German plans for full surveillance of the city, which he does by pointing to a map of Rome partitioned into fourteen sections (Figure 1.11).[70] The detachment from the spaces of the city is evident as the partitions are shown as geometrical abstractions entirely unrelated to established urban divisions and local neighbourhoods. The official explains that every day he walks around Rome without ever leaving his office as he inspects photographs collected in order to identify members of the resistance or any potential insurgent. This approach is in direct contrast to that of the boys of the neighbourhood who are active participants in the resistance and operate through their intimate knowledge of the urban fabric. They take advantage of the state of dilapidation of the city brought forth by the invaders, be these German occupiers or allied bombers. Their notion of the city is not the one charted in maps, nor the one familiar from everyday life. On the contrary, they move in routes of their own making, across roofs, underground tunnels and hidden passageways; moreover, because these routes are contingent and constantly changing, they are absent from the abstracted map of Rome in German headquarters.

Others in the city, those who pursue everyday life against all odds, move within local neighbourhoods, not areas of Rome known for their cultural and religious monuments, but areas that are apart from tourist Rome and yet are full of social and political potential. Indeed, the location shooting was carried out in two nineteenth-century working-class neighbourhoods of Rome, Prenestino and San Lorenzo, both especially active in anti-fascist activities and street struggles against the occupying German armies. Yet these areas do not emerge as distinctive or coherent in terms of their geography. Indeed, it is even difficult to distinguish between the Via Prenestina, in which the church is located, and the Via Tiburtina, where the main Roman characters, including Pina's family, live. Both are large open streets that represent a more modern Rome than the one that tends to emerge from filming in the historical centre. San Lorenzo was the target of allied bombing in 1943, and its dilapidated ruins become markers of recent histories and of potential action.[71] The film thus pursues an idea of locality through location shooting but not one intended to describe the city's stable appearance; rather it evokes a constantly changing urban environment. To further complicate this sense of time, various street scenes are repeated; these remain unexplained by the narrative, and only resonate within the contingent and volatile appearance of the street.

But if the actual city seems opaque and even invisible in terms of the geographies that represent its communities, it is even more divided and fragmented through filmic devices and especially the strategies adopted for shooting on location. In effect there are at least three kinds of cinematic spaces used to represent the city and to activate the role of the witness. Each of these has a very different appearance and thus a different status within the sense of the real that location brings to the film. We propose that these work in relation to each other, rather than as a hybrid mixture of authentic and artificial, as has recently been suggested. The distinctiveness of each emerges through their very juxtaposition.

The indoor scenes are usually the ones that carry the plot, where dramatic action is staged as within a fiction film. It is in these scenes that individual characters take up their place in the drama of heroic resistance. These scenes have a distinctive appearance, being artificially lit and seeming for the most part to take place at night (Figure 1.12).[72] Indeed, the move from indoor to outdoor frequently proves perplexing as the expected continuity of time is disregarded. Thus the gap between indoor scenes, which were shot in film sets, and outdoor scenes, which were shot on location, is made visible through the jarring move from one to the other and back again.

There are a considerable number of scenes that are located in what can be called in-between spaces: communal staircases, courtyards, corridors and ruinous buildings (Figure 1.13). In these spaces a different kind of

Figure 1.12 Interior of apartment building; *Rome, Open City*, 1945.

Figure 1.13 The staircase of an apartment building; *Rome, Open City*, 1945.

film seems to take place, one in which the indoor narrative plot is not directly pursued but the larger implications of the situation are revealed to the viewer. Sometimes, as in the case of the discussion of the future between two characters, Pina and her fiancé Antonio, it is the only space available in which they can leave the plot to muse and worry about the dangers that lie ahead as well as to fantasize about a different world and a new kind of community. At other times, it is taken over by the boys who work for the resistance, move around it at odd hours and argue with adults about their secretive activities. As passageways between the exposure of the outside and the claustrophobia of the inside, these liminal spaces open up complications that cannot be accommodated inside and cannot be revealed outside. It is where conflicts between family members in relation to the struggle against fascism are overheard and where the cohesion of the neighbourhood starts to break down.

The third kind of space is the street, which, produced through shooting on location, turns out to be a very different kind of space. In the street we have moved as far away from the interior scenes that carry the plot as we can. Location shooting seems to keep to the kind of camera shots known from newsreels of the war. Many shots are from above (Figure 1.14) or from a considerable distance as if the camera captures an event without intervening and with the sole purpose of reporting. And indeed various of the street scenes involve group incidents of the kind that might have been reported in newsreels, for example the attack by the hungry crowd on the local bakery; another is the corralling by German soldiers of the inhabitants of a building on the street, which leads to the shooting of Pina in front of everyone as she runs after the German vehicle that carries Antonio away (Figure 1.15). This scene may belong to the plot in so far

Figure 1.14 Exterior view of the street; *Rome, Open City*, 1945.

Figure 1.15 The shooting of Pina; *Rome, Open City*, 1945.

as it moves the narrative action to the next stage, but it also belongs to the street by evoking actual recent incidents that marked Roman streets long after the war was over.

In the exterior scenes, the natural light proves blinding, and one can discern much less than in the interior scenes lit with artificial light. The street emerges within ambient light, which is both uneven and overexposed and seems to wear down the surfaces of buildings and structures even beyond their already decaying state. Seeing becomes a struggle, and oscillates between what is intimately recognisable and what is entirely strange. Recognition does not emerge from landmarks or street names but from the unprepared character of the street and the seemingly transparent recoding of it with the camera. The camera pans across space in long shots that seem to edit nothing out but also to select nothing in particular. The street appears to emerge untouched by filmic procedures, literally pulled from raw matter into an uncertain visibility achieved against the odds. This indecipherability works to keep a sense of becoming or incompleteness that gives the street its life-like appearance but it also makes it strange, ominously dangerous and filled with uncertainty. This is the jarring co-existence of the ordinary and the extraordinary, of the irreversible events of history and the repetitive small movements of everyday life. The gritty appearance of the street, which led to accounts that Rossellini had had to use scarce and faulty film stock, is what produces the contrast between

Figure 1.16 Street ruins, *Rome, Open City*, 1945.

interior and exterior scenes, and in the process offers a non–narrative that
counters the episodic film about resistance.[73]

Shooting on location in *Rome, Open City* ultimately works to reveal the
ruinous state of the street and to activate the ruin in terms of time (Figure
1.16).[74] The constant presence of the ruin, with all of its implications of
past, present and future, both situates the street within the narrative and
detaches it by revealing the uncertainties that surround it. It is the ruin
that opens up unexpected possibilities, evoking the complexities revealed
through time, both back to the conflicts of the war and forward to an
uncertain future. When the film scans across the remnants of bombed
buildings, it is frequently to show how the boys that fight on the side of
the resistance manage to move through the city undetected and carry out
their secret missions. It is as if the ruinous state of buildings allows for
their structure, and by implication the social and political structures of the
city, to gain visibility. The gaps open up opportunities where none had
previously existed, and which may just as unexpectedly disappear.

Urban ruins also become a site in which to consider the contradictions of political sides and the uncertainties of the future. When walking
on the street with Pina, the sacristan asks her if the allies will ever
come or even if they actually exist. Pina points to a bombed building
as proof of their existence, conjoining the destructive power of allied
bombing with the desire for liberation, and the ruin with the uncertainty

Figure 1.17 Attack in front of EUR; *Rome, Open City*, 1945.

of what kind of a future this conjoinment will bring.

One of the most charged ruins of the war in the film is the site of the Universal Exposition of Rome of 1942 (EUR), planned at the height of Mussolini's rule and abandoned after he lost control over the city. When EUR was chosen for location shooting in *Rome, Open City*, it was still being used to house allied forces. In the film, it is a sign of fascism, but as a ruin, it becomes difficult to keep this signifier stable (Figure 1.17). The site is recognisable through its most distinctive building, the Palace of Italian civilisation, which was planned as the focal point of the 1942 exposition. This building was designed to call up the structure of superimposed loggias of the Colosseum but transformed into a rectangular modern form. The building is made of reinforced concrete but is lined with a surface of travertine, and due to its rigid unadorned rows of nine arches appears as a striking surface without depth or substance. If the building has the effect of a shallow theatre set, then the film only accentuates this effect. The over-life-size classicising sculptures of male figures that stand under the arches on the ground floor seem to guard against any threat but also appear as shadows of their ancient counterparts. Their disembodied appearance is in direct contrast to the physicality of the scene of violent encounter in the foreground, in which partisans attack a German convoy. The scene was filmed on the main thoroughfare that runs parallel to EUR, but in many ways it evokes an incident that took place in 1944 in the centre of

Rome, in which a group of German soldiers marching on the small Via Rasella by the Spanish steps was attacked by the partisans and thirty-two soldiers were killed. This led, within twenty-four hours, to the notorious reprisal in which ten Romans were killed for every dead German in the Ardeatine caves near EUR.[75] By 1945 the Ardeatine massacre had become not only the focus of anti-fascist sentiment, but also the source of much controversy in relation to questions of responsibility and collaboration during the war years; moreover, the colossal monument commemorating the incident, which would be built within two years very near to where the scene of the attack in *Rome, Open City* was filmed, was already being planned. Thus the area of EUR is a marker of fascism that visually draws a clear line in the film's plot between the heroic resistance and the brutal fascists, but when considered as a ruin in relation to the Ardeatine massacre, it also becomes part of the post-war internal reassessment of responsibility in relation to fascism.

In the scenes that follow, the film continues to draw on the ruinous urban landscape to interconnect the uncertainties of the past with those of the future. After the heroic deaths of those working for the resistance, the film ends with a location shot, a panoramic view of Rome, which happens to be the only one in the film (Figure 1.18). The overview of the city appears in the distance as the boys re-enter it and confront an uncertain future. But this is not the end, as within this hopeful glimpse of the future is another, one which would appear in another film fourteen

Figure 1.18 Children re-enter the city; *Rome, Open City*, 1945.

Figure 1.19 Children running after a helicopter; *La Dolce Vita*, 1959.

years later. In the celebrated opening sequence of Fellini's 1959 *La Dolce Vita*, a helicopter transports a statue of Christ over the Roman ruins of the Acqua Claudia on the periphery of the city. The camera, in its attempt to keep up with the helicopter, moves from the ancient ruins to the adjacent housing estate, and comes upon a stream of boys that run joyfully in pursuit of the helicopter (its shadow visible on the ground) (Figure 1.19). These working-class modernist apartment blocks are only partly finished yet they are already worn down by use, and thus they are differentiated from the adjacent area, which is an active building site. This is the fascist complex of EUR, which in the early 1950s was once again under construction and being fitted with elegant modernist private villas. This is no mere juxtaposition of ancient and modern, or of fragment and whole. By inter-mixing the deterioration brought by time with the foundation blocks for building into the future, Fellini's film activates two crucial conceptions of the ruin. It is the housing estate in the middle of the sequence that shares the condition of both the classical ruin and the building site. It is situated precisely between the deterioration of the past and the incompleteness of the future, and thus offers the possibility of conceiving of both temporal directions simultaneously. This unsettling mixture of past and future is also suggested by the boys that run in pursuit of the helicopter and by implication towards the centre of the city. The scene evokes the final scene of Rossellini's *Rome, Open City*, only now the boys are compelled by the spectacle of the helicopter rather than their political cause. If a ruin demands a context, a visualised site from which one imagines it was ini-tially snatched, and to which it might be returned in the future, then this scene of the boys re-entering the city might once have been like the one from the earlier film; in time, however, it has like a ruin deteriorated and the boys, no longer motivated by urgent politics, have become distracted by the spectacle of an empty and fragmented culture, revealing the cracks that the earlier version of the scene so forcefully tries to keep hidden. *Rome, Open City* is regarded as the founding film of Italian Neorealism, and thus the symbolic repository of neorealism's claims of innovation and socialist politics. By evoking an ideal of neorealism, lost through the passage of time, the scene in *La Dolce Vita* becomes a kind of ruin, a ruin of film itself.

Moebius (1996)

If in *Man with a Movie Camera* and *Rome, Open City* location shooting opens the street to different forms of critical viewing, in the third film, *Moebius*,[76] the street has disappeared and has been substituted by what lies beneath, the dark passageways of a submerged network of trains. Location shooting has had to move as well, and in the process to confront the disappearance of its usual focus. Instead of the street from which the unexpected might emerge, this film is located in the elaborate underground network of commuter trains in Buenos Aires. The sudden disappearance of a train from the network, a train that cannot be seen but continues to be heard and to affect the network, brings the question of place and location to the forefront. Location shooting is invariably about capturing something that is real, even if frequently it implies the difficulty or even impossibility of doing so. In *Moebius*, the attempt to find 'the real' in urban space entails turning the usual concept of the street on its head, and instead of the material revealing what remains invisible, it is the invisible that must be transformed in order to reveal the material. This underground city, like its external counterpart, is all about transition and the movement of people from one part to another. But instead of operating within a particular urban structure, it begins to operate as infinite and immaterial, no longer able to be found, mapped or represented by any known means including the eye. Drawing on the metaphor of the Moebius strip, in which a one-sided path becomes infinite, the underground network is envisioned as an urban space that no longer has boundaries and for that reason is impossible to reach.

The overt political aim of the film is to insist on the presence of that which has disappeared, on the one hand the public street with its associations of public responsibility, and on the other hand the political dissidents detained and killed in the years of military rule from 1976 to 1983 in Argentina.[77] This historical legacy has yet to be fully addressed by subsequent political administrations and the parallel between this unsettled history and the film's premise of an underground train with passengers vanishing is not surprising. But this metaphor does not in itself reveal how the film addresses the ongoing relation between film and urban space. In effect we are confronted with the disappearance of the visibility of urban space itself, and thus of all the hopes that Vertov's film held for the power of the camera to bring light to all areas of shadow. There are also no longer distinctions between urban spaces through which location shooting asserts its own distinctiveness and brings about a different way of viewing, as in *Rome, Open City*. In the brief scenes in which the above-ground city of Buenos Aires is actually shown, there is virtually no difference from the underground city. A case in point is the only occasion in which the film reveals a panorama of the city, a view that suddenly appears from a dark screen as a bolt of lightning opens up the view that just as suddenly disappears.

Moebius was made within the context of film school training, a project undertaken by students who were completing their studies in 1994 at the University of Cinema in Buenos Aires.[78] Its experimental approach ranged from collective ways in which all aspects of film-making were developed and carried out by forty-five students under the direction of the film director Gustavo Mosquera, to the film itself, which finds new ways to address the changing relationship between film and urban space. The two experimental components are of course not separate. The project was developed from both a literary source, the short story 'A Subway Named Mobius' by A. J. Deutsch, and location shooting that preceded and shaped the final screenplay, which in the film is credited to six writers. The short story is located in the Boston train system, and thus one of the first tasks was the translation from one underground system to another. In Deutsch's story, the division of the city into two relatively separate areas results in the excessive complexity of the transport system that produces the Moebius effect. In the film, the transport system is considered from the periphery, which now becomes the last addition built within what was already an enormous and overloaded system. It was the challenges raised by location shooting within the underground system that proved crucial to this development of the script.

Due to its premise around the metaphor of the Moebius strip, the film is usually classified as science fiction, but we would argue that in its attempts to deal with the legacies of modernity in urban space, it draws on strategies of the documentary.[79] The problems of filming in the extremely busy underground system of Buenos Aires led to the decision to film in sections of train tracks in the periphery, which were made available for filming within limited hours. At the same time the film-makers acquired permission to use an old abandoned station, and to alter it to some degree in order for it to be used for the main scenes on platforms. The strategy of filming was to cover as much ground along the tunnels as possible and to do it with different cameras to achieve multiple effects. The filming was carried out with two early 35mm cameras, and one, a small hand-crank Kinamo from 1926, was modified to be able to shoot with time-lapse techniques.[80] Thus the special effects of movement, including speed, streaking of light and afterimage were produced within location shooting itself and not in post production. Location shooting, then, does not in this instance establish precise locales with particular features; rather it does something counter-intuitive, which is to establish the lack of specificity even as there are long shots that are sustained over long periods of time and over considerable ground. The sense of space is what has been called 'topological', which is to say that it is not characterised by a fixed state, but by the ways surfaces become compliant and adjustable within a constant state of transformation.[81] The location shots are not only repetitive, in that the same shots are reused over and over again, but they also become accumulative; as the film progresses and the missing train increases its speed due to its movement along an infinite path, it erodes further the specificities of location by refracting light that serves to intermesh all surfaces into continuous circuits of light.

The inversion of the city with what lies underneath is the framework used for representing its disappearance. In the scenes that initiate the film, people disembark from an underground train carriage, move in different directions, walk across different corridors, cross different gates, and climb and descend stairs that take them towards different destinations. This process of congregation and dispersal is considered by the voiceover: 'The underground is a labyrinth where in silence we encounter our own without knowing who they are or where they are going . . . we submerge ourselves over many infinite tunnels without noticing that in each exchange we are definitively changing our destiny.' With each change of direction there is transformation as well as transition, a concept of urban space that is articulated repeatedly by emphasising not just distance and speed, but also unexpected and frequently invisible junctures that lead to change in direction (Figure 1.20). The film's titles juxtapose trains in movement with maps that represent different train lines, each displaying all stations, stations that connect different lines, and stations that initiate subsidiary lines. The notion of an urban space that cannot be seen or assessed due to being constantly under transformation is suggested by early scenes that intermix the flow of movement with the mechanisms through which train tracks shift directions, either by opening up a new path or shutting an existing one.

How then does the film attempt to make this kind of transitional

Figure 1.20 Train tunnel; *Moebius*, 1996.
(Courtesy of Universidad del Cine, Buenos Aires.)

dynamic space visible? One strategy is to map out space. The maps of the different train lines are intercut with the mechanisms that enable the trains to stop at a station, to be guided across tunnels, and to change direction at certain key points along the tunnel (Figure 1.21). There are also mappings of the trains themselves, detailed drawings of the carriages, their doorways, windows, seats, and so on. The capturing of these material components on paper only makes the sudden disappearance of one of the trains as it moves through the system all the more palpable.

The attempt to find the invisible train leads the person in charge of investigating to seek out the original plans for the recent additions at the periphery of the system. This search is focused on the public archive, which is conceived as the foundational basis of all knowledge. The return to the source becomes a return to visibility, which is to say a return of the moving image back to the readability of the still image. This attempt to control movement and achieve clarity fails as the investigator, assisted by the keeper of the archive, finds that the original plans are missing. But this is not an unexpected outcome, given that the archive is shown to be as illegible as the system of transport that it should be able to clarify. Vertiginous shelving holding countless overflowing archive folders form the endless corridors of the archive. These corridors are like the train tunnels, entirely indecipherable, the former because they are chaotic, the latter because they are opaque (Figure 1.22). The parallel between the two

Figure 1.21 Underground system map; *Moebius*, 1996.
(Courtesy of Universidad del Cine, Buenos Aires.)

Figure 1.22 The city archive; *Moebius*, 1996.
(Courtesy of Universidad del Cine, Buenos Aires.)

is made overt as the space in which the plans were once located is now empty, leaving a trace of their existence much as the missing train leaves its trace on the transport system. Even when the investigator finally finds the original plans in the apartment of the missing designer, these reveal that the building of the periphery part of the system has taken the system to such an extreme size that it has moved it into the infinite and thus ruptured the system's link to the archive.

If cartography fails to bring the system into visibility, then the moving image fails to return it to the still image. In effect it is no longer possible to return to the point of origin, a point of indexicality that usually holds the potential of location shooting. But instead of bringing visibility to the unexpected and undigested, the film opens up ways of knowing that circumvent the visible entirely. We are obliged to assess the disappeared train through means other than visual evidence. Within the limited site of the city's underground, location shooting operates not by revealing something visually within it, but by activating the other human senses, in particular hearing. The vanished train may not be visible in any of its regular stops, and searches for it may yield no visual evidence of its existence but it still can be heard at certain times. Indeed, it is the sounds of its mechanisms that bring fear to authorities gathered to hear the investigator's report. When those at the meeting hear the train, there is disagreement about whether the sounds came from above or from below. Sound emitted by the missing train is revealed to be mobile rather than stable, and thus in the train tunnels sounds converge, sounds from below as well as sounds from the street above. Through this ambiguity of location, sound serves to link the underground with what remains invisible, urban space itself. In the scene when the investigator goes to the designer's apartment block in search of the missing plans, we are once again prevented from seeing anything but tunnel-like corridors and lengthy narrow staircases, yet it is sound – the threatening ringing alarms and the barking dogs – that fills the void. Sounds, which were mixed with the film after shooting, and which were produced by drawing not only on the facilities of the Universidad del Cine but also those of other universities in the area of Buenos Aires, seem to retain the only fragile connection with what has disappeared.

Electricity, which has effects but is in itself invisible, also reveals the presence of the missing train. When electricity is suspected to be present in different parts of a particular tunnel, someone asks if perhaps the carriages of the train have become unhinged. Light emitted through electricity already defines the location of the underground as tunnels are lit with bluish metallic light that evokes a space of otherness, oscillating between a mechanical world and a world of the dead (Figure 1.23). Lighting is crucial to the distinction between locations, which otherwise seem the same. In contrast to the staid neon light of the subway stations and the warm, inviting hues emanating from the trains themselves, the tunnels

Figure 1.23 Underground tunnel in transition; *Moebius*, 1996.
(Courtesy of Universidad del Cine, Buenos Aires.)

seem like speeding blue light boxes endowed with an uncertain agency. When the electricity in the system is suddenly cut off, everything blue turns deep red and the effect is of a negative rather than a positive of the photograph. Again it is another other, a space that reveals the negative space that usually remains invisible.

With the underground's intricate system of tracks and signals contining to function as if the missing train was still running, everything else in the system is affected by it. We are frequently confronted not with the train but with the effects of the train, the lights that change when the train approaches, the switching of tracks when the train moves elsewhere. This unsettling connection is directly related to the separation between people and machinery. Indeed, even before the disappearance of the train is connected to a boundless system, the separation of people from machines and from each other is revealed as workers try to communicate with each other from separate cabins and to control machinery that is elsewhere.

With the countless additions to the underground system, it has become labyrinthine and thus a parallel to modern urban space. As the investigator explains, at some point in its route the missing train found a node, not an obstruction but a particularity; the new line added to complexity of the system but its location within the periphery did something singular, taking its pursuit of movement and speed to the point where it becomes limitless, as in a Moebius strip. The infinite is conceived in terms of speeding movement, recalling Vertov's *Man with a Movie Camera*. And, recalling the latter, this possibility is attributed to mechanisation, the intermediary that enables the shift from human movement to abstract time, from actual to virtual, and that which is moving forward in time and transforming in the process. The underground system operates to include the invisible train as lights switch on and off in relation to its comings and goings and tracks are adjusted to prepare its change of direction. These are no longer directed by human action and knowledge but by the logic of the system itself. The film, like *Man with a Movie Camera*, starts with the preparation of the machine, which proceeds to pick up speed as the film progresses. By the time the investigator finds himself in the missing train, the speed of the train has increased to such an extent that tunnels with previously readable surfaces have become blurred and vertiginous. The tunnels that were initially lined with moulded bricks and iron tracks quickly have transformed into eerily blue decomposing surfaces. There is no sense of distance between stations, the very shape of the tunnels seems to decompose, and space and duration have become conjoined through the transformative aspects of light. This seems to be the ultimate move towards the limitless, and with it, the breaking up of all boundaries through the machine.

What seems to emerge in *Moebius* is a critique of the legacies of the kind of modernity represented in Vertov's *Man with a Movie Camera*. While the film proposes an urban space moving towards an uncertain future, it is a space that retains a history of industrialisation. In Vertov's film, mechanisation is the primary means through which movement and change is imagined. Trains speed across platforms, one of which has wall paintings with street scenes of Buenos Aires and its history of industrialisation. These optimistic images haunt an underground system that is now not only out of control but also, and perhaps most importantly, productive of a fragmented and alienated social sphere.

The moving train of *Moebius* and the moving camera of *Man with a Movie Camera* offer perhaps the most poignant parallel. Like the movie camera, the train is declared to be about what can be seen and what cannot be seen. The voiceover of the investigator at the start of *Moebius* insists: 'with the underground I discovered the most powerful machine to observe'. As is claimed in Vertov's film for the camera, the train and its system is shown to be without limits. At the end of the film, the investigator finds that the designer is the conductor of the invisible train who declared that the perfect machine's limitless possibilities have turned on those who envisioned its possibilities. One might recall that, in Vertov's film, it is also the train as perfect machine that punctures the screen as the

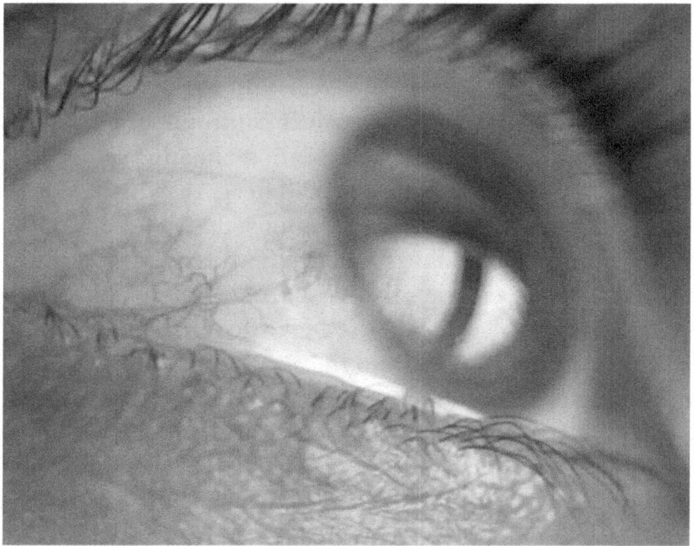

Figure 1.24 The investigator's eye; *Moebius*, 1996.
(Courtesy of Universidad del Cine, Buenos Aires.)

audience watches in astonishment. This train too is absent for it is only particles of light, but due to its motion it had become in 1928 the height of visibility. Vertov proposes to bring about a critical eye through the camera and initiates his film with the preparations and practices that project to that eye what the camera has captured. *Moebius*, however, questions what that eye can see, starting with the breaking down of the mechanisms that form connections and exchanges. Velocity has now become what unhinges sight rather than what releases it. When at the end of the film we see the close-up of the investigator's eye (Figure 1.24), evoking Vertov's human eye (Figure 1.8) and Kino-Eye (Figure 1.9) – and reflecting the missing train in which he is now trapped – we are asked to think about the limits of seeing in the conjunction of cinema and urban space.

There is a long history of claims about the importance of shooting on location for creating a critically engaged viewer. Location seems to anchor the filmic experience in the real world, sustain documentary claims to truthfulness, and position the viewer as witness to (and not simply passive spectator of) events. The urban street holds a particularly privileged place within these debates; as a likely site of the fragmentary and the unexpected it can reveal what is otherwise veiled or opaque in everyday life. The urban ruin is another such site; as an indeterminate materialisation of past, present and future in a dynamic context, it provides an unusual opening for new and unpredictable circuits of movement and thought. We have considered very closely three very different 'street films', and argued that in each instance the claims for shooting on location are negotiated due to the complex relation between the 'real' and the 'constructed' that the conjunction of film and urban space must confront. In all cases we have argued that the critical possibility of location shooting is not tied in any straightforward way to its documentary effect; the distinction between what is real and fictional has always been unstable. There is nothing new about this instability; it is as old as film itself. Moreover, the critical potential of location shooting emerges in different ways in each film that we have considered, not from the urban per se (e.g. the inherent characteristics of the urban street or the ruin) or from the authenticity of location shooting, but from the reciprocal and intertwined relations between urban space, location shooting and other elements, including contrived 'artificial' sets. The criticality of *Man with a Movie Camera*, we have argued, results not from the simple fact that it is created from film footage of actual urban places but because as montage-assemblage it forces critical reflection on the relations between the camera and the human eye, what is represented and the work of editing, urban life and technology. In *Rome, Open City* the space of the ruinous public street works in relation to interstitial passageways and the interior spaces of the film set. In *Moebius*, the disappearance of the street, and the move of location shooting to the virtual/actual spaces of the underground system of transport, drove script development and revealed pathways of movement and thinking that question the separation of virtual space and actual place and demonstrate how one activates the other.

CHAPTER 2

Movement and the Street: the Potential of Cinematic Time

Time and how it is realised is considered to be what makes film distinctive as a medium. Film is inherently about time in that it produces particular experiences of time, and negotiates or even calls attention to the relation between the representation of time on the screen and the experience of time watching the screen. According to Mary Ann Doane, the relation of cinema to time is not only complicated but also contradictory, for cinema brings together multiple temporalities, including the apparatus of film, the representation of time in the image and the time of the spectator.[1] It is not surprising, then, that time has been crucial to conceptions of film's political possibilities. Gilles Deleuze goes as far as to claim that cinema through its evolution has made time visible on the screen, and that together they have 'put the notion of truth into crisis'.[2] Digital technologies may be in the process of replacing analogue film and even the cinema, but film, according to many, has only been able to reveal its full political potential with the passing of time.[3] According to Laura Mulvey, it is now, after more than a century of cinema, that film's privileged relation to time has become apparent, in particular through the unexpected effects of its accumulation and storage of time.[4]

Urban space had a major role in the development of film's relation to time, and thus in its critical possibilities. The city and the cinema are already conjoined in early debates on the time of modernity. Cinematic time was initially conceived as bodily movement, a notion developed in film's experimentations within urban space; together film and urban space forged a critique of industrial modernisation by revealing capitalism's imposition of measured time on the body. In later attempts to challenge the limits of time dictated by the rationalisation of the body, film explored subjective and irrational experiences of urban space. The overt disruption of bodily time and by implication of narrative sequence that would follow was enabled by how new exchanges between film and urban space made visible the uncertainties of memory and the fallacies of established history.

The notion that film introduced time to the still image of photography is a persistent yet controversial aspect of the debates about the distinctiveness of film and its political potential.[5] Indeed, in early forms of cinema, film is conceived as a celebration of movement magically unleashed from the still image. Vertov's 1928 *Man with a Movie Camera* banks on this conception by experimenting with movement through speed, continuity, repetition and reversal. Moreover, this notion is made visible through the intersection of dynamic movement and transformation, be it between the human and the mechanical, or the urban and the cinematic. Gilles Deleuze noted: 'the essense of the cinematographic movement-image lies in extracting from vehicles or moving bodies the movement which is their common substance, or extracting from movements the mobility which is their essence'.[6] In effect, for Deleuze, early cinema does not produce time for itself because it leaves time attached to movement and especially human movement.

Vertov's unleashing of cinematic/urban movement depends on the stillness of the single frame (Figure 1.7) as much as it depends on the proliferation of successive frames to kick-start and intensify movement. The assumption that the still photographic image is the genetic starting point for film led to arguments about film's relation to time, and definitions of film that range from infinite change to coherent narrative sequence.[7] Should film be conceived as an experience of undifferentiated time or serve as a repository of knowledge with privileged moments of significance? In 1907 the philosopher Henri Bergson argued that film's apparatus did not permit it to produce real time as it always depends on a sequence of static states.[8] Bergson argues that time is duration, which means it is always in transition, has no fixed points from which to assess it, and can only have indirect visibility. This is in opposition to the claim that cinema, like photography, holds the potential to capture and store time as in an archive.[9] Ironically, this link between still image and film eventually brought about the recognition that film as archive would evoke the loss of time as much as its storage. After all, the dynamic processes of forming and deforming urban space captured in film would remain, like those of moving bodies, on the screen long after they had vanished from the world.

Even so, the idea of film as continuity became dominant. Cinematic 'real time' was established as the norm once the emergence of sound film regularised the speed of 35mm film to be twenty-four frames per second. Before 1930, films were shot at variable speeds and thus when projected appeared fast or slow in relation to the perceived time of the human body.[10] Conceptually 'real time' suggests no lack or loss of time, even though as Doane explains, 'much of the movement or the time allegedly recorded by the camera is simply not there, lost in the interstices between frames'.[11] The apparent continuity of a single shot, because it is not cut or is edited to seem like an uninterrupted sequence of time, appears as if in sync with the experience of time of the viewer. Cinematic 'real time' became associated with narrative time, and thus unlike Bergson's idea of duration, it was conceived in terms of points of action and resolution, and always located in the here and now.

'Real time', inextricably linked to a normalised notion of bodily movement, proved highly problematic to early advocates of the political potential of film precisely because it was deemed to be inconsistent with the time imposed by urban modernity.[12] For Walter Benjamin and others, montage, in which the cut in the film is made explicit and disrupts any sense of a continuous shot, was a product of film's own apparatus.[13] The post-production editing process, in which separate frames are spliced together and thus affect each of the newly conjoined images, captured a sense of time not limited to the here and now. Benjamin famously argued for a dialectical approach to montage, in which spatial disjunctures of film are developed and serve to re-order the implied temporal sequence.[14] In this instance, the potential of film was not simply that it represented an already existing modern experience of time and space, but that it could serve to change it. In effect, film could disrupt an all too familiar everyday by making it seem strange, as well as unhinge established hierarchies of space and time.

Montage as a property of the film apparatus has had a long and complicated history. Recently it was revisited by Christian Marclays' remarkable 24-hour-long film *The Clock*, in which short clips from different films are spliced together, each showing clocks, watches and other modes of time-keeping registering the particular time at which the film is shown (rather than when it was filmed). The viewer is compelled to project continuity to a sequence of discrete film frames through the continuous marking of time. Instead of the usual denial of the cinema viewer's time, the film demands the self-aware experience of constructing continuity regardless of content. In the process, the film reveals the artifice of narrative since anything that follows will seem to follow in time. Moreover, it shows not only the artificiality of sequential time, but also film's inability to stop time. *The Clock* is composed of films from many decades, thus well-known actors appear in different films at different ages. In effect, it reveals how film itself has contributed to the denial of embodied time by producing a seamless sense of time that both moves forward and denies the passing of time.

Vertov's use of montage had different goals; instead of making the cut

Figure 2.1 Woman washing her face; *Man with a Movie Camera*, 1929.

visible by conjoining opposing spaces and times, the cut becomes a way to extend movement indefinitely.[15] In a well-known sequence at the beginning of *Man with a Movie Camera*, a woman rises from sleep, washes her face and dries it with a towel; there follows a rapidly edited juxtaposition of shots of the woman's eyes blinking (Figure 2.1), the slats of the blinds of her window opening and closing (Figure 2.2), and a camera lens that moves in and out of focus (Figure 2.3). The eyes open, receive and reflect light in relation to the movement of the eye lids, and the implication is that instead of perceiving continuous movement, the eye sees a series of distinct waves succeeding one another after very small intervals. All, including eyes, shutters and camera, are subject to the same blind spots or intervals between each of the still images, which when connected with each other brings about the perception of continuous motion. But while for the human eye the intervals between retinal impressions were believed to be fixed, for the Kino-Eye the implication is that it is possible to increase or decrease the size of such visual blind spots, to employ faster or slower shutter speeds; in other words the camera has the possibility of getting rid of blinds spots almost entirely, the kind of technological improvement that cannot be imagined for the organic body.[16]

According to Deleuze, 'the originality of the Vertovian theory of the interval is that it no longer marks a gap which is carved out, a distancing between two consecutive images but rather a correlation between two

Figure 2.2 Window shutters; *Man with a Movie Camera*, 1929.

Figure 2.3 Camera lens focusing; *Man with a Movie Camera*, 1929.

consecutive images.'[17] With the diminishment of time interval – the gap between frames – it is not only visibility that increases but also movement. Annette Michelson claims that Vertov's film alters the interval from an image composed of multiple separate frames to an image endowed with movement.[18] Deleuze suggests that Vertov's crucial contribution to movement is not to disrupt it but to change it. In the film we are returned to the point where the image moves from a single still image to series of images that produce movement, but not in order to evoke the material evidence carried by the still photograph. Considering this point to be the genetic element of the image, Deleuze argues that this return serves to open up a differential element of movement. Thus the interval between frames does not, as one might expect, terminate the movement but instead accelerates it and changes it. The critical potential of this strategy is said to be its ability to dispel and penetrate the dark through speed and expanse, and thus to move beyond human limits.

Yet the human body is still what defines the movement of the camera. In a celebrated sequence, the camera performs in front of an astonished audience, without the need of a cameraman. The witty performance is perplexing in that its fantastical effects seem at odds with the documentary idea of capturing the real world through location shooting. Yet, the camera through its performance demonstrates its mobility, the very property through which it unveils the hidden in the world, and even concludes its performance by walking away.[19] The audience watches the animation of the camera with the same wonder as the children watch the magician. The camera, however, even as it seeks to surpass the human eye, does not discard the organic and can only imagine motion and progress through human movement.

Deleuze insists that early film always relies on human movement, even when it uses montage, which he claims did forge an image of time, but one limited by being about the totality of time and thus still dependent on movement (especially bodily movement).[20] While recently film historians argue for the experimental approach of early cinema, they also continue to agree that it was limited by keeping to the body as a measure of its temporality.[21] According to Doane: 'Regardless how one assess Deleuze's history of cinema, he is not alone in noting that movement, time and bodies are welded together in the continuity of the single-shot actuality.'[22] There are alternative interpretations. Laura Mulvey, for instance, has proposed that with the emergence of new digital technologies, Vertov's *Man with a Movie Camera* opens up another way of conceiving of time.[23] Analysing the sequence in which the movement of the image freezes and we are suddenly confronted with the still image, Mulvey finds two different temporal dimensions; movement asserts the presence of a 'now' while stillness brings resonance to the 'then'.[24] Deleuze is no less interested in the way that viewers, located within their own time, reinterpret Vertov's techniques of montage, and claims that in this instance montage is not simply the property of post-production editing but also of the audience 'who compare life in the film and life as it is'.[25] Moreover, the material used to assemble the film is already conceived as montage, and its assemblage as part of a modernity of speed, transformation and engagement with the street, 'sometimes very distant or far apart'.

In effect, the different notions of montage have as much to do with different conceptions of the modernisation of urban space as with different notions of film's relation to time. Siegfried Kracauer, who proposed that the modernity of the street was characterised by discontinuity, argued along with Benjamin that film, with its invisible gaps and disruptions, is in sync with modernity's everyday experience of time.[26] The foregrounding of urban space in theories of film's political potential became particularly charged in the years following World War II, when the physical destruction of cities became a site for the reconception of film. Italian 'neorealism' adopted the non-interventionist strategies of the documentary to produce a sense of veracity about the physical and social environment.[27] This brought back to debates on the political film the value of the uninterrupted continuity of the shot, but with an important difference. As one of the early defenders of Italian neorealism, the French film critic André Bazin stated in relation to Rossellini's work:

> [film] must now respect the actual duration of the event. The cuts that logic demands can only be, at best, descriptive. The assemblage of the film must never add anything to the existing reality . . . the empty gaps, the white spaces, the parts of the event that we are not given, are themselves of a concrete nature: stones which are missing from the building. It is the same in life: we do not know everything that happens to others. Ellipsis in classic montage is an effect of style. In Rossellini's films it is a lacuna in reality, or rather in the knowledge we have of it, which is by its nature limited.[28]

In this argument, it is not the overt cut in the film that produces a discontinuity and makes one question narrative as 'real' time. Rather the uninterrupted shot, the so-called 'real time', detaches the interval from technology and brings it to the experience of embodied urban space itself.

Doane points out that recently cinema and cinema debates have rejected the opposition between the continuous and the discontinuous,[29] but that cinema's inscription of time still holds in tension 'the fear of surfeit and fear of absence'.[30] In part this has been accompanied by the new importance granted to the viewer's part rather than to what is inherent in the apparatus of film itself. Deleuze's argument for film as duration makes this kind of move. Deleuze relies on Bergson's notion of time, especially to argue for what is potential in the image of time, but he first must challenge Bergson's own critique of film's relation to time.[31] According to

Deleuze, it is the viewer that makes up for the rupture between each film frame, evoking vividly what seems to be recorded by the camera but is not there. The spectator does not see a succession of still images but instead mobility, as cinematic time is imbued with qualitative change and duration. This is not to say that seeing time itself is easy. For Deleuze, time is not inferred through movement, but emerges as it stops movement from turning into an action and thus into a link in a narrative. The suspension of movement turns something familiar into something akin to Bergson's images of duration, which entail splitting, doubling, fragmenting and imploding; the familiar is intensified instead of simply disappearing into the normalised, and the image of time becomes recognisable by being inscribed with what Deleuze calls 'possibilities'. In this instance, the political aim is not to de-familiarise the world in order to reveal hidden systems of power and oppression or suppressed subjectivities, rather it is to shatter the normalisation of what is all too familiar.

Deleuze argues that time, as opposed to movement, only became visible in modern film, which he locates in the post-war era and its legacies of cities in ruins. This focus on urban space points to the importance of the relation between movement and time in Deleuze's argument, which is not about the replacement of the former by the latter. It is useful to consider why neorealism, which favoured 'real time' to reveal something unexpected within urban space, proved a crucial marker for Deleuze's arguments about the criticality of film. He notes: 'In the city which is being demolished or rebuilt, neo-realism makes any-space-whatevers proliferate – urban cancer, undifferentiated fabrics, pieces of waste-ground – which are opposed to the determined spaces of the old realism.'[32] Out of this, a new kind of time, what Deleuze calls pure time, was produced in film:

> The optical and sound situations of neorealism contrast with the strong sensory-motor situations of traditional realism. The space of a sensory-motor situation is a setting which is already specified and presupposes an action which discloses it, or prompts a reaction which adapts to or modifies it. But a purely optical or sound situation becomes established in what we might call 'any-space-whatever', whether disconnected or emptied.[33]

Deleuze's phrase 'any space whatever', a counterpart to 'any time whatever', which indicates the quality of duration in film, applies to the ways the fragmentation of and voids within the urban landscape disrupted established modes of knowledge, but also unexpectedly opened up new possibilities. It is crucial that this concept depends on the discombobulation of the body and thus the undoing of the naturalised movement of film narratives. But as Deleuze wrote:

> The time-image does not imply the absence of movement but it implies the reversal
> of the subordination; it is no longer time which is subordinate to movement, from
> its norm and its corrected aberrations; it is movement as false movement, as aberrant
> movement which now depends on time.[34]

In this argument the breakdown of bodily movement is crucial to the opening of time for itself, inadvertently revealing the co-existence of diverse presents and of incompatible pasts. The aim is to unhinge time from the expected and falsifying narrative sequence and to make possible thinking that moves outside the constraints of established normalised histories.[35]

When one considers the rich arguments about film and time in relation to particular films, one finds that issues of continuity and discontinuity, of movement and time, and of narrative and duration are ongoing but are negotiated rather than followed in prescribed ways. In each of the films we will discuss, time is overtly announced and produced in the relation of body and urban space, but to different effects. In Vittorio De Sica 1948 *Bicycle Thieves*, the desperate search for a stolen bicycle by a man and his son resonates within the contradictions of everyday time in post-war Rome. The movement of the human body is at the centre of the narrative but the body's increasing inability to retain its co-ordination and timing serves to derail the narrative; yet bodily movement works within everyday time, which is not simply the bodily time of the here and now, but also the accumulation of bodies in time. In the film this accumulation serves both to constrain time and to open up flows of time through urban space that call up unexpected pasts and uncertain futures. In Agnes Varda's 1961 *Cleo from 5 to 7*, a fashionable singer passes time – two hours according to the film's title but an hour and a half according to the units of time recorded on the screen throughout the film – moving around Paris as she waits to learn from her doctor if she has a terminal illness. With a contrast of time as measurable and as experiential – both running out and dragging on –the film produces a distinctive experience of time for the viewer, one of consciously spending time in the film and in the films within the film. *Cleo from 5 to 7* offers diverse screens through which to gauge movement and time in urban space, and these serve to reveal how bodily movement is continuous (and always in the here and now) but time is constantly changing and disruptive, even when urban space seems to remain the same. A very different approach is taken in Jafar Panahi's 1999 *The Circle*, in which a group of women who have been temporarily released from prison negotiate the uncertainties of the street as they move around the city of Tehran as well as in and out of the screen. The repetition of bodily movement is crucial to the idea of a continuous circle of time yet these movements do not affect each other or accumulate within urban space. It is urban space that complicates bodily movement for it is where gaps and hidden dangers emerge and where even the tenuous incomplete narratives of the women are constantly disrupted and become moments of distraction and reflection about other possibilities.

Bicycle Thieves (1948)

In 1949, shortly after Vittorio De Sica's *Bicycle Thieves* (*Ladri di Biciclette*) was released,[36] the French film critic André Bazin wrote a passionate defence of neorealism, which he claimed was fully revealed in this film through the interconnected physical movements on the street of its two main characters (Figure 2.4):

> Before choosing this particular child, De Sica did not ask him to perform, just to walk. He wanted to play off the striding gait of the man against the short trotting steps of the child, the harmony of this discord being for him of capital importance for the understanding of the film as a whole. It would be no exaggeration to say that *Ladri di Biciclette* is the story of a walk through Rome by a father and his son. Whether the child is ahead, behind, alongside – or when, sulking after having had his ears boxed, he is dawdling behind in a gesture of revenge – what he is doing is never without meaning. On the contrary, it is the phenomenology of the script.[37]

Bazin's insight, which would later be developed by Deleuze, offered an alternative to the established idea that this film pursued a social realist

Figure 2.4 Bruno and Antonio crossing the street; *Bicycle Thieves*, 1948.

agenda by addressing the story of a man desperate to keep the job of posting film posters on the streets of Rome. For Bazin, it was not the narrative situated within a time of unemployment and strife in the city that conveyed the 'real' in the situation, but rather what is conveyed through the modes of walking of father and son as they try to find the bicycle required for the job and stolen during the father's first day of work. It is bodily movement, gesture and expression, he argued, that reveals something unexpected and moves the film from a contrived narrative to one that 'unfolds on the level of pure accident'.[38] According to Bazin:

> Its social message remains imminent in the event . . . [and] is never made explicitly a message . . . If this supreme naturalness, the sense of events observed haphazardly as the hours roll by is the result of an ever-present although invisible system of aesthetics, it is the prior conception of the scenario which allows this to happen. Disappearance of the actor, disappearance of the *mise en scène?* Unquestionably, but because the very principle of *Ladri di Biciclette* is the disappearance of a story.[39]

The movement of the body, instead of marking out cinematic 'real time' and defining the sequence of time necessary for the narrative, now serves to undo the story and to forge a link, however tenuous, with the world. It is as if the filmic devices start to disappear, including any preconceived idea of meaning. The film suddenly is located in the moment of embodiment with all of its uncertainties about purpose, direction and capacities.

Father and son, Antonio and Bruno, start their search hand in hand, and led by Antonio they enter the market on the Piazza Vittorio, which is where all kinds of things, including stolen bicycles, are sold and resold. Almost immediately their steps falter and become choppy, and by the time they cross the street towards the bicycle stalls, father and son are already out of step with each other. Urban life works to increase this bodily uncertainty; other people and vehicles keep disrupting their passage, as does the natural environment. Deleuze observed: 'the rain can always interrupt or deflect the search fortuitously, the voyage of the man and of the child. The Italian rain becomes the sign of idle periods and of possible interruption'.[40] When the rain starts as Antonio and Bruno reach the entrance of yet another market, at Porta Portese, everyone scatters in diverse directions and there ensues a prolonged period of confusion. The futile attempts by father and son not to get wet only adds to bodily discomfort and awkwardness. They move back and forth in indecisive steps, with the boy seeking direction from the father who fails to notice the boy's fall and frustrating attempts to take control of his body (Figure 2.5). Their palpable frustration as they huddle against a wall surrounded by a chatty group of German clerics leads to further vacillation. Antonio may be

Figure 2.5 Bruno falling on the street; *Bicycle Thieves*, 1948.

preoccupied with the search but fails to notice most of what is around him, and even when confronted with the young thief in front of the market's main gate, cannot bring himself to react till it is too late.

The chase that ensues once the rain stops and the two run back and forth along the narrow streets around the convent of Santa Cecilia returns one to the comic silent film chase, in which bodily movement seems speeded up and magical in the ways it defines both body and space. But early cinema's use of bodily movement to map out and clarify the space is now reversed, as father and son scurry in and out of little streets, offering the viewer no elucidation of space. Instead, urban space becomes confused and confusing as the two seem to move in and out of the same spaces and return to where they started. The interruption by the father as the boy hides against a wall to urinate is tinged with humour but also sadness; it intensifies an ordinary moment with the recognition of the body's inability to maintain even the most limited sense of agency and purpose.

Bazin's argument about how the bodily movement of father and son serves to undermine the narrative sequence has proved productive and encouraged other interpretations of the film than those pertaining to the narrative structure or the context of post-war poverty. Even so, some recent critiques that the film propagates traditional structures of family and community still persist on foregrounding narrative structure and its prescribed meanings.[41] Deleuze, however, follows Bazin's lead and argues for the ways bodily disruption loosens the linkage between cause and effect and brings the film to the level of the materiality of things and their constant transformation through time. We would like to take up this opening but consider more fully the materiality captured by the camera within cinema's relation to urban space. This materiality is invariably related to everyday life. Bodily movement in the film is located within the narrative structure but also within the time of the everyday, which is not simply the body in the here and now but the accumulation of bodily movement within urban space and its unpredictable effects.

Concepts of the everyday feature prominently in early arguments about the political potential of Italian neorealism. Cesare Zavattini, one of the main proponents of neorealism, who wrote the script for this film based on a 1946 novel by Luigi Bartolini and collaborated with director Vittorio De Sica on various films, argued for the turn to the real through the everyday.[42] Zavattini was certainly much more committed to the subject-matter of social realism than Bazin, but he also criticised conventional plots, which he claimed were intended to make reality palatable or spectacular and, which, most importantly, neglected the historical richness and political importance of everyday life. For Zavattini the question of the 'real' in film became a critique of the usual artifice of studio films. Drawing on earlier theories of political film, he proposed the need to develop films around organic networks within the world and not the artificial genres of cinema. He conceived of the everyday as that which was all around, everywhere and always, but for that very reason had become invisible, and the political potential of the camera was to bring it back into view. Zavattini stated:

> What is so important about a bicycle in the Rome of 1948 where so many bicycles are stolen every day? Yet for a worker who loses his means of support a stolen bike is a very tragic circumstance. Why should we, film-makers, go in search of extraordinary adventures when we are confronted in our daily lives with facts that cause genuine anguish? . . . the smallest details of everyday life [which] are often dismissed as commonplace. The cinema has at its disposal the film camera which is the best medium for capturing this world. It has been said that neorealism does not offer solutions . . . It is enough, and quite a lot, I should say, to make an audience feel the need, indeed, the urgency for them.[43]

Zavattini's approach is to combine urgent social issues with the potential of the cinema to reveal unexpected aspects of ordinary life. His conception of the film is something that is captured between a script and what goes on in the real world. It is not unlike Kracauer's argument for the found story versus the episodic narrative.[44] According to Kracauer the distinction is between stories that emerge from physical reality and thus are found in the process of making the film in the world, and stories that emerge from life but become distinguishable from it as they are shaped by ideas that are not inherently part of physical matter: the latter are episodes. For Kracauer, the cinematic form is undermined by the imposition of a clear sequence of episodes. He argues that *Bicycle Thieves*, while having an episodic narrative, still has the qualities of a found story; it retains an open-ended character that remains permeable to everyday life, neither contained within nor reducible to a singular imposed meaning.[45] In keeping with early notions of the documentary, Kracauer argues for potential meaning in the physical matter captured and verifiable through the camera rather than the prescribed meaning of the textual narrative.

The everyday is typically presumed to be the activities of ordinary people and thus frequently assumed to refer to repetitive unconscious daily movement. Yet there have been extensive debates about the effects of modernity on everyday life. Within one strand of Marxist thought the everyday within capitalist society is conceived as a time diminished due to the alienation of labour, usually accompanied by the containment of the body (including the temporal discipline of the clock). This is an argument developed by Henri Lefebvre, who however departs from Marxist readings of the everyday by insisting that the body holds the possibilities of breaking out of the imposed constrictions of capitalist labour.[46] These and other critiques of modern alienation tend to presume a pre-modern, pre-capitalist everyday that was collective, cyclical and unchanging.

Michel de Certeau, in his influential *The Practice of Everyday Life*, is critical of both the idealisation of a pre-modern collective through the everyday, and the assumed compliance of people, what he calls 'the silent majority'.[47] For de Certeau, the everyday entails a set of relations, not with an individual at the centre, but one in which 'each individual is a locus in which an incoherent (and often contradictory) plurality of such relational determinations interact'.[48] He writes that the everyday is about time rather than space because it entails activities that people frequently carry out in someone else's space, for instance walking, reading and talking: 'it transforms another person's property into a space borrowed for a moment by a transient'.[49] Instead of alienation, de Certeau argues for tactics used by ordinary people to appropriate, however temporarily, the opportunities that come their way. Thus de Certeau's theories of the everyday stress the importance of time and a time that cannot be reduced, either to the individual or to the prescribed time of capitalist society. The time of the everyday is the time of people's tactics as they go about their daily life, and a tactic is not a pre-planned action but what is enacted in the moment and in relation to a complicated set of variables.[50] The reason the time of the everyday is outside the individual or authority is that it is inherently ephemeral, leaving behind the things used or the places traversed, but these are only a trace of the tactic which cannot be reconstructed through the trace. According to de Certeau, if we think of the everyday in terms of the things used to produce it, we are misled to think that the everyday is homogeneous. But this is to miss the time of the everyday, the processes of transit and transition that de Certeau (using a language metaphor) calls 'the phrasing' of the everyday, which is what produces something different.[51] These 'phrasings' accumulate not in the sense of gaining territory but in marking space by producing time: 'Places are fragmentary and inward-turning histories, pasts that others are not allowed to read, accumulated times that can be unfolded but like stories held in reserve, remaining in an enigmatic state . . .'[52]

If the street market has become a privileged site for discussions of the everyday, it is because it is not only a place formed through converging everyday movements but also a space that exceeds the specificities of place by holding within it the traces of movements that extend far beyond its physical boundaries.[53] In the market of Piazza Vittorio these traces are found by father and son in the form of countless bicycle parts scattered across countless stalls (Figure 2.6). The market gives visual confirmation to the complexity of everyday movement, but it also reveals the impossibility of reconstructing just one strand of these movements, the one

Figure 2.6 Bicycle parts on a market stall; *Bicycle Thieves*, 1948.

that concerns father and son. The sight of bicycle parts, disassembled but soon to be grafted onto other parts to form a new assemblage, confirms that within the everyday the material traces are always in the process of transformation and reappearance in another form. The bicycle fragment, reproduced endlessly and filling up every available space, points to how everyday movement is repetitive but also constantly differentiated and extended.

For father and son the search now turns to the concentrated act of observing the evidence of these movements; they look through pile after pile of every kind of bicycle part, seeing more and more examples of the bicycle but knowing less and less about the whereabouts of their bicycle. The accumulation may be made up of bodily movement over long periods of time, but its effects are no longer limited to the individual subject and what can be comprehended and controlled by that subject. As de Certeau has argued, the overall view (within the market) may promise complete knowledge, yet this is illusory for the individual experience is momentary and transient and cannot be fully known through its material traces. What is lost in the case of Antonio's stolen bicycle is its individual history, the time which had marked it and which Bruno is shown to be so attentive to in previous scenes. Film critics have noted that it would have been easier to acquire another bicycle than to find the stolen one, but this would undermine what is at stake for everyday life in the original bicycle. Nothing makes this more explicit than the insistence on the co-existence of fragmentation and proliferation in the representation of the bicycle. When the father stops to question whether the bicycle being reassembled and repainted before his eyes is the stolen bicycle we are reminded that the process of movement and transformation is ceaseless and unstoppable.

In *Bicycle Thieves*, the time flow of the everyday is shown to define the experience of the city itself, which is both separated into parts yet entirely entangled. This is achieved in spite of the fact that the film was, as is frequently noted, not only shot entirely on location but also edited with remarkable attention to the spatial relations of the built city. The separation of parts – the historic centre and the periphery – is made explicit through the transport systems that move people on a daily basis back and forth as they go to work in the early morning and return in the late evening. Yet, as father and son search the historic centre for the thief, the experience of moving on the street is gruelling and disorienting. The progress of the search is constantly obstructed by the very specificities of urban space. It is a harsh terrain, one that has not been re-staged for the film, giving every run-down street and decaying building a startling vividness that does not seem to belong to a constructed narrative. This sense of everyday time, of a time that is repetitive but constantly confronts bodily movement with unexpected challenges permeates the search for the bicycle. Father and son, unlike de Certeau's pedestrian, cannot even complete their own actions, let alone recognise an opportunity if it presented itself.

Contestation at the level of the everyday is what defines the time of the city, which is not only in a state of damage and decay, but also filled with movement, encounter and exchange. Institutions insist on bureaucratic ordering of the everyday but these invariably reveal the conflicts within the collective. The film starts with a group gathered hoping to be assigned jobs by the work office yet the procedures imposed give rise to a quarrel. When the father reports to the office that distributes film posters for his job, it is shown to be a vast enterprise but one divided into separate endeavours with no communication. The work is to be defined within a specific time-frame of work hours as each poster is to be accessible on the street for so many hours before others cover them up. When Antonio starts his new job, he joins a collective that sets off early in the morning on their bicycles carrying a ladder and their posters, an image of labour which seems to hark back to earlier forms of collective bonds, and which is reiterated by the rubbish collectors that gather with their equipment to start their duties early before dawn at Piazza Vittorio. Yet the remarkably joyful scene of Antonio and his co-workers setting off together at a designated hour to post film ads quickly is transformed into the single person unable to find anyone for help after the theft of the bicycle. When Antonio's friend enlists his co-workers, the rubbish collectors, in the search, they incorporate it into the time of their prescribed job. Rather than an everyday time rigidly separated between work and leisure, the film shows the intersection of the two. De Certeau, who identifies this practice by the French term *la perruque*, writes: 'With the complicity of other workers, [the worker] succeeds in "putting one over" on the established order on its home ground'.[54]

Yet these strategies do not seem to point to the survival of community bonds within the bureaucratic organisation of labour. On the contrary, in *Bicycle Thieves*, the everyday carries within it a sense of time that flows in multiple directions, neither the survival of the past into the present, nor the past fully stamped out by the present. Indeed through the flows of the everyday, the film represents a historical moment in which there is no specific present but rather a confluence of past and future. The search for the bicycle reveals a vacuum in the city, and certainly the powers that vied for control over Rome during the war and after the election of the new Christian Democratic Party on 18 April 1948 are virtually absent.[55]

In the years of occupation, the so-called 'open city' between 1943 and 1945, the struggles between fascists (both local and foreign), resistance groups and allied forces divided the city and accumulated autonomous pockets of authority, be it within established offices such as the worker's union or within neighbourhood sectors. After the election of the Christian Democrats (which would then rule for over fifty years), the political situation would change radically with the entry of American capital and the world increasingly organised within and divided between political blocks controlled by the Soviets and the NATO alliance (which led to the bitter confrontation of the Cold War). But between 1945 and the election of 1948 the city was suspended in an unsettled past and an uncertain future. The American-funded Marshall plan had not yet been implemented and its cancellation was threatened by the possibility of the Communist Party being elected to the national government. The film is situated in the tensions within the pre 1948 election campaign, in which the housing shortages and the lack of jobs were central issues.[56]

The everyday struggles of Antonio to keep his job of posting advertisements on the streets of Rome lead directly to the uncertainties of the future. At the time of the theft, he was posting the film poster for *Gilda*, the 1943 Hollywood film starring Rita Hayworth released widely in Europe after the war (Figure 2.7). Indeed, *Gilda* started the large-scale importation of American film into Italy, which became the most visible cultural presence of American capitalism, especially as it quickly threatened the Italian

Figure 2.7 Antonio posting *Gilda* film poster; *Bicycle Thieves*, 1948.

film industry. By 1949, a national law was passed requiring the screening of Italian films on at least eighty days a year. On the street, the poster emerges as a material trace of the everyday; it is put together from pieces, covering posters beneath and itself soon to be covered by others, perhaps the poster for the next Hollywood film. But the presence of the poster also represents the beginning of a new kind of cultural colonisation, one that *Bicycle Thieves* itself sought to counter. From this perspective, the film's argument for a critical outlook is not simply countering traditional narrative time to approximate the real, but doing so in order to challenge new consumer desires that would be constructed through film in the years to come.[57]

The past is no less embedded than the future within the urban paths of the everyday. When the father searches frantically for his son, fearing he might have drowned in the river, he finds the boy at the top of a monumental staircase that is part of the distinctive fascist Duca d'Aosta bridge, located at the northern edge of the city.[58] The bridge is the only overt topographical inconsistency in the film and it is also a moment in which the past suddenly resurfaces in the midst of the conflictual yet mostly silent bodily exchanges between father and son. Within the filmic frame, the tiny figure of Bruno is juxtaposed against a daunting flight of stairs of gleaming travertine (Figure 2.8). Yet when we look closer the stairs are damaged and weeds are growing from below, seemingly crawling upwards and breaking apart its travertine surface. This is indeed a traditional ruin,

Figure 2.8 Bruno and Antonio on the Duca d'Aosta Bridge; *Bicycle Thieves*, 1948.

with the overgrowth of nature and thus of time invading its very matter. The bridge was one of the last fascist urban projects to be completed and the last one formally opened by Mussolini before he left the city in 1943.[59] The bridge carries within it both the fascist restoration of antique ruins for a modernist city, and the subsequent ruination of that restoration. Father and son are reunited but there is no resolution, only a bigger gap between them. This ruin is one that both disrupts the sequential flow of time and space, and flows into another of the everyday paths that father and son activate through their movements.

The loss of the bicycle, then, is what prompts the narrative arc of the film but the everyday intervenes in the narrative and opens up unexpected routes, not only through urban space but also through time. For the narrative, the finding of the bicycle is important, but for the time of the everyday it is important that the search by father and son be no different than other comparable movements through the city and remain within the micro levels of urban life, rather than being endowed with larger social significance. André Bazin argues that it is precisely the uncertainty of why the bicycle is not found that enables parts of the film, through bodily movements, to slip out of the coherent narrative: 'a propaganda film would try to prove that the workman could not find his bicycle, and that he is inevitably trapped in the vicious circle of poverty. De Sica limits himself to showing that the workman cannot find his bicycle . . .'[60] For Bazin, bodily movement, especially its awkwardness, faults and idiosyncrasies, produces a material presence that remains undeciphered and awaits the participation of the viewer. Deleuze on the other hand, regards the discombobulation of the body to be what starts to reveal time itself, no longer delimited by bodily movement: 'in the adult world, the child is affected by a certain motor helplessness, but one which makes him all the more capable of seeing and hearing'.[61] Such bodily disarticulation creates a crucial shift away from motor–action and the body as measure of time by rupturing this continuity and opening a moment of self-awareness through the recognition of disjunctures and misconnections. For Deleuze, the journey of viewing the film is akin to the journey of the search for the bicycle within the film, one in which time starts to split and also re–converge, and through unexpected points of intersection prompts a process of critical rethinking.

In *Bicycle Thieves* the loss of the bicycle becomes a thinking point even before it is stolen, for its theft is anticipated and made palpable from the start. It is as if the future is already always in the present. There are various occasions when the bicycle is put at risk, and the camera invites our anxious attention. When the mother insists on visiting the *santona* (the seer who had predicted that her husband would get a job), her husband leaves the bicycle on the street under the observation of young boys that loiter nearby and come and in and out of the screen frame. Is the impending theft a question of chance, luck or timing? The bicycle has entered into a dialogue with the viewer, not so much about who will take it or why but about how time opens up unexpected paths, paths that are within everyday time and which keep reappearing and disappearing through its entanglements. When near the end of the search, father and son revisit the *santona*, her prophecy is already not in the present and yet not entirely in the past ('you will find it immediately or not at all'). It seems to predict what we already know, that the bicycle will not be found, yet immediately when the two leave the building they literally bump into the young thief. Of course it does not change the result, but it raises the possibility of a new 'now' while retaining the idea that there never was a 'now' invested with opportunity ('not at all'). Thus it provides a suspension of narrative time (time as action and effect) in favour of new opportunities to think about contradictory conceptions of the present. Each unexpected turn alters the possibilities for new interpretations.

The time of the everyday, a time that is forged from the constant urban processes of movement, fragmentation and transformation, is also what produces the constant disassemblage and reassemblage of the film. This potential for thinking and rethinking about time itself is one reason that *Bicycle Thieves* has been so unusually generative.[62] Of course the story of a family struggle against the odds has held a continuing appeal as a film narrative. Yet the film's constant opening of gaps in the narrative in which action stops and thinking is activated about the contradictory pathways of time has been an important factor, one that has only become more evident with the passing of time.

Cleo from 5 to 7 (1961)

Cleo from 5 to 7 (*Cleo de 5 à 7*) is all about time: the time of the body, the time of the street, and most of all cinematic time, which links the time of the film and the time of watching the film.[63] Agnes Varda's 1961 film is explicitly about the relationship of cinema and time but does not follow a prescribed route. Its approach to time, signalled initially by the delimiting of time in the title and by a structure in which scenes are divided into carefully measured consecutive units of time, seems at odds with the radical approach to narrative espoused by Varda's contemporaries.[64] For the French New Wave, the rejection of sequential time that characterised Hollywood film was crucial and led to the decisive unhinging of narrative time. Varda's film, however, insists on the measurement of time within a precise sequence that is underpinned by the movement of the body. The film was shot in chronological order and for the most part at the time represented within the film.[65] Part of the pleasure of the film is recognising the consistency between the time on the screen and the time at the viewer.[66] The implication is that the two are caught together in time, and that there is no time during which the two are apart or can hide anything from each other. The time spent by fashionable pop singer Cleo waiting to receive the results of a medical test does not play out exclusively on the screen. Cleo's intense experience of time on the screen and the spectator's time are impossible to extricate from each other, although they are not the same.

Cleo and the viewer spend time together but the experience proves to be quite different. The title marks out two hours, although the film takes up an hour and a half, from 5 to 6.30 p.m. The term 5 to 7 denotes an illicit afternoon affair,[67] yet the time spent by Cleo is anything but the French concept of a stolen 'time out of time'. Instead the time frame is determined by the modern organisation of carefully measured time. Cleo is obliged to wait for a precise appointed hour to learn about her physical condition and her future. Modern time-keeping is contrasted with superstitions about time, but these too organise and delimit time in ways that are not that different from bureaucratic concepts of time. They may be presented as opposites, rational and irrational, yet both project a sense of time that will only be revealed later, in the future. Both raise fears about the unknown within time itself, giving it a daunting presence that is imposed externally but experienced as embodied.

If for Cleo the film's time frame produces a sense of waiting that is slow and protracted, for the viewer it becomes a race against time. The film is divided into small time units, each announced on the screen and usually six to seven minutes, although some are shorter (Figure 2.9). Clocks appear constantly on the screen and some, like those on the shop window that Cleo passes on the Rue Rivoli, remind one of the ticking clock that is the screen. At Cleo's home, the many clocks that decorate the sparse space lack arms, and seem suddenly to stop time; time restarts when Cleo abruptly departs from the music rehearsal and chooses a chain with a clock to put around her neck. Time seems to come at the viewer from all directions, interlinking the near with the far: Cleo puts the ticking clock on her body while the radio news in the taxi brings the time of Algeria into Paris

Varda wrote that the marking of time throughout *Cleo from 5 to 7* works to bring the viewer back from any sense of being lost in the film (as in

Figure 2.9 Cleo from 17.05 to 17.08; *Cleo from 5 to 7*, 1961.

Hollywood cinema) and that this 'creates a distance towards the characters'.[68] Timekeeping, then, is a means of prompting awareness of the film as film rather than as escape from the world. The marking of time in *Cleo from 5 to 7* invites the viewer not to watch a film but to consciously spend time in a film, and to experience time through the heightening of its limits. Instead of the cinema's usual erasure of actual time in order to transport one into another world, this film is entirely concerned with what it means to be 'in time'.

Cleo shares this experience with the viewer, in that her own confrontation with the possibility that her time might be coming to an end due to an illness prompts her to confront her experience of time. She becomes sensitive to how her body feels in time and space, something evident as she moves through the city and tests out its effects. And it is this testing out that increases her dissatisfaction, even if in the course of the film those around her interpret her dissatisfaction as self-indulgence and even narcissism. Cleo begins to be aware of blind spots that have kept her from recognising herself in time and these emerge in moments of self-confrontation in mirrors and glass reflections, evoking in part the illusion of glamour and celebrity produced through cinema itself. Just before Cleo and her new acquaintance Antoine reach the hospital at the end of the film, she says to him, 'You have answers for everything. It is strange, I have questions for everything. Today everything amazes me. People's faces next to mine.' Cleo has crossed over to the viewer's space, and has become attentive to viewing time, just as the viewer has become attentive to filmic time.

Cleo from 5 to 7 offers multiple conceptions of time, from the measured and concrete to the elusive and intangible; these coexist in, circulate around and – as we hope to show – realign the relation of urban space and time in early 1960s Paris. In Varda's film, time is propelled forward through measurement, but measurement is always in dialogue with bodily movement, the time it takes Cleo to move from one place to another. For most of the measured time, Cleo moves across the city by foot, car and bus. Her three walks define the film in terms of bodily movement, but these are interspersed within three car rides, which emerge more explicitly as cinematic sequences, what we would argue are a set of potential films within the film. These 'filmic' sequences also pertain to bodily movement and time but now shown to be transformed through the film screen. Increasingly the filmic sequences adopt a playful mode, in juxtaposition to, and serving to modify, the unsettling relation of bodily movement and urban space. By setting a tone that is distinctly different from the expected seriousness of film that aspires to critical potential, *Cleo from 5 to 7* alters the viewer's engagement with the screen and brings to the 'spending of time in the film' not only unexpected pleasures but also a more dynamic sense of time in the city itself. We propose that through the different sequences, the film reveals changing time in a city that through its enduring myth has been defined as always the same. The spaces of modern Paris produced through Cleo's bodily movements initially seem ensconced in a mythic past, not unlike perhaps the image of glamour in which Cleo finds herself contained. But through the cinematic screens produced within the film, time is shown to be always changing, even if there are entrenched idealised images of the city that prevent one from recognising it. Cinema is at the centre of this process, for it is both the producer of the myth (as it is the producer of glamour and celebrity) and that which might prompt viewers to question it and recognise the vibrant and uncertain aspects of time.

In the film, urban space seems to afford unlimited potential for movement, circulation and transition, yet the film keeps to a fairly limited circuit of Paris. Cleo starts her first walk on the fashionable Rue de Rivoli on the right bank, although on the eastern, less-elegant side of the street where fashion shops intermingle with transient clothing stalls and other shops. This thoroughfare was redefined as a boulevard in the nineteenth century by the addition of arches that blur the distinction between the inside and outside of buildings, but it predates the system of boulevards that came to define central Paris. When Cleo and Angele take a taxi home, it entails crossing Pont Neuf, entering the left bank and driving across the sixth arrondissement, which is dominated by the university and the student-oriented narrow streets around the Odeon theatre. As the taxi moves further south and reaches the area of Montparnasse, we are back on the wide boulevards, although, unlike those on the right bank of the city, these were associated with artistic and intellectual communities. This is where Cleo lives and where she takes her second walk, apparently directionless but reaching the celebrated Dôme Café. Cleo wanders within the café much as she does on the boulevard, haphazardly intermingling with people, overhearing snippets of conversations on artistic issues and revealing her frustration with most of what she encounters. She suddenly visits a nearby artist's studio where her friend works as a model, and this prompts the second car ride. During this car ride, transitional spaces emerge, especially the train station of Montparnasse in which people's movements as they exit the station seem to exceed the boundaries of the left bank of Paris and of the city itself. There is another taxi ride and then finally a bus journey that covers considerable ground very quickly. Together with Antoine, Cleo travels north across a number of interconnected boulevards, first reaching and traversing the important roundabout at Place d'Italie, and continuing down the broad Boulevard d'Hospital.

One might well suppose that urban movement is associated with the mythic nineteenth century Paris of the boulevards.[69] The boulevards that now define central Paris are part of a nineteenth-century initiative to modernise the city by introducing wide tree-lined avenues, many of which became associated with new kinds of leisure and consumer activities, including large department shops, cafés and bistros.[70] It was the civic planner Baron Haussmann who devised a way to reorganise the entangled streets of the city by opening up boulevards at the centre, and organising the space in terms of broad thoroughfares with standardised monumental facades punctuated with balconies and conjoined with slate roofs. The effect of such a radical transformation was to alter urban space, turning it into a stage for the emergence of consumer culture and the technologies of surveillance.[71] The association of the boulevards with promenading is a long one but in the later nineteenth century walking became associated not only with new leisure time but also with consumerism in all of its manifestations.

Perhaps for this reason one of the consistent interpretations of Cleo is as a female *flâneur*.[72] The late nineteenth-century literary figure of the *flâneur*, usually male and well to do, strolls and loiters through the new shopping arcades, not as a consumer of things but of the street itself.[73]

In Walter Benjamin's influential theorisation of the *flâneur*, which is informed by Baudelaire's essay 'The Painter of Modern Life', the stroller is someone who was intoxicated by the spectacle of the street and yet managed to retain a distance that produced thinking and knowledge about it.[74] In Benjamin's arcades project, the *flâneur* is conceived as abandoning himself to the street and transgressing the boundaries of the body by stepping at will into the bodies of others.[75]

Yet Cleo's movements around the city are not like those of the *flâneur*. For Cleo walking on her own is unusual, as she tells her friend, and her walks take her out of her comfort zone. We watch Cleo on the move, and frequently do not know where she is going or why, and most of the time neither does she. For this reason alone, a more apt concept of her walking may be the *dérive*, which was described by Guy Debord in 1958 as when people 'during a certain period drop their usual motives for movement and action, their relations, their work and leisure activities, and let themselves be drawn by the attractions of the terrain and the encounters they find there'.[76] The *dérive*, proposed in the late 1950s by the avant guarde anti-art collective Situationist International,[77] entailed drifting through the city in ways that disregarded the city's official organisation, especially in relation to modern consumerism. Cleo's walks, rather than establishing a temporary relation to the street, as is usually claimed for the *flâneur*, keep her within a constant state of uncertainty. For Cleo, walking around is perplexing rather than engaging, whether she walks in her own neighbourhood or crosses one of the main boulevards. She is never compliant in urban space but neither does she overtly challenge established orientations.

An important parallel between Cleo's walks and the *dérive* is that the goal was not to master the street, but rather to activate one of its many possibilities.[78] Cleo's walks, while seeming to repeat what has already transpired, change direction and pick up speed. Her wanderings may initially evoke the received nineteenth-century notion of Paris as a city of boulevards open to the constant flows of people and the spectacle of commerce, but increasingly, especially through the imposition of cinematic time, urban space starts to produce another sense of time. Within the internal film screens, the city no longer seems ensconced in the imaginary elegance of nineteenth-century Paris but rather speeds up and is shown to be constantly in the midst of change, one brought on by transport, colonial relations, international markets and the beginning of mainstream tourism. Although the film was made just before the construction of the (still only) high-rise building in central Paris, the Montparnasse tower, and the completion of the Boulevard *Périphérique*, the circular motorway around Paris, key urban changes are already in the kind of time produced through the ways the film screen alters the appearance of urban space.

Initially, cinematic time seems very close to the body, something that for Deleuze limits cinema's critical possibilities. Drawing on non-interventionist devices associated with the documentary – the hidden camera, the unexpected movements captured by such a camera, the long duration of shots with apparently little or no editing – the flow of the film seems to take place within the actual life of the city and to be produced by that life. When Cleo first steps out onto the street from the claustrophobic room of the fortune-teller and walks along the Rue Rivoli, the camera follows closely behind but then widens the view onto the full expanse of the boulevard (Figure 2.10), capturing its transitional and dynamic states as if from an invisible place. The camera evokes a disjointed mode of urban seeing, the constant glances in multiple directions and the failure to conjoin multiple and changing perspectives. The focus on shop and café windows signals a change from post-war hardship to a new proliferation of goods and services, but these reveal a fragmented population, not only through the discussions overheard in various scenes in cafés but also in the use of reflective surfaces that split the surface of the screen and evoke the time of urban space to be incoherent and incomplete. While this may recall Walter Benjamin's argument on the *flâneur*, the camera produces a much more disrupted space through the inability to retain a consistent frame within which to hold in the movements of the street.

Figure 2.10 Cleo on Rue Rivoli; *Cleo from 5 to 7*, 1961.

It has been argued that Cleo's interest in her reflection as she encounters it when moving from place to place pertains to her self-obsession and even her desire to turn herself into a fetishised object.[79] Yet this turn to the reflective surface also evokes, as already suggested in relation to Cleo's image of glamour and celebrity, the film screen itself. The film screen is constantly evoked in the film, becoming explicit when Cleo and Angele take a taxi home from the Rue de Rivoli. A sudden change of viewing point is suggested first through spatial transitions: from walking to riding in an automobile, from the right to the left bank across Pont Neuf, and from the broad boulevard to narrow and intimate streets. The viewing point is now from the interior of the taxi out towards the street. Our view, coinciding with Cleo's, is framed by the windows of the car, which become a kind of film screen through which everything is seen and transformed into a continuous sequence of time. The car's consistent movement, in spite of obstructions along the route, allows the screen to suggest an acceleration of speed while the images projected through the window (or on the screen) are increasingly fragmented and disjointed. In effect, this is an earlier version of Christian Marclay's *The Clock*, in which the splicing together of film frames produces a sequence of time even with entirely disparate frames.

While in the taxi, Cleo becomes the spectator of her own film and we become aware of how the film frame produces speed beyond the limits of bodily movement and simultaneously brings coherence to the dispersed matter that is the street. The boundary between screen and viewer is made overt when a man in another car tries to get Cleo's attention and touches her hand as it rests on the window frame. She pulls it away, startled that this boundary could be breached. Compared to Cleo's earlier walk, in which she is interconnected with others and is not always able to see but keeps pressing around and against bodies, the car ride offers the possibility of being more detached from urban space and yet more attentive to its visual stimulation and distortions. For Cleo everything suddenly appears strange and unfamiliar, as if seen through a screen on which a montage-like sequence of film frames are projected. One presumes that Cleo has travelled the route from Rue Rivoli to Rue Huyghens in Montparnasse, where she lives, many times before, but now it is as if she has never seen it before. The displays in shop windows perplex her and even startle her, as in the case of the African masks (Figure 2.11). When the taxi is suddenly surrounded by students who are performing a carnivalesque mocking ritual, Cleo, unlike Angele, is unsettled as if encountering a threatening situation. Cleo's inability to see things as 'normal' may be part of her moment of anxiety but it also reveals an awareness of the changes that are

Figure 2.11 View from the taxi; *Cleo from 5 to 7*, 1961.

all around but cannot be fully deciphered. The city seen through the film screen offers moments of confrontation that suspend all held assumptions about oneself and the world.

Cleo's second walk, which takes place after her music rehearsal is interrupted, presents a much more visceral engagement with unexpected aspects of the street. In this instance the camera again follows and even stalks Cleo as she tries to move away from the crowd gathered around a street performer that swallows and regurgitates frogs; she disentangles herself, only to encounter a man piercing his flesh with needles. Even the people gathered on the street push and stare aggressively at her, and whatever was left of a safety zone around her is shattered. By the time she reaches the Dôme Café she is no longer able to stop and take her place, because, as de Certeau has suggested, 'to walk is to lack a place'. Cleo no longer belongs in what was previously familiar space. She is unable to settle at any table as the snippets of discussions around her show an incoherent cultural scene in which her own achievement in pop music is regarded as part of the problem.

With the second car ride, with Cleo's friend at the wheel of an open-top car, the film moves to its most dynamic cinematic sequence. This imaginary move from life to cinema proves decisive for it seems to bring Cleo back into the world in a new way, and through the apparatus of the cinema. The sequence is primarily filmed from the outside in, instead of from the inside out as in the taxi ride. Thus the windshield of the small

Figure 2.12 Cleo and friend in the car; *Cleo from 5 to 7*, 1961.

sports car evokes the shape of the cinema screen that holds the two protagonists within it, especially since the camera frequently cuts out the rest
of the car (Figure 2.12). Not that the screen is entirely autonomous, of
course, as the arm gestures to indicate left and right turns wittily persist
in transgressing its boundaries. For this sequence, the film was shot with
fewer frames per minute than is usual, producing the effect of being
speeded up a little, as if generating an increased level of energy.[80] This
effect is only compounded by the screen (the windshield) being enmeshed
within a dynamic urban environment that brings many speeding circuits
into contact with each other. As already noted, the car zooms across a
set of streets around the train station of Montparnasse, which produces
movement and speed through different modes of transit. At one point, the
screen of the car is itself entirely framed by a local train, a long-distance
train, many cars and buses all crisscrossing simultaneously in different
directions. Within this space of multiple transitions, the car's speed
appears to overcome what might be conceived as bodily limitations and is
even unleashed as a force by daring to confront physical limitations. The
sequence produces an exhilaration that must be attributed to the cinematic
screen itself. Whatever was weighty and disruptive in Cleo's walks has
now become light and agile. But it also transforms Paris itself into another
city, one no longer located in its mythic image of elegant boulevards and
shopping arcades. The heightening of sensation through the speed and

intensity produced by the screen both opens the body to the imagination and brings visibility to the relentless changeability of time. Perhaps what is being claimed for the cinema screen's production of time is that time is not exclusively a property of the body, yet it can unleash an awareness that the body is also always in time and this awareness must include the life force, but also death.

It is in this context that Cleo and her friend stop at the cinema where the friend's boyfriend is showing a short silent film. Entitled '*Les Fiances du Pont MacDonald*', this film within the film turns back the clock on the city of Paris and features Jean Luc Godard and Anna Karina as lovers that enact two possible futures. Shot at sixteen frames per second, the film appears speeded up and, as with silent film,[81] it revels in the wonder of bodily movement itself and film's ability to intensify and reverse movement and time. The two sequences in the short silent film are inversions of each other, both staged by Canal Saint-Denis on the staircase of the bridge by Boulevard McDonald.[82] When Karina leaves her lover, she descends a high flight of stairs, falls flat on the ground and suddenly dies, but when the sequence is repeated – after her lover takes off his dark glasses (Godard was known for always wearing dark glasses) – the tones change from black to white and she not only lives but there is a happy ending for the lovers (Figure 2.13). The difference, then, is attributed to the effect of the glasses and thus to seeing. Within this humorous take on the innocence and whimsy of the silent film, there is, no doubt, a satirical take on the preten-

Figure 2.13 Woman descending stairs in a silent film; *Cleo from 5 to 7*, 1961.

sions of New Wave film, and with Godard's lofty claims about film. Yet the film also offers a succinct version of what other films within the film aspire to reach. The glasses become another version of the cinema screen, a means to see and to transform not only the view but also oneself. Both the glasses in the silent film, and the film screens evoked in the film, share what has been called 'the transformative power of looking', and its effects have been with Cleo as she moves through the city, and with the viewer as they have been spending time in her film.[83] For both the experience will be transformative and entail a new attentiveness to time, exuberance and pleasure unleashed by the cinema itself.

Thus Cleo's increasing sense of her body in time and in the world around her (demonstrated in the last bus journey) is attributable less to an internal transformation through exchanges within urban space, and more to a transformation within the time produced by the screen in relation to urban space. The result of this new exuberance is a performative self, comfortable within one's body but aware of its limits. On her way to Park Montsouris, where Cleo opts to visit after dropping off her friend and before heading for her medical appointment, she asks the taxi driver to slow down in order to watch her friend as she joyfully rushes up a set of monumental stairs twirling as she ascends (Figure 2.14). This is the performance that Cleo herself will give, in reverse, when she first enters the park and finds in a lavish nature-draped staircase a space that finally she can occupy with some certainty but also awareness (Figure 2.15). Cleo's

Figure 2.14 Cleo's friend rushing up the stairs; *Cleo from 5 to 7*, 1961.

Figure 2.15 Cleo descending the stairs in Park Montsouris; *Cleo from 5 to 7*, 1961.

performance as she descends the stairs is also another version of the silent film, although now filled not with the wonder of cinema's production of bodily movement but with cinema's unleashing of a life force through the production of time. Antoine informs Cleo that this very day is the longest of the year being the first day of summer, something Cleo now understands through her recent bodily experience of waiting. Antoine also announces that this is the last day of his break from the Algerian war to which he must return, recalling that time in the film – the time the viewer has been particularly attentive to – has run out. Once again the time of the film and the time of the viewer are inextricable connected yet retain a critical difference. When Cleo finally, but almost accidentally, meets her doctor, he provides no resolution either way; he confirms her illness but suggests a way forward. But by then Cleo has already come to terms with herself in time, perhaps by having accepted her bodily time to be part of a larger sense of time, primarily by seeing herself in the film screen not as autonomously framed but as animated in time and re-engaged with the changing world.

The Circle (1999)

Cinematic time in Jafar Panahi's *The Circle* (*Dayereh*) is produced primarily through the choppy continuity of the hand-held camera shot, one that evokes circular movement while seeming to move haphazardly across urban space. This circular orientation intertwines the plight of women on the streets of Tehran, and it detaches this plight from the predictability of narrative time and its prescribed interpretation.[84] It becomes a circuit that enfolds urban space within the film screen where it is extended, constricted and reconfigured. In *The Circle* this constantly changing circuit is time itself, and it works to interlink that which is unconnected – the circumstances of separate women – and to disrupt that which is continuous – bodily movement and its ways of revealing space. In the process, it opens up unexpected possibilities.

The Circle has been widely recognised as explicitly political; it was banned in Iran for its references to prostitution, and in its international release it was discussed as introducing issues and forms of film-making that had been officially excluded from recent Iranian cinema.[85] A persistent claim is that the film departs from the traditions of Iranian cinema by using visual images with particular cultural and national charge, but now detached from those expected meanings.[86] The release of the film was entangled in highly publicised political conflicts, including the incident when Panahi,[87] on a trip to Buenos Aires to attend the screening of *The Circle* at a film festival, was detained in New York when he refused to be photographed and fingerprinted.[88] In 2010, Panahi was arrested in Iran and convicted of threatening the country's national security and of propaganda against the Islamic Republic, receiving a six-year prison sentence and a twenty-year ban on making films. While a large number of filmmakers and other supporters, both inside and outside Iran, have voiced their protest against Panahi's incarceration, his clandestine film-making while under house arrest, especially the recently smuggled *This is not a Film* (2011), has also generated critique; the Iranian film historian Hamid Dabashi has written that Panahi's disregard of the ban on film-making has in effect served to threaten the possibilities of Iranian film as a whole.[89]

Given its overt political context, the film itself has received relatively conventional interpretations. As the title suggests, the film draws on the concept of the circle, implying linked sequences that at one point join up with the first sequence and starts again. The circular structure of the film begins with the opening of a window within an enclosed space and ends with the shutting of a similar kind of window in another enclosed space. At the start, a woman approaches the shut window and once it is opened asks about her daughter who has just given birth (Figure 2.6). The mother's primary concern is with the sex of the newborn and the news that it is a girl prompts her sudden departure from the building; the camera begins to follow her but suddenly focuses on a younger female relative who also comes out to the street. This discontinuity in terms of people and continu-

Figure 2.16 Shut window in medical ward; *The Circle*, 1999.
(Courtesy of Celluloid Dreams, Paris.)

ity in terms of movement will remain the pattern through which the circle is formed and changed, again and again. When one woman disappears from the camera's view another will take her place, until the last scene in which a woman re-enters what might well be the same institution featured at the start of the film. The camera follows the woman into a cell, and as it slowly pans around we recognise all the women that have been seen throughout the film on the streets of the city. A window opens and a guard calls the name of the woman who gave birth at the start of the film, but we are told that she is no longer there as she has been moved to a nearby ward. The metal window shuts suddenly almost like a trap. The circle has closed but has something not changed in the course of this one day?

With such a charged image of closure, one might well concede that the situation of these women (or of women in general) is and will remain the same. The circle may well imply cyclical time, which is repetitive but unchanging and is thus associated with biology or nature. By locating the precarious and even perilous situation of women within fundamentalist Iranian urban culture within the idea of the circle, the film sets up an overdetermined proposition, which appears to have very few places to go if it seeks to raise new possibilities. The film has been praised for dealing directly with women's situation within Iranian culture, and for making the fraught issue of women's visibility the central theme.[90] Yet, in film reviews, the idea of the circle is frequently discussed as a formal visual device, suggesting that aesthetic concerns override political ones.

We consider how the idea of the circle works in relation to time, and we start from the premise that the circle and its varying repetitions serve to make us think about the multiple possibilities of time and *within* time. In particular these possibilities pertain to women's fraught relation to space – urban space – and thus time, and the sequence of time, is always produced through a close examination of the relation between internal and external experience of urban space.

Three women on a temporary pass from prison seek to leave the city of Tehran but encounter obstacles at every turn. In their attempts to get money to buy bus tickets, they interconnect with other women whose circumstances are not the same yet who also find themselves in a web of diminishing or even disappearing options. In the film the women confront their situation by walking, running, hiding, all in the effort to remain invisible within urban space. The issue of seeing and being seen is central to film in general, but in *The Circle* it is particularly fraught. If one takes into account that the veil or hijab has been regarded as one of the most charged signs of Iranian cinema, the basis of the circle as a process of seeing and being seen brings the film directly into the terrain of this controversial issue.[91] The veiling of women, a system imposed by the post-revolutionary Islamic government, has been discussed as standing for the nation in problematic ways and requiring innovative strategies from Iranian film, especially as cinema has inscribed within it the pleasures of spectatorship.[92] It has been argued that in *The Circle* the veil has become at least partially liberated from official meanings.[93] Yet from the start the engagement between viewer and screen is all about the intermediary of the veil. After the arrest of their friend, two of the women try in every possible way to remain unseen from authorities and by implication from the viewer. They hide behind a nearby huge sport utility vehicle and peak around it to see what is transpiring on the street; they watch, glance, turn their heads this way and that way to look, not as a way to control their environment but as a way to be attentive to its dangers. When they are unable to assess the situation, they try to conceal their prison clothing by putting chadors over their heads as they escape down the street (Figure 2.17). For the camera this becomes a sequence of undulating fabric fluttering in the wind as they make sudden turns, around people, vehicles, street corners. These circular motions bring visual form to the opposing potentials of flight and entrapment, potentials that evoke two opposing modes of time. In some ways this recalls the urgency of seeing for survival in *Bicycle Thieves*, and even the failures of sight in negotiating a dangerous urban space. And while the urban culture of consumerism and spectacle in *Cleo from 5 to 7* offers different pleasures to the viewer, it too raises the question of the collusion between the film's implied critique of objectifying

Figure 2.17 Women fleeing; *The Circle*, 1999. (Courtesy of Celluloid Dreams, Paris.)

modes of seeing and what is on offer to the viewer. But in *The Circle* the contradictions multiply and the critical perspective on seeing and being seen requires to be refracted through cultural differences, which will be different depending on audiences, as well as through traditions of the film apparatus.

The camera reveals unexpected strategies and prompts the viewer to think about 'seeing' again. With the camera keeping for the most part to long shots, which appear to be unframed and haphazard in their continuity, there is a sense of by-passing the film apparatus and capturing what is real on the street. Yet the camera, by moving in unexpected ways, also announces its function as a technology of seeing. What the camera does not do, however, is construct the viewpoint of a character in the film or bring to that character the qualities and appearance of a subject. In fact, the camera treats everything in front of it the same, retaining a disinterested perspective that creates a distance, even when it is photographing someone close up. It does this by flattening out the view and catching everything equally, rather than privileging facial features or the perspective of a character. The use of long shots that meander across urban space as if unedited for lengthy periods of time create the sense of unplanned spatial orientation. Rather than following a character (as in *Cleo from 5 to 7*) or even revealing bodily movement (as in *Bicycle Thieves*), the camera produces the sense that what has come into visibility is in some ways by chance. This approach brings a vividness to whatever the camera captures, to the point that the materiality of things become as vibrant as human action, and everything on the street seems as present as the particular women to whom it devotes most attention. In a well-known effect of the documentary, the view offered by the camera is not limited to the people with which it happens to spend the most time, people who in any case become visible (and thus meaningful) in very tenuous and disjointed ways.

This is not to say that narrative components are not caught by the camera's moves. After all, while the women that come in and out of the film screen do not become characters with the kinds of motivations and subjectivities of traditional film narratives, their circumstances and shared urgent situations are revealed. This is done as if by chance, in snippets of conversations and in the way the camera encounters and pursues them. As paths cross, we begin to recognise that they are linked on a chain, one that conjoins desperate personal situations but not laden with emotional narrative surplus. This circle, the narrative circle, emerges as tenuous and disjointed and only through the presence of the camera does it gain some visibility. Indeed the screen both reveals the links of a narrative circle and shows them to be entirely transitory and lacking in symbolic weight; there is no indication that the links in the circle make the circle stronger or serve to forge any sense of comradeship between the women. On the contrary, fear and uncertainty seems to constantly undermine collectivity, and we are left with urban circuits that resemble each other through their circularity without repetition or completion.

But what does the camera capture as it follows someone, more often than not someone trying to escape from being seen? The camera spatialises much more than it describes or characterises the women in question. The uncertainties of the women's way of occupying urban space is given increasing attention as the camera itself disrupts the stability of that occupation. This is achieved not only when the camera follows women who run and seek to conceal themselves, but also when the camera suddenly stops and waits for a particular woman to consider their situation in space. As already noted, the camera, whenever possible, moves around things bringing a sense of physicality to circuits of space, which is to say to time's presence in space. But the camera also goes out of its way to reveal the women's own experience of space through circular motions. In a remarkable instance, the young Nargess anxiously waits for her friend in an open internal courtyard of a factory filled with garment and textile workers who move across the camera in all directions. By the time she looks upwards towards the extended curving staircase, the camera has already gone there, following her friend back and forth as she seeks to connect with someone she perhaps knows. Suddenly the camera returns to Nargess and stops, for now it is she that reiterates the orientation of the camera when it fol-

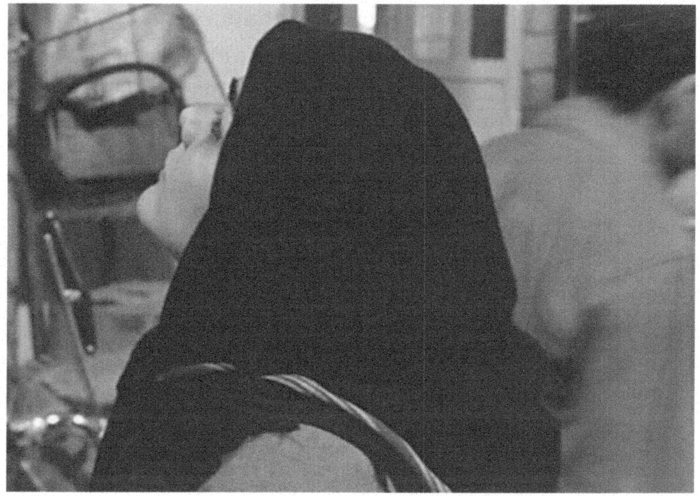

Figure 2.18 Nargess turning around; *The Circle*, 1999.
(Courtesy of Celluloid Dreams, Paris.)

Figure 2.19 Nargess turning back; *The Circle*, 1999.
(Courtesy of Celluloid Dreams, Paris.)

lowed the shape of the stairs (Figure 2.18). Nargess moves around and the still long shot shows her from every angle for a full 360 degrees (Figure 2.19). In this sequence, unlike the one that the camera activated by moving across the curving stairs, the movements and noises in the building suddenly recede, still visible but opening up a different kind of space in the foreground where Nargess is situated, one entirely embodied but also imaginary and outside the narrative moment of urgency.

In effect, the camera activates time throughout the film, and reveals it in a way not usually expected from the continuous hand-held shot. Time becomes palpable but also unpredictable and incomplete. There is always an uncertainty to the time frame during which the camera becomes attentive to movement on the street, and brings attention and even visibility to someone in the midst of traversing urban space. This attention can be intense, as the person is brought into extreme close-up shots and their conversations are overheard, but then something will interrupt the intensity and for no apparent reason it will turn elsewhere, pre-empting continuity and resolution. These indeterminate circuits of the camera produce time as duration, which is not at the beck and call of bodily movement but is produced through an unpredictable and transient viewing point. As already noted, time as duration does not offer the resolutions warranted in narrative sequence and it always has within it the potential for change, fragmentation and dispersal. Yet duration does produce the idea of a circle, although not one limited to the movements of a single body or even a number of interlinked bodies. This kind of circle is indecipherable for it has no beginning and no end. Thus although the structure of the film implies an unbroken circle forged through bodily movement, the screen shows another idea of the circle, one about time as fragmented, inconsistent and potential.

The camera, then, looms large as it moves across urban space, yet through its idiosyncrasies it also reveals an inability to penetrate urban space and bring it fully into visibility. Indeed, the relation of camera to urban space is fraught, and although it does not appear to seek to conceal anything in particular, it also tends to cut off spaces, make sudden turns and pass over spaces in ways that leaves one wondering what has been missed. Within this surface of the city, life in Tehran seems to be no different from life in any modern city. It is activated through busy streets, market exchanges and systems of transport that move people from one place to another. One might consider the initial situation of the three prisoners to be exceptional, the matter of film narratives. Yet it does not take long to recognise that they are not exceptional and that for many, especially for women, and even more for some women, survival is always in question.

Given the political character of the issues addressed in the film, the street and urban space in Tehran is a crucial component in the interpretation of the concept of the circle. In comparison to other cities discussed in this chapter, Tehran presents a very different kind of urbanism.[94] The city is shown in extreme close-ups not enabling orientating overviews or interrelations between spaces. The historical core of Tehran was altered through a process of modernisation that has been compared to the Haussmanisation of Paris.[95] A division emerged between the opening of boulevards and broad streets outside the historical core to accommodate new forms of transportation, and the narrow streets and pathways within which domestic buildings were located. With the opportunities presented by oil resources, Tehran was transformed through industrial production and the influx of foreign products and global exchanges. As a consumer city, Tehran developed a middle class that opted to relocate in new residential areas while the historical core continued to be occupied by poorer communities, including displaced agricultural communities that migrated to the city once industry developed to work in the factories. In the film there is a mixture of the busy thriving modern city, overcrowded due to large vehicles, and the quiet secluded alleys and passageways that seem to exist apart from the pressures of modernisation. These become spaces both of concealment from the movements of the city and of entrapment as constraining family bonds are shown to operate outside the purview of public space.

Urban space emerges as unreadable but also as permeated with danger and violence. Fear of authority is not reserved for certain kinds of places where one might presume surveillance and exposure, but is always potential within urban space as a whole. Dabashi wrote:

> violence in Panahi's cinema is like a phantom: you see through it, but it lacks a source or physical presence – who has perpetrated it is made intentionally amorphous. The result is a sense of fear and anxiety that lurks in every frame of his film, but it is a fear without an identifiable referent.[96]

There is no safe place, whether public spaces of the market or the train station, the deserted narrow alleys of domestic residences, or the enclosures of shops, hospitals or cars. Violence is what underlies the physicality of urban space and it is just a matter of time as to when it becomes visible.[97] Within the first few minutes that we encounter the three women who have just been released from prison on a day pass, they are separated as they encounter different forms of authority that question their presence on the street. The attempt to connect with someone they knew from prison through her father at a newsstand only serves to disrupt the everyday movements of the street as they bring suspicion to those around the newsstand. While narrative components constantly appear and disappear, the circuits of the street continue to emerge and to bring doubt and uncertainty about what is to come and how it will come. Nargess, left to her own devices, manages to find out where the father of their friend lives, and enters the small alleyways that appear to provide refuge from the open street. But as she reaches the house, it is the violence within that becomes more threatening and compels her to return back to the main street and thus to become separated from the camera that had followed her there.

In effect, the gaps of knowledge constantly registered in relation to the narrative turn out to be primarily gaps in urban space. Unlike *Cleo from 5 to 7*, in which filmic transformations through framing and speed change our view of time in urban space, in *The Circle* it is not the apparatus of film that produces discontinuitty. The breaks in continuity and thus in comprehension are within the conditions of urban space itself.

When considered in relation to urban space, the linkages within the circle are not only fragile – in that it is not held together by narrative sequence – but also intense – in that they are both prompted and broken by the sudden eruption of violence. But there are disruptions to this permeation of violence within urban space. The first time the camera stays with a character for any length of time, it does so when Nargess is first separated from her friend and is uncertain what to do. The intensification of urban space through the expectations of violence is suddenly disrupted as she starts to notice her surroundings, which is to say the things going on in urban life that do not have to do with her own situation. She looks and listens in ways that seem to suggest an entirely different space. She observes a man decorating a car, apparently for a wedding, and becomes entirely engrossed in small details: how he touches the decorations, drinks from a water fountain and splashes the embroidered wedding shirt that he is wearing.

When her friend returns, she is less interested in what has happened to her friend and insists on showing her a painting that is amongst many objects for sale in a market. She interprets this painting, a copy of Vincent Van Gogh's 'Blue lilies', for her friend as an image of her home in Raziliq with its surrounding hills. The young woman explains that it is a paradise to which they must return. Her visual attention extends to criticising the painting for failing to include a certain patch of flowers that are to be found in her home town. And it is not just visual distraction but also audial as she hears a group of traditional musicians playing as they walk along the market area and follows them, again becoming distracted by the shop windows and all of their varieties of visual pleasures.

These distractions might recall Deleuze's argument about how the unhinging of narrative brings forth purely ocular and audio cinematic moments that in effect interrupt the non-cinematic narrative and produce another kind of time. Indeed these moments of distracted observation remove Nargess from the immediate danger on the street to the larger problem of belonging, and perhaps to her realisation of the impossibility of returning home. But she is also engaged with the street and her moments of distraction return to the life of the street, which offers a kind of in-between space and prompts her to encircle the space and attempt to find a way out, even if unsure of where she is going. When she is back to paying attention to the dangers of the street, she seems to be unsettled to the point that she does things that make the return home literally impossible. Her friend Arezu puts her in the bus to the bus station twice and in every instance the young woman follows her friend out. When she finally reaches the bus station and after many obstacles manages to buy a ticket, she suddenly decides to buy a present even though the bus is to depart in ten minutes. Again she is distracted through the shop windows, apparently oblivious to the passing time, and suddenly stops at a shop when she sees the embroidered shirt of the groom and goes in to buy one. When after many delays she acquires it and suddenly realises the time, she rushes, only to be stopped by a police search of those boarding the bus.

The visual reminder of incarceration, of prison bars, is constantly evoked in the film and also works to produce another idea of the circle, in this instance as literally jail. Perhaps the most striking is when Nargess suddenly realises that she will miss her bus and runs across an upper gallery of the train station (Figure 2.20). Her sense of urgency is intensified as she runs around the circular gallery composed of vertical partitions that stress the circularity and mobility of the scene while simultaneously framing Nargess in a kind of prison. She is running to the bus but also away from the modes that seek to imprison her. Or is she running towards imprisonment?

The Circle manages to maintain a striking tension between the fear of incarceration and the fear of abandonment. In the film these seemingly opposite conditions are entirely intertwined and associated with location in urban space. The second occasion when the camera lingers over someone is when it focuses on Pari, the daughter of the man with the newsstand; Pari is a prisoner who we find out escaped together with the women let out for the day. In this instance we are offered considerable narrative detail as she explains to various friends how she ended up in jail with her lover who was then executed. And we learn that she left the prison in order to get a permit to have an abortion since without her husband's permission she cannot have one. While this sequence of the film, mostly located in a large hospital, verges on a structured narrative, the attempts by Pari to appeal to a former prisoner to get the permission from her new doctor husband conveys very effectively the

Figure 2.20 Nargess running across the station gallery; *The Circle*, 1999.
(Courtesy of Celluloid Dreams, Paris.)

tenuous narrative links between the women but also the shared precarious position within space, in this instance internal space. The constant presence of surveillance in these spaces is evoked in shots of Pari waiting for her friend to return from seeing the doctor. The view through a window into the surgery space returns us to the start of the circle and will lead to its endpoint. Each instance is a stop towards incarceration but also towards abandonment. Pari leaves the hospital in what is now night, making concealment both more possible and more frightening. And as if to drive the point home, it is at this moment that Pari herself observes another woman trying to abandon her little daughter on the street.

As in *Cleo from 5 to 7*, women's relation to the street is not the same in the course of walking as when moving inside a car or bus. In *The Circle* the car is no less dangerous but it does give rise to opportunity. The mother that leaves her child walks straight ahead on the street determined not to look back, and as she does unseen cars slow down and their occupants proposition her. When she finally gets into a car, again determined to get away from the site of the abandonment, the camera shows her from the windshield staring only ahead. Too late she realises, as do we, that she has been entrapped by a police officer and will be arrested. When he stops where another police car has detained another woman, a moment of interruptions enables the first woman to slip out of the car and into the darkness of the city, all while the second woman looks on and gives a gesture of recognition and acceptance that on this occasion it is the other woman who can get away. It is not coincidental that the interruption is partly caused by traffic including a car with a bride and groom, which evokes the earlier car decorated for a wedding. The car is itself a contested space, offering various kinds of entrapment and opportunity.

Given the dangers of becoming visible within the urban environment of Tehran, it is particularly intriguing that the last time the camera follows someone around for any length of time it is a woman who spends most of this time rejecting the eye of the camera. At the end of *The Circle* the woman who gets arrested for prostitution is moved to a van that will take her, together with several male prisoners and guards, back to the prison. In this sequence nothing actually happens other than the camera focuses for a long period of time on the woman who looks straight ahead and away from the camera. This refusal of her look forces us to look at her with some intensity. She is no longer imbued by fear of her environment and in fact seems to accept what is ahead. But even this non-narrative moment presents its opportunities as she smokes a forbidden cigarette made possible when the others in the van are distracted by singing. When she enters the jail cell in which all the other women are found, she finally looks around and her sweeping, circular view is projected through the camera. The circle is now literally a prison, but filled with all the other circular circuits that have opened up the circle to the unpredictability of time.

The three films discussed produce cinematic time that is inextricably connected to their engagement with urban space. These are not films that use urban space as context, but films that through the relation of film and urban space show the importance of time in offering new political possibilities. *The Circle* may be different from *Cleo from 5 to 7* in revealing the gaps within the time of urban space itself and pointing to its uncertainties. The latter, meanwhile, gives prominence to the cinematic apparatus in forging a new and potentially enhancing experience of the time of modernity. *Bicycle Thieves*, perhaps more than the other two films, seeks to find a way to consider the fraught relation between bodily movement and urban time, and to convey that the gaps between the two can become a site of thinking about new possibilities.

Remembering to Forget to Remember: the Persistence of Memory and the Cinematic City

In his influential writing on history and memory, Pierre Nora mused that 'we speak so much of memory because there is so little of it left'.[1] With massive historical transformations, among the most significant being the disruptions associated with urbanisation, collective living memory has given way, he argues, to a different kind of memory, which is 'above all, archival'.[2] Modern memory works through various sites and systems of retrieval that are 'intensely retinal and powerfully televisual'.[3] In this regard, he notes the 'omnipotence' of imagery and cinema.[4] Recent debates on the archive have complicated the question of memory even further by arguing for the importance of the processes of memory in relation to images rather than the contents of the archive itself. These debates ask: what is the value of retaining the past through images and how does it serve the present or even the future? Jacques Derrida in *Archive Fever* proposes that the archive can work as a critical tool to think about how our present and future is shaped as we persist in thinking that we are dealing with the past. He argues that the form of archived materials is crucial to the kind of memory that it is possible to forge within it. Analogue film is quite different than more recent digital technologies in making us think about what it means to remember the past. The Internet, now the ultimate archive, is a site of rampant amnesia as well as a site from which information can never be erased and thus never entirely forgotten.

Memory and physical place also have a long-standing link, including the tradition of memory palaces.[5] In this mnemonic system, the things to be remembered are associated with specific physical locations, and it is through spatial relations that memory is nurtured and maintained. In early modern memory systems the link between place and memory was not intended to be static, but rather to engage the reader in a constant process of revisiting places in order to rework memory and deal with the challenges of the present. Film has taken up this link and used it to produce critical thinking about how memory mediates our relation to urban space in the present and even the future. Christopher Nolan's 2000 *Memento* is a case in point. This film follows a man with short-term memory loss as he moves around the city, apparently looking for the man who killed his wife. In his movements, the man uses places in the city not to remember his past – something he is keen to forget – but to constantly recharge his short-term memory. In doing so he takes Polaroid photographs, upon which he then writes some piece of information. We (the audience) see the process backwards, a device made evident through the Polaroid photograph in which the image disappears rather than appears. Through this mixture of the filmic and the photo image, we start to see how memory is forged always within the contingencies of the moment rather than as a verifiable truth. In the process the film makes visible the splintering of time into multiple surfaces, what Deleuze in his discussion of memory and film has likened to the shimmering facets of a crystal.

In this chapter we consider different ways in which film works as a kind of archive or materialisation of various forms of memory. We consider film as a repository of images from which new histories and memories keep re-emerging in unexpected ways; as a medium not just for representing but evoking nostalgia; and as a technology that mediates the indeterminacy of trauma, as a means of forging memory in the present out of the indecipherable and unstable remnants of memories from the past.

Archival Memory and Urban Space:
Los Angeles Plays Itself (2003); *The Exiles* (1961)

Archives are where fragments of the past are housed. They mediate our relationship to the past by stimulating memory, serving memory and structuring what can and cannot be remembered. Despite the modern compulsion to archive, not all material is archived and archives are places where authority – legal, state, colonial, patriarchal – resides, through the literal materials assembled there and the classificatory systems that structure them. The archive is fundamental to liberal forms of governmentality and the formation of the liberal subject, and to modern notions of 'the public'. Patrick Joyce has argued in the British context that the free publicly accessible library was essential to the formation in the nineteenth century of the self-observing and self-governing democratic liberal subject.[6]

Though the limits of liberalism and the disciplinary potential of the archive are most often emphasised,[7] critics recognise that the archive also functions as a potential site of agonistic politics. Early public library collections, for instance, were constituted with the 'sociologising' intent (parallel to the 'anthropologising' intent of the colonial archive) of providing information about the condition of 'the people'. This has meant that, as well as being used to plan and manage the population and create the conditions for traditions of liberal governance through individual self-help, the archive has been and continues to be a resource for radical social critique and collective agitation. So too, the classification schemas that structure the archive are haunted by their exclusions. In colonial contexts, Ann Stoler has proposed that archives are not simply sites of skewed or biased colonial knowledge but are 'condensed sites of epistemological and political anxieties' where one can read colonial worries about what can and cannot be known about colonial subjects. The archive, as a site of colonial administration and control, simultaneously can reveal unexpected voices, what Stoler calls 'disabled histories'. This occurs, for instance, when she detects in the Dutch colonial archive 'a few brief words in Malay, seized from a "native informant", not given the due of a narrative at all'.[8] In a related vein, Michel de Certeau has argued that, by revealing bodily evidence such as stammering, forgetting and repeating, the archive holds within in it embodied memory that cannot be inscribed into text as history. Emergent experiences, bodily evidence and momentary eruptions of the voices of the marginalised can destabilise the archive and offer glimpses of a 'world out there shot through with other strange worlds'.[9]

The utility of the concept of the archive, in Thomas Osborne's view, is an elasticity that allows us 'to oscillate between literalism and idealism'[10] Tracing the etymology of the term, Jacques Derrida locates the origins of the archive in the domicile of the magistrate; hence the close links he traces between the archive and the administration of law. Joyce, as noted, in the first instance locates the archive in the public library. For Michel Foucault, the archive is not an empirical concept but a functional one, a system governing the classification of thought.

Within this unsettled oscillating concept of the archive, the city itself keeps emerging as a key archive and site for articulating memory. Writing about a local historian's interest in uncovering a hidden history of the Jewish community in Bransk, Poland, for instance, Eva Hoffman notes that his desire to pursue this project came through traces in the urban landscape: 'he kept stumbling on mysterious stones beneath his feet'.[11] At the end of his close reading of the design of British public libraries as archival spaces, Joyce asks: 'But what is the archive?' and concludes, 'It is about the city and the meanings and uses of space. Therefore the street is my archive, the built environment is my archive.' And while the public library 'certainly archives the street and the built environment . . . it does not exhaust their meaning, which is produced out of the experience of these things, an experience refracted through memory . . .'[12]

Not surprisingly some of the same tensions that emerge in relation to the archive in general shape discussions of the city as archive. Monuments are official sites for remembering official history and simultaneously forgetting or erasing counterclaims to space; they are often dead zones that close off the possibilities for urban politics and contestation.[13] But for some theorists the city archive of monumental spaces – like all official archives – is haunted by what is repressed.[14] The entire urban fabric is a sedimentation of the past that can be richly evocative of memory, and these memories can destabilise the present by giving uncanny inklings of other possible worlds that have existed and can be made to exist in the same space. Shared urban space can provide the means of developing and living – in concrete, material, mundane, routinised ways – shared collective memories; disruptions to and destruction of shared space can occasion and stimulate critical thought and action.[15]

The utility of the archive as concept and practice has not been lost on film-makers or film scholars[16] and Charlotte Brunsdon makes note of 'an archival turn' in the recent literature on and practice of making films on and about cities.[17] This takes the form of film historians studying early film industries, tracking down and archiving long-vanished film locations, re-releasing archived films on DVD and/or the exploration of 'the archival power of film' by contemporary film-makers. We focus here on how this archival power might work in relation to memory in and of cities and film.

While we wish to explore some general arguments, we are not legislating where the radicality of the archive lies – in this or that particular use – in part because a critical use of the archive might take shape differently in different contexts, or differently in the same context at different historical moments. Cities are unique sedimentations of urban development with particular social and geopolitical histories; they afford different possibilities and provoke distinctive responsibilities to remember at different times. The criticality of Patrick Keiller's filmic installation/exhibition, *The City of the Future*, for instance, has to be understood in relation to the cities on view – British cities filmed between 1896 and 1906. Keiller describes *The City of the Future* as 'a virtual landscape'[18] created from sixty-eight single-shot 'actuality' films, each roughly three minutes in length. Whether and how Keiller's critical intent has been achieved is a matter of some dispute[19] but in most instances critics locate its potential in a disruptive and uncanny familiarity the viewer may have with the old city fabric (and a recognition that past utopic ideals are unrealised in present-day cities), and the simultaneous strangeness and familiarity of the past.

Not only can the preoccupations of the present (such as globalisation) be detected in the past, to see the buildings on one's street or in one's city living a different life in the past denaturalises the present and 'exposes a profound disjuncture between society and space'.[20] There is a potential within Keiller's project, critics argue, to reawaken a sense of open-ended possibility and 'de-create the real'[21] in a way that might provoke aspirations for a different future. The point may seem trite but this critical reaction to Keiller's film and the use of archival material in this way depend on both a contemporary urban infrastructure in which Victorian architecture endures, and memories of empire, in which earlier processes of globalisation resonate.

We have elected to think about the archive and memory in the context of a very different urban form, Los Angeles, through Thom Andersen's 2003 documentary film *Los Angeles Plays Itself*. In the case of Los Angeles the issue is not so much the ways in which the tensions between filmic and actual remnants of the architectural past provoke memory and critical reflection on the present and future but the systematic erasure of whole sections of the downtown infrastructure and the ways that this is intertwined with the construction of memory through film in both non-critical and critical ways. Andersen created his 169-minute filmic 'essay' by stitching together a vast archive of mostly Hollywood film; his film is largely a montage of extracts from 217 films dating from 1913 to 2001, all filmed in Los Angeles, with voice-over first-person narration of a text written by Andersen and performed by Encke King.

Andersen's film, which Madison Brookshire likens to 'a manifesto' and 'something like a new film theory',[22] is in the first instance an exposé of an inadvertent collusion between Hollywood film-makers and the production and erasure of collective memory in Los Angeles. Andersen quotes approvingly a remark that film critic, Richard Schnickel, made about the noir classic *Double Indemnity*: 'You could charge LA as a co-conspirator in the crimes the movie relates.' The reverse can be said, Andersen seems to say, about the history of urban development in Los Angeles: the vision of LA that the movies relate has been a co-conspirator in the crime of urban development. More often than not Los Angeles is invisible or entirely malleable as a cinematic place: we are shown Los Angeles cast as picturesque Switzerland, as rice paddies in China, as Chicago. In Norman Klein's felicitous phrasing, 'Los Angeles remains the most photographed and least remembered city in the world'.[23] But Andersen also uses archival film footage to uncover a darker tendency to distort history by consistently rendering certain landscapes and architecture, for example modern architecture, as villainous and decadent. The pervasive influence of film noir

Figure 3.1 Bunker Hill as shown in *The Exiles*. (Courtesy of Milestone Film & Video.)

and crime dramas served to create the impression of Los Angeles as 'world capital of adultery and murder'. 'Nowhere else is evil so banal.' Many of these films were shot in downtown Los Angeles, in particular Bunker Hill (Figure 3.1), and Andersen, like Norman Klein and Mike Davis, argues that the portrayal of downtown in Hollywood film is not incidental to its vulnerability to urban renewal: 'noir cinema, like noir literature, reinforces the primitivist fantasies of anti-tourism, the lingering panic that erases neighbourhoods in yet another way'.[24] In a massive restructuring of downtown that began in the late 1950s, the houses in Bunker Hill were raised, the hill levelled, and a landscape of skyscrapers was built in its place. Other downtown neighbourhoods – Chinatown, Little Italy, Chavez Ravine – were similarly levelled 'without a trace';[25] 'virtually no ethnic community downtown was allowed to keep its place'.[26]

If noir and crime movies of the 1940s and 1950s created the atmospherics that supported the common sense of urban renewal, Andersen argues that Hollywood films took on the city's problems explicitly in the 1970s, after the riots in the Watts neighbourhood in south Los Angeles in August 1965, in ways that reshaped collective memory and political consciousness. Although he claims that Los Angeles always has been 'a city with no history' in which nostalgia is the 'dominant note', what changed in the 1970s in his view was that Hollywood films began to explicitly engage with the history of Los Angeles and search for explanations of what had gone wrong. The iconic film is Roman Polanski's *Chinatown* (1974), a fictional account of personal greed, moral decay and civic corruption around water and land development. Andersen, as do many others,[27] argues that this film has been read – inaccurately – as a docudrama. While scholars such as John Walton point to the fact that environmental activists nonetheless have used to good effect the popular belief in the veracity of this film, Andersen is less sanguine: *Chinatown* and films like it (e.g. *LA Confidential* (1997), *Who Framed Roger Rabbit* (1988)) suggest that there is a secret history to Los Angeles that lies beyond public memory and public influence. These films intimate that cynicism and political inactivity are rational responses in the face of a collective memory of backroom deals, collusion among elites and police corruption.

Very little of a sustained critical scholarly nature appears to have been written on *Los Angeles Plays Itself* and not all of what exists is positive. Film theorist Paul Arthur felt that Andersen focused too extensively on Hollywood film and not enough on alternative urban visions of the city's avant-garde (which is perhaps to miss the point of the film).[28] Richard Lippe felt that Andersen's premise is too simplistic: 'the overriding implication seems to be that just about everything produced within mainstream cinema is dishonest and reactionary. This position needs a more developed argument than he provides.'[29] Nick James says the film 'enters well-worn fields of complaint about Los Angeles, most of them rendered by Mike Davis' book *City of Quartz* (ironically a book whose factual basis has been called into question. . .)'.[30] What is particularly striking about the latter two criticisms is how literally these critics are reading the film as text. But how does *Los Angeles Plays Itself* work as a film and not simply as a didactic argument? What distinctive opportunities for the production of counter-memory arise from a filmic archive?

Certainly Andersen uses the archive in a traditional way – as evidence. As an evidentiary resource, the archive 'confers credibility' and 'ethical authority' to those who use it.[31] To substantiate his claims about the destruction of the lively neighbourhood of Bunker Hill, Andersen turns to a vast film archive to document its manufactured destruction. Because 'the movies loved Bunker Hill', Hollywood films unwittingly documented its transformation: in the 1940s it appeared as a solid working-class neighbourhood; by the 1950s it was a favourite location for noir films and was represented as home to crooks, artists and prostitutes, a representation, as noted above, that was not incidental to its demise. Andersen places alongside these latter representations portrayals by independent film-makers in the 1960s and 1970s of on-going racialised communities in central and south Los Angeles: an urban Native community located in Bunker Hill in *The Exiles* (1961), a Mexican community in *El Norte* (1983) and African American communities in Watts in *Bush Mama* (1975), *Bless Their Little Hearts* (1983) and *Killer of Sheep* (1977). These films, he argues, 'prove' that 'there once was a city here before they tore it down and created simulacrum.'

Andersen's film is a montage of film extracts; as such it clearly reveals its own constructedness. It also works to de-naturalise both film and the city in a more fulsome way. Andersen sutures extracts from different films that use the same site in very different ways to make visible the fact that film is an unreliable archive of anything but itself; there is no trustworthy relationship between filmic representation and place. At the same time, Hollywood film has so penetrated the actual landscape that the reliability of the built environment is itself questionable. Andersen takes us on a tour of buildings scattered around the city that we would read as having a 'real' function but are actually permanent film locations, for instance a McDonalds that is a dedicated film set. The built environment is shown to be misleading, difficult to read and thoroughly intertwined with filmic representation.

But how is the film archive used in more subtle *filmic* ways to de-naturalise and re-orient popular memory in Los Angeles? How is Andersen's film pedagogical in a less didactic way? A film extract is not the same as a text or even a photograph lodged in an archive. As a moving image it brings the past alive in quite a different way. Capturing the body in movement, it possibly has a greater potential to 'stammer' in the ways described by de Certeau. In theorising the aliveness of film, Mary Ann Doane,[32] as do many other film theorists, focuses on the temporal aspect of film, the way that film immerses the viewer. Doane argues that film brings the viewer into an experience of time that is lost within modern capitalist societies; in the latter, time is rationalised and systematised by the discipline of the clock. The immersive experience of film offers a 'counter dream' of full presence. In *Los Angeles Plays Itself* we enter this dream in some of the extracts of films made by independent film-makers, which were shot in a neorealist style. Alert to the fact that a more militant film tradition was shut down within Los Angeles, David James criticises these neorealist films for framing minority histories in Los Angeles within a liberal humanist appeal for sympathy and understanding.[33] Nonetheless, films like *Bush Mama* immerse the viewer in another world and temporality, what Andersen (explicitly paraphrasing Deleuze) describes as 'spatialised, non-chronological time of meditation and memory'. What also needs to be restated is that these films immerse the viewer in places that also have been swept away through the forces of capitalist development. Actually immerse the viewer. Such an immersion can activate the question: to whom do these landscapes belong? The film is a montage of different knowledges of the same place; by bringing them into tension within the same film, Andersen destabilises one way of knowing, remembering and taking possession of a place.

Doane discusses at length another potential of the film archive for simultaneously opening the past and future: films are full of noise and this noisiness is aligned with contingency and the possibility of there emerging something interesting and unanticipated within the film itself. She argues that this is especially true for early actuality and neorealist films because the long take allows more opportunity for the unexpected to appear on film and for the eye to explore the image in order to detect it: the length of a long take 'situates it as an invitation to chance and unpredictability'.[34] What Andersen reveals is that we can read the archive of Hollywood film in this way as well. He states at the beginning of the film that movies are not about places; they are about stories. If the viewer is paying attention to place, he states, they are not following the story. He invites the viewer to re-engage their 'voluntary attention' to look at Los Angeles as represented in fictional film and to read fictional film as a kind of documentary archive. He does this in the didactic way described above but he also reads the noisiness of even Hollywood fictional films. Looking closely at a scene of *The Atomic City* (1952) as a crowd of fans leave Gilmore Field, which was a minor league baseball park destroyed in 1958, Andersen notes that real baseball fans were used in this scene, not professional extras. This is significant because production regulations, which would have been in play if professional extras had been used, prohibited any scene showing social intermingling of white and 'coloured' people. As a long take lingers over a clearly racially diverse crowd leaving the stadium (Figure 3.2), Andersen

Figure 3.2 Leaving Gilmore Field; *The Atomic City*, 1952.

ventures that Los Angeles was perhaps more comfortably integrated in the 1952 than it is today, a profound disruption of the meliorative version of history told within liberal multiculturalism.

Los Angeles Plays Itself has itself become part of a film archive and has been newly disruptive of urban memory in unanticipated ways. Andersen declares Kent MacKenzie's *The Exiles* to be the best movie made of Bunker Hill and shows a number of clips from it. *The Exiles* is a docu-drama, filmed in a style referred to as 'dirty realism', structured around the lives of three Native-Americans living in Bunker Hill. It was created from extended interviews with non-professional Native American cast members. In *The Exiles*, three main characters narrate monologues that they developed themselves in voice-overs as events unfold over the course of a single night (Figure 3.3).

MacKenzie, a non-Native American independent film-maker who was then a student at the University of Southern California film school, sought out participants/cast members who did not see their relationship to society or themselves as problems but were, rather, 'just living their lives'. Nonetheless, the production and reception of the film have not been without controversy and critical readings of the film locate this particular filmic archive as a site of colonial knowledge production and power relations.[35] Alcohol consumption became a central theme in the film[36] and whether the film confirms stereotypes about drunken Indians or is a realistic and nonjudgmental representation of the lives of many urban Native Americans at that time is a matter of dispute. The film

Figure 3.3 The morning after a night on Hill X, returning to Bunker Hill; *The Exiles*. (Courtesy of Milestone Film & Video.)

most clearly breaks away from these stereotypes in relation to the main woman protagonist, Yvonne, who does not drink alcohol and articulates (frustrated) ambitions for herself within the urban context. The film also reinscribes a familiar colonial geography, in which authentic Native life is segregated within the rural reserve. This occurs most obviously through a memory flashback of one of the three main protagonists. As Homer reads a letter from his family, his family members appear on the screen, apparently living a simple and contented existence on a romanticised reserve located in a sweeping foothills landscape, oddly familiar from Hollywood westerns.[37]

At the same time, the film remains to this day one of few films centred on urban Native Americans living in Los Angeles (or any city for that matter). Although Los Angeles alone had a population of 146,000 Native Americans in 1960, which was the largest urban Native American population in the United States, by the 1990s there was almost no trace of a Native American landscape 'anywhere near downtown'.[38] *The Exiles* is considered by some to be 'a rare archive of the urban Indian experience and a primary text of how urban relocation [from reserves] is remembered and recreated as urban memory'.[39] It is claimed to show Native Americans practicing a 'respatialisation of the urban,'[40] not only by coming together in a new pan-tribal urban community but by inhabiting urban space in a distinctive way. One of the last scenes of the film, for instance, is a '49' that takes place on 'Hill X', an isolated location overlooking the city (now Dodger Stadium). In a commentary on the film, Native American film-maker, poet and author, Sherman Alexie, portrays a 49 as 'a party and also something religious', 'a contemporary version of ancient tribal tradition'; because it gets 'mixed up with drinking' it is 'profane and sacred at the same time'. He states that it has its origins in Native boarding schools when residents had to 'sneak off' to drum and sing and that the 49 retains the trace of being a subversive act. While the 49 is still a 'ubiquitous event' within Native American culture, the ten-minute scene in *The Exiles* remains, in Alexie's reckoning, 'extraordinary'; 'this remains the only extended 49 I have ever seen in a film'.

The Exiles was never widely distributed and, until Andersen's film, it was 'screened mainly in college classrooms by instructors who had recordings copied from other battered copies of the film'.[41] The sampling of the film in *Los Angeles Plays Itself* led Cindi Rowell of Milestone Films to locate the only existing 35mm print, deposited in the University of Southern California Cinema archive, and eventually to its careful restoration and release in 2008. It is now easily obtained from, for instance, Amazon.com. Andersen's film, then, has reactivated other films that have been left in the past, exemplary of the fact that archives are not static and that their political effects are indeterminate.

The Exiles reinserts Native Americans into the official history of Los Angeles[42] (albeit not in unproblematic ways) and it radiates within memory in less obvious ways as well. As Sherman Alexie comments on the film in an audio-recorded interview included with the film in the recently released DVD, there are parallels between characters on the screen and his own friends and family in Spokane: 'that guy looks like Homer, a friend of mine'; 'she has a rez accent . . . when I heard that, even the sound of her voice, that accent, I was so excited when I watched the movie for the first time . . . it felt so real', 'Once again I sat up in my seat . . . to see her walk into this room, and this communal living [space], you know, I grew up on the reservation but we lived in Spokane the city at various times and this is very familiar to me, a bunch of Indian guys sitting around listening to rock and roll, unemployed, drinking and wondering what they are going to do that night' (Figure 3.4).

While the film may prod Alexie's memory, it does not allow any viewer to fully absorb the characters or scenes in the film into private memory – it provokes a livelier, unstable and more open-ended process. Because the voice-over monologues run parallel to the action on the screen and do not explain the actions that we view, the film both distances us from the action and invites our active engagement. Again in the words of Sherman Alexie as he watches a scene involving Homer, one of the three central protagonists in the film:

Figure 3.4 Homer and his friend; *The Exiles*. (Courtesy of Milestone Film & Video.)

We don't really know him well enough to make any judgments . . . We are not given that . . . these are all strangers that we are trying to learn. The film is asking us to try to learn these people. Try to get to know them. We enter into a relationship with them, a brand new relationship and we are not given anything. We have to work hard. We are active, we have to be active to deal with this stuff.

Andersen forces us into this relationship as well. The intermission built into Andersen's 169-minute film is signalled by a clip from *The Exiles*. Yvonne, an Apache woman and another of the three nonprofessional actors around whom *The Exiles* is built, sits alone in a cinema. The lights come up and Yvonne looks up, down, and then away, smirking to herself in a self-conscious and despondent way (Figure 3.5). Addressed so directly and elusively, it is difficult not to respond to her gaze. It is perhaps no surprise that at the point of releasing the film as a DVD in 2008 there was a great deal of curiosity about the circumstances of her life and how it had taken shape over the fifty years since *The Exiles* was filmed.[43] Traces in the archive, Andersen has shown, can reactivate other memories and a curiosity about not only other worlds that are now past, but the present and what might be. Writing about the ethics of remembering aboriginality in the Australian context, Chris Healy[44] notes that memory is no cure for forgetting; memory and forgetting are unstable and intertwined processes. Perhaps the most politically productive remembering and forgetting, he suggests, occur when we are forced to live with (or sit through) the artefacts of colonial culture (as *The Exiles* no doubt is) in ways that allow us to simultaneously acknowledge and mourn the past and present, and develop a curiosity about a different past (than the one we think we know), along with a commitment to a different future.

Figure 3.5 Yvonne at the cinema; *The Exiles*. (Courtesy of Milestone Film & Video.)

Nostalgia and Looking Towards the Future: *24 City* (2008)

A number of commentators note the current obsession with memory and loss in popular culture and scholarly writing. 'The twentieth century began with a futuristic utopia,' writes Svetlana Boym, 'and ended with nostalgia.'[45] Nostalgia refers to a preoccupation with the past as a site of longing, regret and desire, literally a painful longing (*algia*) to return home (*nostos*). When it was first coined in 1688 to describe the melancholy of Swiss military conscripts stationed far from home, nostalgia was conceived as a symptom of an afflicted imagination rather than a form of memory. Although no longer medicalised,[46] the whiff of pathology clings to the term. Often considered to be bad history and an irrational and inaccurate form of memory, nostalgia is also 'a sort of political crime'.[47] Romanticising or sentimentalising a non-existent past, a nostalgic frame of mind seems to whitewash the complexities and violence of the past and offer a fantastical escape from the present and future. A long line of political philosophers, from Kant, Hegel through Marx, Levinas to Fredric Jameson have condemned nostalgia for its reactionary effects of preserving the status quo of class (and patriarchal) privilege, instilling political passivity, inciting reactionary nationalisms and blocking historical understanding.

And yet, against 'these figures of dismissal',[48] recent thinking draws attention to the political possibilities opened by nostalgic longing. Nostalgia registers unease or disappointment with or estrangement from present circumstances and thus can provoke rather than suppress oppositional thinking. The challenge that nostalgic thought poses to understandings of history as linear and progressive, of such concern to its critics, is also its great potential. Nostalgia is said to mourn 'distances and disjunctures between times and spaces'[49] and to be a reaction to the ruptures and displacements of modernity and globalisation. As such, 'nostalgia stalks modernity as an unwelcome double, a familiar symptom of unease in the face of political and economic transformation'.[50] But it simultaneously actualises alternative temporalities and spatialities that challenge modern notions of standardised time and legible space. Nostalgia reverses and displaces time and brings the past to the present in confused, dream-like ways. Rey Chow asks of nostalgia: 'Could the movement of nostalgia be a loop, a throw, a network of chance, rather than a straight line?'[51] Nostalgia is a waste of time, a meditation on time passing, decidedly non-productive; it thus instantiates a pause in the modernist march toward progress. Boym claims that nostalgia articulates a yearning for the particular as opposed to the universal, Edward Casey that it conjures a 'plenum of places', 'a world full of places', rather than an empirical place given in a specific moment. In this sense, claims about the veracity of nostalgia are beside the point because a different sense of time and place are evoked within a nostalgic mode of memory and imagination. 'Perhaps it is this paradoxical interplay of the definite and indefinite in space as well as in time,' muses Casey, 'that gives rise to nostalgia's baffling combination of the sweet and the bitter, distance and proximity, presence and absence, place and no-place, imagination and memory, memory and non-memory.'[52]

But what political potential comes from rupturing or stalling modernist time and space? Simply: it creates a feeling of discomfort and some time and space to critically reflect on the present. Nostalgic memory can conjure other worlds and other ways of living. In the present context of economic precarity, privatisation, outsourcing of formerly public services, there is good reason, Matthew Hannah argues, for a productive engagement with the 'ruins' of previous social systems that seemed more attuned – however imperfectly – to sociality, solidarity and the life of the population.[53] Not as historical records but as hauntings that might re-enchant the present and our hopes for the future. As Ken Loach says of his 2013 documentary film, The Spirit of '45, which draws on archival film footage and sound recordings to celebrate the year that Britons 'embraced social democracy' and created the National Health Service and other traditions of public ownership that have been systematically dismantled since the Thatcher years: 'we need to remember and learn from the lessons'.[54]

Nostalgia has a special relationship to the two keywords that define this text – city and film. As a literal longing to come home, for what Casey calls a world-under-nostalgement, it is inherently tied to a sense of place.[55] The plenum-of-places evoked by nostalgia creates its 'characteristically multi-layered structure'.[56] Physical places also embody nostalgia and cities are often rich contexts for nostalgic remembrance. Nostalgia is frequently marketed through a place-based heritage industry. So too the claim has been made that 'the cinematic image, because of its visible nature, becomes a wonderfully appropriate embodiment of nostalgia's ambivalence between dream and reality, of nostalgia's insistence on seeing "concrete" things in fantasy and memory.'[57] Fantasy, forgetfulness, temporal reversibility and other distortions of linear time can be built into fragmented narratives as well as the structure of a film, through uncanny doublings and juxtapositions, ghostly presences, voiceovers that embody nostalgia by simultaneously reflecting, recalling and anticipating the future in the present, and cinematography that alters the viewer's experience of time by slowing or speeding or suspending action, sometimes all at the same time. Films can both show nostalgia, for instance through characters that dwell in the past or by integrating ghostly images, and draw the spectator into a retrospective or nostalgic mode of viewership.

There is another sense in which film-place-nostalgia are intertwined: that is, nostalgia is a response to and takes form within specific historical and geographical circumstances and can only be evaluated as such. Whether nostalgia is celebratory and sentimental or critical is not usefully adjudicated in the abstract.[58] In the case of filmic nostalgia, it has taken shape differently in different contexts and the term can be used to refer to very different modes of nostalgia. Fredric Jameson, for instance, identified a proliferation in the 1970s and 1980s of nostalgic Hollywood films, which romanticise the past and invite the viewer to consume it as fashion, style or glossy image.[59] In these films, Jameson argues, the past is mobilised in an allegorical way that blocks rather than enables a historical understanding of the present. Jameson is very clear that this type of nostalgia film is 'in no way to be grasped as passionate expressions of that older longing once called nostalgia but rather quite the opposite: they are a depersonalized visual curiosity and a "return of the repressed" of the twenties and thirties "without affect".'[60] In other contexts a proliferation of that 'older longing' has been the focus of attention. Rey Chow declared that 'the nostalgia we see in Chinese cinema may well be the episteme of Chinese cultural production in the 1980s and 1990s. Nostalgia links together the otherwise diverse intellectual and artistic undertakings of the mainland, Taiwan, and Hong Kong.'[61] Processes of dislocation are neither uniform nor entirely distinctive across these places; feelings of nostalgia at work more generally within consumer culture (including the type criticised by Jameson) interlace with specific conditions of massive social and economic and urban transformation: for instance, in Hong Kong a history of colonialism and 'the handover' to China in 1997; in mainland China, the transition to post-socialist market economies and an extraordinary destruction and reconstruction of urban space. As a messy amalgam of different types of nostalgia, of longing and desire, Jean Ma argues that Chinese cinema opens a different perspective on debates about memory, history and nostalgia that 'challenge, on the one hand, its easy dismissal as a devolution of history into the culture industry and, on the other hand, its valorization as a locus of self-evident, experiential truth'.[62] Ma explores this in her book-length project on the films of Hong Kong-based director, Wong Kar-wai, and two Taiwan directors, Hou Hsiao-hsien and Tsai Mingliang. Wong, for instance, has been credited with transforming Hong Kong into 'a city of sadness'[63] in which anxieties about the future are considered through nostalgic interpretations of the past and an obsession with time and memory. Many of his characters are trapped in memory, and the materiality and structure of his films often disrupt linear time and position the viewer in a retrospective mode.[64] Rather than revisiting Ma's (and others) impressive engagement with the nostalgia of Wong Kar-wai's films, we turn to think further about the mobile politics of nostalgia[65] in relation to the widely available *24 City*, a 2008 film by Chinese film-maker Jia Zhangke.

Jia is associated with a group of Chinese film-makers that emerged in the mid-1990s, known as the Sixth or Urban Generation.[66] They have been preoccupied with the intensity of social and economic change in China through the 1980s and 1990s, as the country has moved from a planned economy to a market economy and capitalist modes of management. Cities have been highly visible and concentrated nodes of these changes and of the emergence of a globalised mass consumer culture. In the 1990s, Zhang argues, 'the relentless urban demolition' ushered the economic reforms of the 1980s 'to points of no return' and 'the ubiquity of the bulldozer, the building crane and the debris of urban ruins' became 'the trademark' of Urban Generation cinema.[67] These film-makers have tended to focus on the uneven social impacts of the massive socio-economic transformations and on those who have been uprooted or displaced in the process: marginal urban populations adrift in post-socialist China, such as disaffected youths and the 'floating population' of migrant workers who lack official residence status. Coming to Beijing from Fenyang in Shanxi province, Jia has described himself as a migrant-worker director and the extensive use of digital video technology by Urban Generation film-makers has both opened opportunities for the creation of more independent film and legitimated claims to producing 'amateur' or 'unofficial' cinema. Their style has been called post-socialist critical realism;[68] it is rooted in documentary aesthetics and is often documentary in effect, using on-location settings, amateur actors and naturalistic sound. The turn to documentary has itself been grounded in the urban experience, and in particular the rapidity of urban change. Explaining his shift to documentary in his more recent films, Jia explains:

> There have been changes in China in the past one or two years that have come so swiftly that if I don't film as fast as I can I will never be able to catch up. I feel the need to use documentary to record the changes we are experiencing right now . . . I must use documentary to tell my stories and prevent not only the disappearance of memories but also the disappearance of the architecture, the buildings, the disappearance of the whole generation of people after 1949.[69]

On the face of it, 24 City may seem an odd choice to think about the critical possibilities of nostalgia, given Jia's strong claims that it functions as an archive of collective memory. Writing about the origins of the film, Jia states that since 2000 he had wanted to make a film about state-owned corporations and workers' experiences of the transition from a planned to market economy; indeed, he had written a fictional script on this theme. And then in 2006 he heard on the news about a state-owned factory in Chengdu that employed 30,000 workers and sustained roughly 100,000 dependent family members. The Chengfa Corporation (also known as Factory 420 and first created in 1958 as a top-secret production facility building military aircraft) was devolving its resources to China Resources Land Limited, a state-owned property development corporation (listed on the Hong Kong Stock Exchange as red chip stock) that would demolish the factory and redevelop the land as high-rise residential towers and retail and office space.[70] 'This news report made me aware of the fact that the industrial memories of 50 years of the New China needed to be confronted . . . I suddenly felt this was a gigantic allegory . . . this was a story about the system, a story of the collective memory of all Chinese people.'[71] Mixing fictional with documentary 'aspects', as he does in 24 City, 'makes me feel that my films belong to real life experience, that they are indestructible evidence'.[72] Looking back at the Cultural Revolution of 1966–76 he observes that 'you don't get to see a lot of unmediated images', meaning memory and history outside of a highly controlled official version of it:

> I really fear if I don't do something right now to document the change right now in China we're going to have something similar, 10 years of Chinese history that just disappear from the face of the earth in terms of individual, not official governmental histories. This is what is driving me at this time.[73]

And yet *24 City* is neither entirely documentary nor fiction; it has been argued that the merging of the two privileges memory over linear or official history.[74] Jia grounds the film in his own nostalgic memory: locating his childhood in a county town 'with a strong rural flavour', he remembers helping his classmates with the wheat harvest in the summer. At the end of the day, 'when with great effort we straightened our long-bent backs and wiped away our sweat, we would turn our eyes afar'. In the distance, 'against the sunlight, the chimneys of the diesel engine factory proudly billowed white smoke. This is when I understood why everyone wanted to enter the factory and become a worker.' He recounts that at the end of the 1970s if a child was able to get a job in the factory, 'this was considered a glorious event for the whole family, because it meant a stable monthly wage; it meant distribution of tea leaves and white sugar in the summer, and a heating subsidy in the winter.' 'The factory's subsidized housing, the unshakeable pension payments to come, represented not only material benefits, but the inner pride of an entire class.'[75] Pheng Cheah has written of his 2004 film, *The World*, that it is 'part ambivalence, part lament, part nostalgia'[76] and Jason McGrath that his earlier film *Platform* could 'easily be read as a product of nostalgia'.[77] A review of *24 City* in *The Wall Street Journal* states that some critics have interpreted this film as 'an apologia for harsh policies of the past'.[78] But if *24 City* is nostalgic about the past, it is, as McGrath notes for *Platform*, a complicated nostalgia, neither complacent nor transparent, nor reassuring. McGrath frames Jia's nostalgia within Boym's distinction between restorative and reflective modes, the former attempting to restore a lost home, the latter opening the possibility of inhabiting different places simultaneously and experiencing a multiplicity of 'planes of consciousness'; he claims for Jia's work the latter.[79] Jia's nostalgia, he argues, arises from within ambivalent personal memories and it 'embraces ambiguity, distance, irony and fragmentation as inseparable aspects of its object of meditation'.[80]

How does this work in *24 City*? At one level, the film moves through linear time, with the opening scene recording a crowd of workers flowing through the factory gates and jostling up a stairway into an auditorium to attend the ceremonial announcement that their factory will be closed. As the film progresses the machinery within the factory is dismantled, the buildings emptied and demolished, the grounds excavated, and new luxury high-rises arise in their place. The focus shifts from the older workers who are retired or made redundant to a younger generation of workers making their way in the new economy. And yet other temporalities disrupt this linear time. The opening shot of the workers entering the factory (Figure 3.6), for instance, pays homage to the first film of the Lumière brothers,

Figure 3.6 Workers entering the Chengfa factory. (Courtesy of Cinema Guild.)

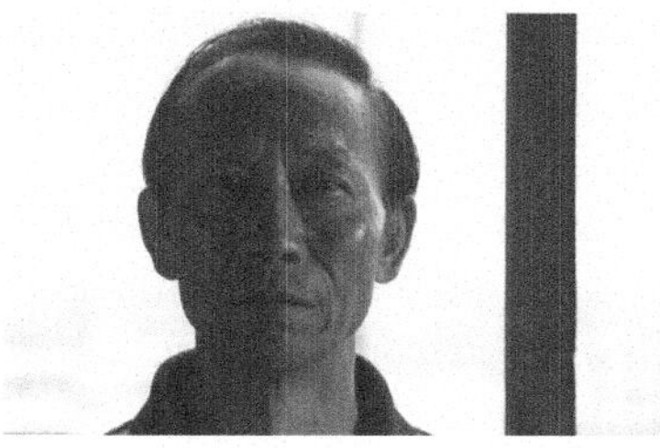

Figure 3.7 A portrait of He Xikun. (Courtesy of Cinema Guild.)

Figure 3.8 He Xikun haunts an emptied room. (Courtesy of Cinema Guild.)

Shot on This Day in 1895.[81] What follows this opening are life sketches of nine different individuals: five are created through footage of interviews with actual workers, the last four performed by actors. The first three life-sketches work within a straightforwardly nostalgic mode.

We are introduced to the first worker as he climbs an empty staircase, the ceremonial speech announcing the factory closure still audible. In the next shot (the first of many such portraits), we are brought very close to and into visceral relation with He Xikun as he stares directly into the camera and swallows with some difficulty slowly and loudly; his image fades as the room is emptied of his ghostly presence (Figure 3.7 and Figure 3.8). Silence. On a black screen appears what is identified as an ancient poem:

The cherished hibiscus of 24 City.
  in full bloom
Chengdu shone and prospered

When we return to He Xikun, he is now seated in the room from which he was made to disappear, and he tells a story about his former supervisor Master Wang. Smiling fondly he reminisces about his supervisor's frugality and industry. He tells of throwing away a tool one day, some fifty years ago, which he considered to be worn out. Master Wang retrieved it.

Then Master Wang said 'Xiao He, you know that this small thing has come into our hands through those of many others. It can still be used.' . . . I was so impressed. People like me were too immature. We had to learn not to be wasteful. Old masters like Master Wang knew: 'Waste not, want not' . . . He was right and I learned that from him.

The interviewer who sits just outside of the frame, presumably Jia, repeats: 'He knew. How many hands our tools have passed through.' He Xikun then confesses that he feels guilty and sad about speaking about

Master Wang because he has not visited him in recent years. Sighing deeply and looking away, a long shot rests on the stillness of He Xikun for what feels like a very long time.[82]

Jia takes the circumstance of the film to create the opportunity for He Xikun to visit Master Wang in his apartment. He finds a much diminished Master Wang who, after some awkward attempts at conversation, states self-consciously that his cognitive functioning has declined: 'My brain's rusty. Too slow. It was okay before. I used to remember things well. But not now.' The awkwardness of the present encounter recedes when Master Wang begins to reminisce about the past and recount details of his great industriousness and dedication as a worker. When his memories run out, the two men simply sit in silence and He Xikun strokes Master Wang in silence. In an intimate close-up that has all of the characteristics of haptic visuality,[83] the camera moves slowly from Master Wang's hand being stroked by He Xikun, up his arm to his face, his head now caressed tenderly by He Xikun, along He Xikun's arm, to rest on He Xikun's face, which eventually looks down in sorrow. It is difficult to read the ten-minute sequence involving He Xikun as other than a sentimental yearning for the vitality of youth and a past of firm moral grounding and solidarity, affection and respect among workers.

Nostalgic remembrance gets considerably more complicated as the fourth and remaining characters tell their stories and this is especially so for the four women who do so. Most of the scenarios are set up to invite nostalgia. The fourth, for instance, begins with eleven young men rushing towards a bus, presumably at the end of their shift. A solitary woman stands in the idling bus and the bus pulls away just as the young men reach it, to their obvious annoyance. She then tells her story seated in the bus as it drives around the city without stopping, evidently outside of time and the work-a-day schedule of the city. But if this is a time-outside-of-time of nostalgic reminiscence, they are mostly bitter memories that she recalls, told through tears. Laid off from Factory 420 at age forty-one she speaks of her determination through aphorisms: 'We call that smiling through your tears'; 'Come rain or shine, I must go forward.' Jia transforms and monumentalises one of her observations into an aphorism. In a conversational way the woman states that she likes her current job of sewing at home in part because she believes that working forestalls aging. Jia ends her sequence by writing her words as an inter-title — white letters on a black background: 'If you have something to do, you age more slowly.' The stories are both nostalgic and not, at once sweet and bitter, generalised and specific. Speaking of the process of making the film, Jia states that his views changed through the course of interviewing over 100 workers as part of the process of making the film. Going into the project critical of 'the pressure and constraints exercised by the system on individuals', his views changed as he interviewed workers because he 'realised that when they had chosen to work in the system, it was often a very idealistic choice, a very pure and humane choice, because they wanted to change China, to remake the human being, to bring individuals happiness'.[84]

Jia holds us within this ambivalence towards both the past and the present. The last sequence emerges from a cloud of dust thrown up by the implosion of Factory 420 as it falls to the ground. Out of the dust, an image of Su Na (played by Zhao Tao, a constant within Jia's films) appears, applying lip-gloss before she leaves for work (Figure 3.9). Fashionably dressed, including a trademark globally recognisable Burberry plaid scarf, she eventually tells her story in an old classroom of one of the now vacated high schools within the Factory 420 community, a location that draws her into beginning her story in her childhood (Figure 3.10). She grew up in the factory community, failed her college entrance exams, 'hung around on the streets' for a while and eventually found her niche in the new economy as a personal shopper who goes to Hong Kong every two weeks to purchase expensive designer clothing for 'rich women with time on their hands' who 'like fashion' but have 'no energy to buy'. She points to a tower in the skyline and tells the off-camera interviewer that she has a friend from Malaysia – 'I met him on an airplane' – who wants to take over the revolving restaurant in the tower and hire her to manage it. 'I've never worked in catering, but there's no harm in trying. Maybe I'll become a powerful woman!' The future may seem bright and full of possibility but her tone shifts when she explains why she has

Figure 3.9 Su Na emerges from a cloud of dust. (Courtesy of Cinema Guild.)

Figure 3.10 Su Na reminiscing in her former classroom. (Courtesy of Cinema Guild.)

taken a loan to buy an expensive car, necessary, she feels, to maintain her credibility with her clients. Unlike her friends who expect to receive the fruits of their parents' labour in the form of apartments and cars, she must purchase her car on credit. Her mother was laid off from her job at Factory 420 in 1995 and now works part-time at a telephone-pole factory. Her father is retired from Factory 420 and deeply depressed by his loss of status. For a long time she no longer went home because she 'felt the mood of failure and depression'. She runs through a list of boyfriends with whom she has lived instead, not in terms of their personal qualities but by the name and quality of the real estate that they temporarily cohabited. Needing to find her mother one day she is forced to seek her out at her factory, where she is repulsed by the noise, the uniformity –'the workers were all wearing blue uniforms' – and the demeaning and dehumanising work that her mother does there: 'I didn't even know whether it was a man or a woman when I approached'. It is this day that she 'suddenly felt grown-up. I began to care for my parents.' She now focuses her ambitions on making 'lots and lots of money', with the objective of buying an expensive apartment for her parents on the site of their former life – 24 City. 'I know it will cost a lot. But I can do it. I am the daughter of a worker.' Neither the past nor present nor the future are bright: one is associated with difficult, degrading, repetitive labour and social conformity, another with the emptiness of commodities and commodified relationships and the last with idle consumption – an apartment in 24 City. But they double back on each other to extend critiques in all temporal directions. The past offers the only meaning to be found in the present: a web of interpersonal relationships, empathy, responsibility, loyalty, kindness and a sense of determination and belonging rooted in a romanticised identification as child of a worker. Certainly the past is open to manipulation: although Jia is likely the constant interlocutor throughout the film he only appears briefly and unannounced in one scene, lingering in the background against a wall to witness a marketing agent explaining to a news broadcaster that the name of the 24 City development originates in an ancient poem. Easily domesticated, romanticised and knowingly commodified as heritage, the past nevertheless offers political possibilities and it is the juxtaposition and jumbling of the satisfactions and dissatisfactions in different temporalities that might lead the viewer to ask what it is to have a meaningful life and find threads of ideas in different times and places.

The film also positions us, not just as witnesses to other people's complicated nostalgic narratives, but also potentially as nostalgic witnesses. Some of this nostalgic mode of viewing is internal to the structure of the film. For instance, a sense of loss is instilled when a shot of an outdoor neighbourhood basketball court in use is followed by one of an excavated building site; the text overlying the image of the building site tells us that this is exactly where the previously viewed basketball court recently stood. Throughout the film we return to the same spaces within the factory in slow panning shots as they are cleared and laid to waste. The narratives of the nine individuals are sequenced roughly in chronological order, in the sense that they move from oldest to youngest character, but they in no way follow a single narrative and the different memories and time orientations sit alongside one another. Chris Berry argues in relation to Jia's earlier film, *Platform*, that 'one loses a sense of when a shot will end or exactly what it will cut to, and this is quite different than a certain sense of progress invoked by ideologies of modernity, be it driven by the socialist command economy or the alleged socialist market economy of the new era';[85] the same might be said for *24 City*. The narratives are interspersed with long, still portrait-like shots of various individuals, some are of the interviewees but others of workers we will never come to know, all staring directly into the camera (Figure 3.11). These portrait shots force the viewer, Navarro argues, into another temporality of viewing and to contemplate 'not what has already taken place but what might still happen'.[86] They simultaneously bring us into a somewhat uncomfortable experience of time endured in the present[87] and forcefully create a time for contemplation. Random sounds from the street often intrude into these spaces of stillness, dividing attention and creating a sense of multiple places and tempos co-existing in real time – the slow time of the supposed focus of attention and the noise and chaos of the street and everyday life.[88]

Figure 3.11 A portrait of a retired worker. (Courtesy of Cinema Guild.)

To a Chinese viewer, the green tinge of the film may be evocative because of associations that they bring to the film; in this case, nostalgia would be working in an entirely different register. The green tinge was introduced during post-production and comes from Jia's memories from the 1970s and 1980s when many families in northern China apparently painted the lower metre of their interiors walls in green: Jia recalls,

> To a child who was short, as I was, that green was the colour I met everyday. Moreover, the colour not only appeared on the walls of homes but also in all kinds of workplaces. Everywhere, in hospitals, offices, classrooms, all sorts of public places had their walls painted this colour. When you went into state-run factories, you would see the green colour on those machines and walls. To me, this green colour comes from real life. It represents my memory about that old system, the China that dates from more than a decade ago certainly.[89]

Jia's body of work forces an entirely different kind of reflection on politics and nostalgia as well. He has been positioned as an organic intellectual[90] and has claimed for himself the responsibility to create transformative films. His modest rural upbringing, the thematic content of his films and his critical approach to both the recent past of state social-ism and contemporary Chinese society, the fact that he was placed on a blacklist and banned from making films in 1999 after the screening of *Xiao Wu* – these factors have all established Jia's political authenticity. Since 2003, however, the ban has been lifted and Jia's films can be distributed in China, with his agreement to submit to a streamlined script approval and censorship process. *24 City* opened in more than 100 theatres in China. In Jia's view, this reflects the fact that the Chinese state began to view the film industry as an economic opportunity rather than fear the political and disruptive effect of the films themselves. Jia has had immense success within the international film festival circuit and there was a retrospective on his work at the Museum of Modern Art in New York in March 2010, the first mainland Chinese film-maker to be honoured in this way for over twenty years. He has now set up his production base in Hong Kong to attract international investors and for respite from state censorship. A piece on Jia in *The New Yorker* magazine in 2009 begins at Jia's first fashion photography shoot for the Chinese version of *Esquire* magazine. As Pheng Cheah notes, 'it is highly doubtful that Jia can transcend the circuit of commodification'.[91] In Cheah's view, this 'is the aporia faced by the organic intellectual today' in the context of contemporary globalisation, with very large implications for 'counter hegemonic struggles at the level of culture'.[92] Opening to transnational flows is crucial for struggles against the territorial state but these flows are almost inevitably intertwined with and contaminated by flows of capital.

Perhaps the best we can do is to work with the kind of ambivalence evidenced within debates about the politics of nostalgia: transnational circuits of cultural production and the territorial state create openings to the inevitable closures of each. A risk of the kinds of openings that we have detected within the nostalgia of *24 City* – moral conduct, familial bonds, affection and respect, solidarity – is that these values could be appended to a new improved Asian model of capitalist development and replace rather than transcend universalising and chauvinistic versions of European modernity. If nostalgia is to be critical, ambivalence about its politics seems essential rather than problematic, so that it can do its work of unsettling the present.

Remembering Now: *Caché* (2005)

Referring to cinematic images of memory, Deleuze wrote 'attentive recognition informs us to a much greater degree when it fails than when it succeeds'.[93] Deleuze thus connects the critical potential of the film image with the breakdown rather than the retention of memory. When we cannot recognise an image and cannot figure out how to read it, the senses, according to Deleuze, become suspended; the image does not automatically link up with a familiar narrative and instead enters an uncertain circuit of connections, one that might well provoke thinking. This proposition can usefully be considered in relation to Michael Haneke's *Caché* (*Hidden*), a film that does not take visibility for granted, either in the past or in the present.[94] This is a cinematic film, which is to say that it compels the viewer to look,

Figure 3.12 Surveillance shot of the street; *Caché*, 2005. (Courtesy of Artificial Eye.)

not simply to access the narrative but to think about how looking itself works. Yet seeing is no easy task as many of the film's sequences remain perplexing and indecipherable. The first shot has become celebrated for maintaining such a high level of ambiguity that its effects as filmic sequence and as an image of surveillance (the primary way in which it has been considered) are still under debate. Interestingly enough this is a long uninterrupted shot of a well-to-do residential urban space, which by being static, unframed and undifferentiated offers little guidance as to where to look or what to look for (Figure 3.12). But given how long the sequence lasts we are compelled to think about what it is we should be seeing and recognising. And this frustrating experience never lets up; throughout the film characters look at images and wonder what they mean; discordant frames are intercut within continuous shots, surprising the viewer and raising questions about what one has seen or not seen. This uncertainty has generated countless debates that still persist on the Internet about what the film shows or does not show.

What most critics have seen in *Caché* is that it takes the form of a psychological thriller and that the mystery is about how videotapes left on the doorstep of a family house pertain to the father's past, and specifically to a childhood incident.[95] Unlike Andersen's *Los Angeles Plays Itself*, *Caché* has been inundated with interpretations, what has been called 'a tsunami of thematic discussions' about memory – individual and collective, personal and national, traumatic and constructed – and what it means to refuse to remember the past and to take responsibility for one's actions. Inevitably, this refusal of memory has been linked to France's colonial history in Algiers, and located within a broad sense of national memory that raises questions of guilt and responsibility.[96] We will take a different approach and consider what is productive about the inability to recognise and remember. Instead of tracing a clear line of individual responsibility about a collective French past, we will argue that in *Caché* the inability to remember is connected to the indecipherability of images not simply in the past but in the present, and that it is in the present and not in the past that memory is forged. The film itself produces a circuit of images that begin to reveal connections not only between politics of the past with those of the present but also between politics and images; these circuits, however, always operate at the level of the image and thus remain unstable and have the potential to keep turning and changing.

For some time now the interest in memory has put memory into a conflictual relation with history as well as with the archive. In his 1971 essay 'Nietzsche, Genealogy, and History', Michel Foucault argued for freeing history from the model of memory, seeking instead to challenge humanist history by turning history into a counter-memory.[97] But memory turned out to have a bigger future, becoming a means of critiquing official history as exclusive and disembodied. The focus on memory rather than history pointed to the instability of the past, especially in relation to psychoanalysis that had long been concerned with the complex nature of memory in relation to consciousness. According to Jacques Derrida's influential *Archive Fever*, the archive is not the initiation of a secure place for the past but actually 'occurs at the place of originary and structural breakdown of the said memory'.[98] This psychoanalytic process of forgetting followed by disavowal of the past and denial of that disavowal is not part of Foucault's conception of the bureaucratic work of the archive, which tends to stress the gaps in the retrieval of knowledge.[99] In post-colonial studies, however, the archive as an official site of domination and subjection continues to be accompanied by processes of suppression and disavowal necessary to maintain something irrational as rational.[100]

The use of trauma theory is what has given Derrida's archive both its possibilities and limitations. Theories of trauma have recently come under considerable critique. Within the field of history this critique has focused on the limiting of history to melancholic culture, and reducing the past to Freud's debatable notion of the subject.[101] In another strand of this critique, the concern is that trauma, now an accepted idea of national collective memory and even of national identity itself, has been produced in retrospect, even through scholarship. For instance, the association of trauma with certain visual forms – photography of particular historical events – has now been attributed to the development of the study of photography itself.[102] But there are also arguments that scholarship has undermined trauma, as in the claim that the term 'Holocaust' has served to obliterate trauma by putting the study of it in its place.[103]

It is interesting that while writings on *Caché* tend to focus on trauma theory, they condemn the main character's refusal to acknowledge what happened in the past (and by implication France's colonial histories) as if recalling was self-willed. Perhaps this is because the director Michael Haneke has said that the film is about the moral dilemma of how one can bear the condition of being guilty and knowing what to do about it.[104] But he also said that the film could have been set in other places and that it is not particular to the Algeria-France conflict. In other words, the film is about the implications of the breakdown of memory rather than about the particular historical legacies of France's colonial past. Indeed, trauma theory, while imposing a specific psychoanalytic process on diverse histories, did make it impossible to think of memory as a conscious reserve within the person that can be brought back willingly through the act of recalling. In the film Georges and Anne consider why they have been sent videotapes of their house and street, and immediately the focus is on Georges because he is a television personality. While various possibilities are considered, and more images are sent, the uncertainty is scattered in all directions and it is Georges himself who starts associating the tapes with the memory of a certain childhood incident. But this is not a fully formed memory that he is keeping secret even from himself. At first Georges does not know if this incident is meaningful and if so in what way. When he visits his mother he tells her that he was surprised to have had a dream about Majid, a boy he had forgotten about even though his parents had almost adopted him after Majid's own parents – Algerians who worked for Georges' family – disappeared while attending a demonstration against the French bombing of Algiers in 1961.[105] The presumption is that they were among the over 200 Algerians killed by the Parisian police and later found in the river. Georges' surprise extends to the realisation that his mother too had forgotten Majid, although when she explains why ('not a very pleasant incident') it is uncertain if she means the deaths of the parents, the change in the plan to adopt the boy, or Georges' part in this decision. Georges becomes unsettled as his vague memory of the boy becomes intertwined with the relationship with his mother; after talking to her in a somewhat distracted manner, she points out that he seems strange and should be careful. That night he has a dream of a small boy, presumably Majid, cutting the head of a cockerel and blood splattering on the boy's face as he comes with the hatchet towards a second boy, presumably Georges. By the time Georges brings up the possibility that Majid might be behind the videotapes to his wife, he and Anne have watched yet another videotape, one shot as the camera moves along a street in a much more modest neighbourhood, and then through a corridor in a humble and dingy building. When his wife insists that he tell her his theory he says 'I can't tell you because I don't know. It is only a hunch'. Anne, who tries to take a direct approach and asks questions in the manner of a detective, cannot conceive that Georges could know and not know at the same time.

It is not coincidental that the association of the videotapes with an incident in the past revolves around the drawings that start to appear together with the tapes. The first drawing is on the piece of paper in which the second videotape is wrapped, and it is of a schematic round head, with a splash of red emanating from the area of the mouth (Figure 3.13). Initially, both Anne and Georges find the drawing perplexing; he wonders if it is a child's drawing and she says she would not know. The same drawing, extended to include a schematic body, reappears in a card sent the next day to Georges' office and to his son at school. While looking at this second videotape – showing the same view of the street but at night – another version of the image in the drawing appears. This image, of a young boy in a dark room with blood gushing out of his mouth, is only visible for a few seconds and then the previous shot of the street continues (Figure 3.14). It is precisely at this point that in the voice-over we hear

Figure 3.13 Drawing of a head with bloody mouth; *Caché*, 2005.
(Courtesy of Artificial Eye.)

Figure 3.14 Boy with a bloody mouth, *Caché*, 2005. (Courtesy of Artificial Eye.)

Anne asking Georges what is wrong, and when he fails to answer she asks again till she gains his attention. The interruption in the videotape occurs at the same time as a sudden interruption in Georges' concentration; the viewer, meanwhile, does not see him, but sees instead the image that seems to have flashed through his mind and that somehow has emerged as he was watching the videotape. Thus the drawing – both sketchy and bold and thus an image still to be realised and with the potential to be realised – connects with the hallucinatory image suddenly present within the videotape. And it also connects with the posted cards, as well as with the dream that Georges seems to have while at his mother's house. The next drawing, the one found together with the tape put at the front door during a dinner party, is similar in format but shows the head of a cockerel and the splash of red is around the severed neck. The schematic drawings are images in the making, in the sense that they are yet to be fulfilled. In this instance one might turn to Derrida's strategic use of trauma theory and his argument that archival material is neither in the present nor in the past but remains in a kind of uncertain state, and for this reason becomes entrancing and even hallucinatory.[106] Within the archive this evidence has yet to be turned into knowledge and instead of having gaps (Foucault) or being suppressed (post-colonial) it remains in a state of waiting for attention.[107]

Thus, instead of outright denial of the past, Georges is in the process of producing a memory, one that seems to be prompted by the tapes but that starts to emerge from the images that are located neither fully in the past nor totally in the present. But even when he does start going down this route, and pursues the possibility by linking one image to another, he is uncertain about how to assess the situation. Again turning to Derrida's archival argument, there is a disconnection between the event and knowing how to feel about it. Just as the archive harbours this ambiguity, Georges is not simply perplexed about the incident in his childhood that suddenly emerges and starts to be fleshed out, but is also perplexed about how to feel about it, especially as he now attributes it to a distant childhood time. The confusion is partly because the memory is not a memory in the sense of having been stored in the past and kept hidden or repressed. Instead it has been forged through an uncertain circuit of images that hold resemblance and difference, some real (drawings), some dream-like (Georges' dreams) and some hallucinatory (the scene that emerges suddenly within the surveillance tapes).[108]

Derrida's argument about the breakdown of memory claims that trauma is not passed from one person to another but through different representational and technological forms; the archive itself produces knowledge as it shapes it through its particular ways of storing documents.[109] He is interested in writing, and especially the idea of the post script, a form of writing that refers to the future in which there is something unexpected and perhaps violent still to come.[110] In *Caché*, the production of memory is situated in circuits formed through different technologies of seeing – television, film, digital video – and the viewer is challenged to consider how different technologies affect and produce seeing. As is often pointed out, in the family home a large television is situated in the middle of the sitting room, inserted into a wall of built-in bookcases filled with a variety of storage formats: videotapes, DVDs, picture books, novels. The most pointed juxtaposition is that between book and television, implying the loss of substance and attentiveness from one to the other. This juxtaposition is repeated in the television studio in which Georges conducts his interview show, and in this instance the books are literally abstracted shapes, further stressing the ways that television has emptied out depth in knowledge of the world. But television comes under stronger attack as its ability to hold the couple's attention only works when the television is used to project the videotapes. Otherwise, the television screen, which is always filled with violent images of disasters and conflict in different parts of the world, is the invisible background to Georges and Anne's exchanges. Television's violent images, themselves potentially the site of trauma, have become mere surface image and entirely stripped of connection or meaning. Unlike the drawings, which are aporetic and prompt puzzlement and contradiction, the television images seem overdetermined, already located within a set of rehearsed global relations. The film makes ethical demands on the viewer precisely in the confrontation with unresolved propositions, with something that is neither fully past nor fully present, neither of one place or of the other.[111]

Television is also compared to the videotapes, and is shown to be manipulative, with ordinary time sacrificed for the sake of the spectacular or sensationalist. When Georges appears in his television show, the film suddenly rewinds, and we realise that Georges and a colleague are editing the show, reminding us of the videotapes, although now the images are projected through digital technology rather than the more antiquated videotape. The goal of the editing is to cut out anything potentially complicated ('too theoretical') and to highlight the sensationalist ('homosexuality') to the point that the very words spoken by the participants are manipulated and changed. The videotapes, on the other hand, are said to last for hours regardless of how little happens. According to Derrida, the loss of memory has always been accompanied by 'the dream of perfect technical reappropriation of the past'.[112] In effect, the videotapes, despite (or because of) their associations with surveillance, especially urban surveillance, seem to hold this promise. Surveillance banks on complete and uninterrupted vision, and in the film, it is the surveillance videotapes that seem to be a counter to the reduction of seeing and thinking within television.

How do the images of surveillance function in relation to *Caché*'s call for ethical forms of viewing and questioning?[113] In the film, the videotape is initially offered as a mute image, in the sense that it is presented entirely undefined as to what it is and how it should be seen. Indeed, it takes some time before we realise that the first sequence of the film is in fact a film within the film, a videotape left at the door of the house where Georges, Anne and their son live. Georges and Anne look at the tape, rewind it, look at it again, talk about it and as uncertainties emerge the semblance of normality in their daily evening routine begins to break down. Georges is attentive to the cassette tape as object, wants to see the bag in which it was left, where was it left, was there a note? Why a cassette when this kind of technology was already being supplanted by the DVD? Of course the videotape cassette had become known as a form for home screening, and the mode of rewinding the tape moves the entire screen backwards in a linear way, marking it horizontally with overlapping moments. This gives the image a physicality as it moves backwards or forwards, at least when it is being manipulated by Anne or Georges; otherwise it is identical in appearance to the rest of the digitally shot film, and for this very reason causes confusion between the two.[114]

It is by capturing public space within a static shot extended over a long period of time that the film within the film resembles official surveillance footage used to police urban space (Figure 3.11).[115] In this kind of surveillance, the curtailment of individual liberties is usually justified as being for the sake of the larger 'public good'. *Caché* initially positions the viewer not only as the eye of surveillance by having access to the tapes, but also as the focus of surveillance by seeing the tapes alongside Georges and Anne. This ability to occupy both sides of the exchange is achieved by keeping to surveillance's so-called neutral eye, a viewpoint that is not immediately informative and frequently only meaningful in retrospect. In surveillance footage, the image usually works to verify something rather than to reveal it in the first place. But Haneke's film compels the viewer to think about the footage before its meaningfulness is evident, and thus not as a site of evidence and truth but as a site of sensation, projection and consideration. Rather than making the image suspect, as has been suggested,[116] it turns the image into a productive conundrum. For such a mute image, it is remarkable how much noise it generates. After the revelation that what we are watching is a videotape, which has been focused on a particular house, we join the film's narrative of two characters coming out onto the street, and thus to the same site as in the videotape only later in the same day. They walk to the cross street in front of their house from where the video seems to have been taken, a street that happens to be named Rue des Iris. It is indeed the eye that marks this space as the couple tries to find the exact place from where it must have been filmed, the traces of the filming that might still be there, and ultimately why it is that they cannot answer any of their queries. It will not be the last time they turn to the street to try to find answers. When their dinner party with friends is interrupted by the door bell, Georges opens the front door and, finding no one there, yells at the street as if the exterior world itself has turned against him; only then does he find that another videotape has been left on the doorstep.

Of course the street does not answer Georges' angry accusations and the videotape only starts to resonate once moved inside: inside the house, inside family relations and inside the individual person. It is within Georges and his troubled interiority that most of what is produced in the course of the film can be located. As Foucault has argued, relations of power are produced not only within webs of relations, but also within the contradictory pressures that mobilise the individual subject.[117] Practices of surveillance invariably involve the complicity of those under surveillance, which tends to account for the acceptance of these practices and even for the internalisation of surveillance. The sensation of being observed, especially by those one conceives as relevant to one's place in the world, has been associated with self-awareness and the rethinking of how one might conceive of one's actions and thoughts.[118] The surveillance tapes work between circuits of relations (familial, professional, social) and within the self. While the latter is presumed to be where secrets are hidden, in the film both form the conditions under which a memory is forged. For Georges, it becomes less about revealing or confronting something concealed within himself and more about reworking a sense of self through the encounter with the lens, one that brings into play questions of personal and political responsibility. Rather than remembering something that was already there, Georges is in the process of producing a memory by starting to see outside of himself.[119]

The question of who has made and sent the tapes may be crucial to how the film works as a thriller, but it soon becomes the wrong question to ask. As has been noted, every attempt to find the answer is met not only with uncertainty at the level of the narrative, but also because the impossibility of making the tapes becomes increasingly apparent. Within the narrative there are hints of this as Georges and Anne look on the street for the source of their surveying eye. Even so, there is still the possibility of an outside perpetrator as the first tapes are from the street, either in Georges' neighbourhood or Majid's; the video of Georges' former family home is also from the exterior, although because this is from a distant past, its status as an actual image begins to raise questions. By the time the surveillance tapes show Majid's apartment, they have moved into the interior, and not only in terms of architecturally built space. Even more than the exterior shots, these seem impossible in terms of the production of the footage itself. The camera would have to occupy the place where walls are expected to be, unbeknown to Georges who stands next to it, or Majid who we are beginning to realise knows nothing about it. According to Anne, the two-hour videotape of this incident is primarily of Majid crying after Georges' departure. When Majid calls Georges back to the apartment and immediately kills himself after Georges arrives, we are shown the scene from the same angle as the supposed videotape of the previous encounter of the two in the apartment. We have now entered a very different order of image, one that is surely produced from Georges' viewpoint but not necessarily one that he can assess within rational terms. It evokes Derrida's argument that the archive (in the film, the surveillance videotapes) is not only mnemonically unreliable but also becomes hallucinatory and thus defies all pragmatic and ethical explanations.

The performative aspects of Majid's suicide, staged for Georges' attention, has been rightly criticised as something that has little to say about the position represented by Majid himself, and by implication the political position of Algerians in relation to France.[120] Indeed this scene is so intricately connected to the hallucinatory aspects in the formation of Georges' memory that it disregards any other subjectivity. Moreover, it is all about sensation rather than information, and thus exceeds its existence as real, imagined, videotape or anything else. Derrida suggests that trauma is itself susceptible to self-destruction since trauma cannot confront itself and wants to get rid of itself. But in *Caché,* the enactment of the suicide is played out as an extension of earlier manifestations: the child-like drawings, the dream of the young Majid cutting the head off the cockerel and coming towards the young Georges with a knife, the images that merge within the surveillance videotapes through Georges' projections. This circuit of images, all evoking a bloody cut, is what produces the specificities of the memory, which is increasingly conceived as being in the past but which nonetheless refuses to stay there.

Even in the earlier videotapes, the possibility of being generated externally comes into question. A subject of much discussion in the scholarly literature is the hidden clues left within the film itself. There have been suggestions that Haneke purposely positions himself and his camera as the source of surveillance. And indeed in the second videotape in which the street is recorded at night, the light of a car reveals for a short moment the unmistakable shadow of the camera, the film's own camera. Is this a sudden reminder that it is all constructed and that the status of this videotape is no different from the one that seems impossible within Majid's apartment? Or does it bring a similar kind of hallucinatory feel to the urban scene? Georges is obsessed with finding the place of the surveilling camera, but the actor playing Georges (Daniel Auteuil) passes by the camera and fails to see it because as an actor the camera remains invisible.

In the film, the surveillance videotapes are characterised by a still and prolonged view, one that seems ambiguous in terms of what is to be seen but also rigorous in demanding close attention. While looking for clues, and finding none, what we begin to see is the street itself, or even urban space, in a well-to-do residential area of Paris.[121] One can reverse what Thom Andersen states in *Los Angeles Plays Itself,* which is that if one is looking at the location in which a film is set, one is ignoring the narrative. In *Caché* one is left with no recourse but to look at the location emptied of narrative.

Is it not, then, the street itself that emerges from these shots of surveillance? Or perhaps it is the separation of the street from interior space that is accidentally recorded. The street that we look on is orderly and still, so much so that we welcome the rare movements that we catch as a car goes by or a person rushes out of their house to get into a car. This is a very different image of the Paris street than we encounter in Agnes Varda's 1961 *Cleo from 5 to 7*, in which motion, energy and curiosity is of primary importance. The silence of the street in *Caché* is deafening, and it is this emptiness and lack of engagement within urban space that becomes increasingly visible through surveillance.

The surveillance tapes provide a view outwards while seeking to penetrate the interior. This is a view of an empty street, a street that has become a non-space and no longer contested because it is already under control. In a way, the surveillance videotapes reveal the results of their own work of protecting the private over the public. The camera that films the street that we see with both puzzlement and intensity is directed to a particular house, but even this is unclear as the front door is mostly covered by a strategically located bush and is behind a reinforced metal grill gate. Even so, it is only through the surveillance videotape that the outside becomes of concern to the inside, and the only reason that Georges and Anne venture out. So in this respect, the surveillance videotape reminds the interior world about what is outside, as much as it produces and shapes a memory from a distant past.

The street is indeed a no-go zone for the parents of the family but less so for the son. When Anne and Georges decide to report the videotapes to the police, they come out of the police station and almost instantly clash with a man on a bicycle that is going down the street. This is a shocking encounter because of its suddenness, but also because of the immediate escalation of conflict between Georges and the man on the bicycle. The conflict is ostensibly about who was in the wrong about the traffic regulations of the street, but it is in fact about who belongs and who does not belong within urban space. The young man on the bicycle is dark skinned, and thus there has been a tendency to explain the conflict in terms of France's attitude to immigrants and the liberal hypocrisy about acceptance of difference. But what is rarely mentioned is how assertive the young man is about his claim to the space of the street, bringing to the film some sense that there is another side to the orderly street that the couple inhabits. This contemporary encounter contributes to the ongoing forging of Georges' internal memory of the past, but it also reveals the struggle for urban space itself even when, or especially when, official and private control of the city seems to be on the ascendancy. Once again the street – as public space, however imperfect – emerges as the counter to the privileges claimed by a liberal intellectual elite. And it is ironic that the very forms used by authorities to produce this privileged sphere, visual surveillance, becomes the means through which the viewer of the film is compelled to examine and perhaps remember earlier hopes for public space.

Figure 3.15 Surveillance shot of the school; *Caché*, 2005. (Courtesy of Artificial Eye.)

But what about the other much-discussed shot in the film, the final one, which is as static, unframed and elusive as the first one (Figure 3.15)? It might as well be another surveillance videotape. In this instance the camera opens a wide-angle view into the front of the school of Anne and Georges' son Pierrot. This shot is an inversion of the shot of the street that commences the film. The boundaries of the space are ambiguous and it is crowded with young people that appear and disappear, loiter and rush around, converse with others or wait for others to show up. Again we are compelled to look attentively without knowing what it is we should find. Many viewers have not found anything in fact, while others have noticed that amongst the young people that come and go are Georges' son and Majid's son who can be seen momentarily chatting to each other and then going their separate ways. According to Derrida, memory is never about an opposition between remembering and forgetting but about what is coming.[122] In *Caché*, the breakdown of memory becomes a way to think about the present and how the present remains in some ways invisible if we persist in not questioning the forms through which we understand the world and continue to see it through normalised prisms. Could it be that the surveillance videos serve to reveal not the hidden interior of a particular subject but the world around us? The world we share is actually much more difficult to see than the kind of interiority privileged by trauma theory. This world is not only always in the process of change but it is also constantly interpreted and reinterpreted through technologies of viewing – including those of surveillance – with the goal of manipulating and controlling our view.

We have argued that *Caché* draws on the opportunities offered by the breakdown of memory in theories of trauma. However, we also proposed that the film is not seeking to locate memory in relation to a traumatic subjectivity, be it that of the character of Georges or of the collective memory of French colonialism. Instead, the breakdown of memory and the reconstitution of memory becomes a way to examine the process of viewing itself, and puts pressure on the ethics of viewing across different technologies at the beginning of the twenty-first century. The history of surveillance is all about curtailment and control, but perhaps one can differentiate between surveillance as a practice and the images produced through surveillance. The image, after all, does not always do what it is told to do. While images of surveillance fail to make truth visible, and have been said to 'potentially make truth *indeterminate*' and thus feed a culture of suspicion, they also open up, due to this very indeterminacy, the co-existence of diverse and contradictory views not only of the past but perhaps more urgently, of the future.[123]

The indeterminacy of the images makes critical assessment of the ethics and politics of film that much more urgent. In *Los Angeles Plays Itself*, Andersen insists that filmic images of urban space matter, even if many of the films he uses were produced by a film industry that exploited urban space to suit its own (mostly financial) interests. In this case it is a personal and collective commitment to urban space that seems to drive a politics concerned less with the status of the film than with what it can reveal in spite of itself. This is an argument about reading film against the grain, informed by the politics of the corporatisation of urban space and the persistence of everyday life. The ambivalence of memory is present here as if it is in *Caché*, and through this ambivalence the films insist on an ethical approach to viewing (*Caché*) and on a politics of urban film-making (*Los Angeles Plays Itself*). For Jia's *24 City* ambivalence seems to be located not in the film's representation of memory but in its politics. Drawing on personal and collective memory to evoke a knowing sense of nostalgia, *24 City* risks co-optation at the level of politics but counts on the personal and local to challenge, however tenuously, established global relations. This film too has the potential to be read against the grain, but the uncertainties of nostalgia mean that it will continue to be a site of political debate.

CHAPTER 4

Cinema and its Publics:
Between the Screen and the Street

Notes from Vancouver, July 2013

I was returning from an interview with a central protagonist in the film, *Fix: the Story of an Addicted City*, a film that was arguably a decisive factor in the 2002 Vancouver city election and instrumental to the opening of North America's first (and only) supervised injection site. By chance, I meet on the sidewalk Peeroj Thakre, co-founder of Urban Republic, a Vancouver-based arts society responsible for the 2008 pop-up cinema featured on the cover of this book. She is interested in talking about where the possibilities for creative interventions in the city lie; in her view pop-ups now are so ubiquitous that it is time for something new.[1] I then came home to a pleasant email in response to some previous grumbling about a work-related disappointment:

> Well then you will be happy to hear that one of my clients James Ong is Board Chair of the Vancouver Queer Film Festival and said he would give us a guest pass to accompany him to a film or films at the festival so you can talk with him. He said it is interesting that that particular festival survives when others fail as it is seen as a 'family affair' for the gay community.

The sender of this email had recently volunteered at a festival called Indian Summer, at which the Bollywood film *Little Zizou* was screened after dusk in a somewhat notorious Downtown Eastside park. In the exuberance of the moment, one of the other volunteers declared that the experience of viewing the film in this context had altered his sense of the city. As I sit reading the email I am within ten square blocks of a video store that has its own memorial blog (dearvideomatic), created when it closed in spring 2012,[2] as well as two recently closed neighbourhood theatres, each with its own Facebook page. On the Facebook page of The Ridge Theatre is posted a short video commemorating its closing night (Figure 4.1).[3] On the marquee of The Hollywood Theatre (now a – literal

Figure 4.1 Farewell from the Ridge Theatre, Vancouver, 2013.
(Courtesy of Elizabeth Lee.)

– Church at the Hollywood) there is posted a phone number along with an entreaty to donate to the restoration of the facade. The Church at the Hollywood webpage reveals the opportunity to express one's love for the Hollywood Theatre by donating online, using VISA, Mastercard or American Express.[4]

There is nothing particularly remarkable about these encounters and events and similar stories could be told about London or Rome, the other cities where we reside. Or likely about the city in which you live. Film and cinema are part of the life of many cities and we live with cinema and film in everyday sorts of ways. And yet this lived, embodied and placed aspect of cinema is rarely part of the narratives told about its critical possibilities (and limitations); too often these potentials are seen to flicker across the screen and emanate from film itself. Indeed this has been our approach in earlier chapters. It would be untrue to say that spaces of exhibition and viewership are never tackled within film studies; weighing the experience of viewing single channel artist videos in a cinema as opposed to art gallery space, for instance, Laura Marks writes of the 'enormous epistemological and political consequences' of the context in which the film is shown[5] and there is a vast literature contemplating the significance of viewing film in the cinema, on the television or the Internet screen. But consideration of the contexts of exhibition and reception is a minor literature within film studies, the spaces examined tend to be generic: the cinema, the art gallery, the home, the Internet, and the critical potential of these spaces is typically considered separately from the film on view.[6] In this chapter we follow the impulse to think about the spatiality of exhibition and viewership more fully, looking into actual places and contexts of the city and into current debates about the politics of urban possibility. We do this by focusing on three interrelated questions or concerns: first, how might we think of film in relation to critical publics; second, how do the spaces of viewing (and in particular the cinema) function as and in relation to critical publics and public urban space; and third, how might we think of the criticality of film and urban space together?

Cinema and Alternative Public Spheres

A defining assumption of film studies is that film 'is a cultural artifact endowed with transformative potential' that '*matters* because it has social consequences'.[7] While it is widely recognised that not all of these consequences are radicalising (spanning from incorporation into mass consumer culture to critical reflection on the same), Judith Mayne has observed that the politicised audience has been a spectre haunting spectatorship studies and that 'one of recent film theory's most persistent fantasies is the fusion of critical spectatorship with political engagement'.[8] This fusion and tension between criticality and politics lies at the heart of the concept of the public, understood as a domain of critical discourse among private persons in civil society that occurs apart from, in relation to and sometimes opposed to the state and state power on the one hand, and the private sphere of the conjugal domestic family on the other.[9]

Cinema as Public Spaces

Cinema as a time-place has a chequered history in relation to this public. Miriam Hansen has detected within early cinema (1895–6 to 1909) the formal conditions for an alternative public sphere.[10] Early cinema was a critical time-space, she argues, for groups – women, new immigrants and the recently urbanised working class – that had little access to existing institutions of public life. Hansen makes a close study of the openings and cultural accommodations made possible through the films themselves, as fantastical spaces that allowed otherwise marginalised people to 'organize their experience on the basis of their own context of living'.[11] She has no illusions that the engagements between audience and film were necessarily or even typically radicalising: projecting images of material abundance, mobility and self-transformation, 'the cinema to some extent absorbed the functions of the utopian imagination, albeit in a diminished, alienated, and depoliticized form'.[12] And yet the situation of exhibition and reception – as a time-place – created new and critical possibilities for public life, and these 'effects on the viewer were determined less by film itself than by the particular act of exhibition, the situation of reception'.[13] With no fixed schedule of film screenings and continuous admission, for instance, the cinema offered the working class 'refuge from the time discipline of the factory'.[14] Early film exhibition emerged out of nickelodeon and vaudeville formats and involved alternating film and non-film acts such that audience absorption into the fictional world of film was intermittent and the space of the theatre ever present. Cinemas attracted diverse audiences. Strong claims have been made, for instance, about the significance of this space for women: 'more than any other entertainment form, the cinema opened up a space – a social space as well as a perceptual, experiential horizon – in women's lives, whatever their marital status, age, or background.'[15] Hansen argues that cinema served a 'threshold function' between family and mass entertainment and thus was able to draw a particularly heterogeneous audience. This created an unusual space for experiencing diversity, for what Hansen frames as 'civil interaction among strangers'.[16] The active sociality of the non-filmic activities, such as sing-alongs, ensured that the cinema experience was in some sense collective.

The structural conditions of viewership and the characteristics of film itself had changed by the First World War: narrative film increased the propensity for audience identification and absorption into the space of the screen, film distribution was more fully industrialised, film presentation more regulated, non-filmic elements and attractions were largely

eliminated, and an interactive audience was disciplined into a mass of
mute individual spectators through rules of silence; all of these factors led
to a cinema experience that was less improvised and locally contingent,
in short one that had fewer of the characteristics of a vibrant alternative
public sphere. The architecture of the cinema itself became more concentrated on the screen. First screening venues were typically converted
spaces such as town halls, churches, schools, storefronts and vaudeville
theatres. Only as the logics of industrial film distribution were stabilised
did fixed-site cinemas emerge: between 1914 and 1922 roughly 4000 new
theatres were opened in the United States.[17] Many of these were so-called
movie palaces: ornate, opulent and sometimes fantastical spaces that were
attractions in themselves. Anne Friedberg quotes a quip made by the
movie exhibitor Marcus Loew in the 1920s: 'we sell tickets to theatres, not
movies'.[18]

One of these prosperous cinemas is featured in Vertov's 1928 *Man
with a Movie Camera*, which includes the space of the cinema as a crucial
component in the political potential of the film itself. Vertov initially was
concerned about the effects of new urban cinemas on audiences and even
wrote that the proletariat must be saved from what he called 'cinema
churches'.[19] In the case of his first newsreels, he initiated the idea of a
'mobile cinema' that would be taken from place to place, and would suit
a new kind of radical film because the film would now be shown in the
original context in which it was shot. Of course *Man with a Movie Camera*
does just that, in that the screen and the space of the cinema are continuous and reflexive. Vertov's insistence that the cinema should not obliterate
the conditions of urban space but rather create a dialogue between them
is achieved by the unprecedented attention given to the conditions of
viewing that this new cinema space produced and by making these conditions a topic for the viewer's awareness and consideration.

Friedberg traces a different argument with respect to the permanent
cinema in the 'tirades' and manifestos of the 1920s that rejected orna-
mentation as a distraction that undermines the potential absorptive
power of film; in the case of cinema a modernist design impulse was thus
interwoven with arguments about spectatorship and the opportunity that
a modern design, rid of distracting elements, affords the spectator 'to get
lost in the imaginary space of the screen', in an 'imaginary, *endless space*'.[20]
By the 1960s, when film theorists came to theorise the apparatus of the
cinema and cinematic spectatorship, the darkened theatre and the immersive screen had become defining features of 'the' cinema. And so Roland
Barthes could describe the 'cinema situation' as 'pre-hypnotic' and as a
'twilight reverie' in 'a veritable cinematic cocoon' of 'a dim, anonymous,

indifferent cube'; 'how many members of the cinema audience slide down into their seats as if into a bed . . .!'[21]

Against this backdrop of a torpid viewer glued to 'the mirror'/screen, Barthes is nonetheless aware of the public nature of the occasion; private film screenings hold no interest for him and of television he says only that it has 'doomed us to the Family'. Ungluing himself from the kind of passivity envisioned by spectator theorists of the 1970s and 1980s[22] involves for him not 'ideological vigilance' or a critical intellectual response, but a fuller appreciation of the embodied affective and vaguely erotic context, 'by letting oneself be fascinated *twice over*: by the image and by its surroundings'. 'I complicate a "relation" [between spectator and the screen] by a "situation"' which includes 'the texture of sound, the hall, the darkness, the obscure mass of other bodies, the rays of light entering the theatre, leaving the hall'.[23] Barthes (refreshingly) complicates the presumed narcissistic and passive spectator by acknowledging a fuller spatial and urban context. His is hardly a vision, however, of an engaged alternative public sphere.

Few such claims have been made by film theorists for modern cinema spaces. The tendency is to emphasise the darkness of the theatre and the overriding power of the screen. In her discussion of the materiality of the screen, Friedberg shapes her discussion around Hiroshi Sugimoto's extraordinary photographs of movie theatres (Figure 4.2). Sugimoto's concern was to photograph time itself. To this end, he left his camera aperture open for so long that the images on the movie screen vanished and in their place appeared a luminous empty white screen. Friedberg notes, 'But what remains here, despite the ephemeral instability of the cinematic image, is the materiality of the theatre.'[24] Friedberg nonetheless goes on to argue that the fact that Sugimoto created these photographs as an extensive series – photographs of screens and movie theatres throughout the world – reveals 'a structural similarity: each theatre is a synchronic exemplar of the constants of the architecture of spectatorship . . . Despite variations in theatre architecture and films projected, what remains – constant and haunting – is the screen.'[25]

And yet if one goes to a website of one of the movie houses shown in Sugimoto's photographs – and it is notable that so many cinemas now have their own websites or Facebook pages – a different representation of materiality emerges beyond the screen, one that dwells on the uniqueness of the place. The Canton Palace Theatre in Canton Ohio, one of the movie palaces photographed by Sugimoto, for instance, is in the midst of a 2012/13 capital campaign: by 2013 $887,510 had been secured from local foundations for renovations that have been ongoing since October 2012, and the goal is to

Figure 4.2 Canton Theatre Palace, Canton, Ohio, 1980.
(© Hiroshi Sugimoto, courtesy of Gallery Koyanagi.)

raise a further $310,290 through individual 'community member' gifts. The webpage is replete with 'Palace Stories', mostly sentimental reminiscences of both the place and films viewed there: for example, 'Having been raised in Canton, I love this place. Celebrated my son's 8th birthday here! Four generations of my family had been there, too. Volunteered many years ago, and still have commemorative brick . . . somewhere. Awe inspiring to the young, memory invoking to the not so young!'

Similar stories can be told in many cities. In Vancouver in 2012, the Heritage Vancouver Society named neighbourhood Movie Theatres as second in its list of top ten endangered sites in the city. The Society considers the loss of the Hollywood and the Ridge to be 'a tragedy' and outlines in great detail why historic movie theatres are significant.[26] They are 'intimate' and 'independently-run' 'everyday reminders of the past,' 'architectural treasures' that are 'much loved' features of 'community life'. They contribute to the 'special character' of the area and are 'neighbourhood community spaces' that are 'unlikely' to be replaced if lost. They contribute to the 'identity, character and vitality of the city's neighbourhoods' as 'landmarks and community spaces'. The Hollywood theatre is undergoing its own restoration and fund-raising campaign: the objective is to raise $20,000 for restoration from private donations to supplement the grant already received from the Vancouver Heritage Foundation.[27] The restoration is in line with the City of Vancouver's Cultural Heritage Plans for Vancouver as 'a city of vibrant creative neighbourhoods'.

It needs to be remembered that these are not fully public spaces: accessibility typically requires paying the price of admission. Cinemas have in many contexts instantiated ethnic, racialised and class divisions, in some instances informally (as in the ethnic-identified neighbourhood cinemas described by Hansen), but in many cases through restrictive scheduling, racially segregated seating arrangements and pricing.[28] And just as Hansen notes for early cinemas, most of these restored cinemas likely are not and will not become revolutionary public spaces – indeed the constant reference to the family in the testimonials on the Canton Palace Theatre website would drive Roland Barthes to despair.

But some of the other language of the Heritage Vancouver Society is worth attending to. There is an implicit critique of the corporatisation and homogenisation of programming associated with Cineplexes and there is an astute awareness that these are privately-owned but nonetheless community spaces that are unlikely to be replaced despite the function they serve as quasi-public spaces.

One need only read memoirs of those for whom access to a cinema is difficult to re-enchant the cinema as a public space of strangers sitting together in the dark. Raja Shehadeh writes of his grandmother's friend Esther Jallad, who went daily to one of three movie theatres in Ramallah:

> Esther carried one passion with her: she loved to go to the movies . . . Every afternoon at three-fifteen, dressed to the hilt, her pursed mouth heavily lipsticked, eyelids smudged with pink eyeshadow, her large handbag dangling from her crooked arm, she would walk down from her house to the cinema as though on a rendezvous that could not be missed . . . What did Esther make of the films she watched? She never discussed them, never spoke of what she saw. Her movie-going was a solemnly solitary affair.[29]

This was an affair that came to an abrupt end when Israel occupied the West Bank on 6 June 1967. When Esther's husband died, 'all her children abroad and no cinema to escape to', Esther moved to Amman to live with her daughter. A caring granddaughter bought her a video player with which to watch her favourite movies:

> To her amazement, Esther never used it. It was not for the films that Esther would go to the cinema: rather it was being in the dark, watching films with others,

young and old, who came for all sorts of reasons, and then leaving the emotionally charged, smoky hall for the other world outside, having made that other world seem different.[30]

The cinemas did reopen for a time in Ramallah but were forced to close down a few years after the First Intifada in 1987 'when the Israeli army began storming the darkened theatre to arrest suspected activists who were taking time off from resistance'.[31]

In the context of the Iraq–Iran war in 1988, Azar Nafisi writes of going to the cinema in Tehran to see a Tarkovsky film:

> the most amazing feature of the day was not the heavenly weather, not even the movie itself, but the crowd in front of the movie house. It looked like a protest rally. There were intellectuals, office workers, housewives, some with small children in tow, a young mullah standing uncomfortably to the side – the kind of mix of people you would never have found at any other gathering in Tehran . . . Inside . . . [t]here was a sense of wonder at being in a public place for the first time in years without fear or anger, being in a place with a crowd of strangers that was not a demonstration, a protest rally, a breadline or a public execution.[32]

At issue is not the distinctively absorptive experience of watching a film in the modern cinema[33] but the extent to which, in much film theory, a fuller experience of viewership has been collapsed into the screen. The predominant narrative is one of increased individuation and privatisation of viewership within the multiplex (where film viewership is often elided with shopping and consumerism and the potential for critical engagement seems slight)[34], in the home or in front of the computer screen.[35] What potential the actual spaces of viewership hold – at present – for the critical possibilities of cinema and film reception remains an open and uncertain question and is an issue to which we return.

Documentary Film as Public Discourse

But first consider this: perhaps the space of the cinema is not essential to film's capacity to build critical publics. In his otherwise appreciative discussion of Hannah Arendt's theorisation of public life, Michael Warner feels that her focus on speech and action now seems 'fairly antiquated' and reflects her 'unfortunate faithfulness to the metaphor of the polis rather than a complex understanding of how politics happens'.[36] For Arendt, being seen and heard by others is deeply significant because individuals see and listen from different positionalities: 'This is the meaning of public life, compared to which even the richest and most satisfying family life can offer only the prolongation or multiplication of one's own perspective with its attending aspects and perspectives.'[37] Retaining as a defining characteristic the notion that the public is a relation among strangers, Warner nonetheless rethinks the spatiality of the public in mass-mediated societies. For Warner, the public comes into being only in relation to texts (including filmic texts) and their circulation; it is an ongoing social 'space' of discourse, organised around nothing other than discourse itself. A public is a self-organised voluntary association, constituted by active uptake of a discourse or text. A public discourse 'promises to address anybody. It commits itself in principle to the possible participation of any stranger.'[38] Warner contrasts this to a concrete audience, a crowd witnessing itself in visible space, on the grounds that such a public has a 'sense of totality bounded by the event or by the shared public space'.[39] For Warner, a public is less spatially bounded.

We will want to reconsider Warner's assumptions about the spatially bounded nature of any audience; while it is the discourse that moves, the space of the theatre may be significant to its propulsion. But let us follow Warner's argument one step further. In his view, the kinds of texts/discourse/speech that publics might organise around are many; the only quality that Warner specifies is that their address must be both personal and impersonal: this 'gives a general social relevance to private thought and life'.[40] Within film studies a particular type of film has held the promise of organising publics; this is the documentary or non-fiction film. Jane Gaines writes of a 'mythology on the Left . . . that documentary film has a legacy of social change'.[41] As to whether there are grounds for this mythology, there is some doubt. She recounts a study done in 1995 by Kirwin Cox of the National Film Board of Canada in which he polled forty-eight film scholars and film-makers for their opinions about documentaries that 'changed the world'. 'In the end, they settled for films that had had some local "influence" for want of examples associated with cataclysmic change.'[42] Repeating this exercise among colleagues and associates, Gaines reports that they could list documentary films that moved them personally but were uncertain about larger claims. 'As I anticipated, they argued that it was only in connection with moments or movements that films could be expected to make a contribution to social change, and that in and of themselves, they had no power to affect political situations.'[43]

The lines between non-fiction and fiction film are now very blurry and the effectiveness of documentary film tends no longer to be tied to claims to realism or objectivity.[44] There remains, however, an understanding that the term documentary refers to a specific relation between the film and the world beyond. Jane Gaines theorises this through the concept of mimesis, arguing that radical film derives its power from the events it depicts; the worldliness of documentary film footage acts in a distinctively mimetic way on the bodies of the viewers. This is what moves audiences collectively 'to get up out of their theatre seats and take some kind of group action'.[45] Vivian Sobchack argues that the term documentary can be thought more radically as a particular mode of subjective relation to a cinematic 'text', that is, as an experience rather than a genre or thing. It is a mode of consciousness and identification with the cinematic image/sound that involves considerable traffic between the image/sound on the screen and the world outside. She draws upon the psychologist Jean-Pierre Meunier's tripartite distinction between the perception of home movies (the experience of which she thinks is more aptly expressed in French as *film-souvenir*), documentary and fiction film. With a *film-souvenir*, one already knows the object represented in the film and the cinematic image is a marker of one's own experience; it is a prompt to memory. With fictional film, we only know the objects represented in the film though the film and thus we are entirely dependent on the screen for knowledge. The documentary is somewhere in between and involves bringing personal and cultural knowledge to the process of viewing: we 'see beyond the screen's boundaries and back into our own life-world'.[46] Sobchack's insistence that the documentary mode of attention and learning about the world exists in a pre-existing relationship between the screen and already available cultural knowledges (rather than being a characteristic of the cinematic text itself – the film might be a documentary or fictional film depending on what the viewer brings to the experience) suggests that the type of mimesis that Gaines attributes to documentary film may exceed the conventions of genre. Or as Anna Godas, the CEO of Dogwoof, the largest distributor of documentary films in the UK, put it: 'I hate those festivals that throw all kinds of documentaries together as if the category made them all the same. [It is important to understand] the film in relation to the world out there.'[47]

Whether and how the circulation of discourse shapes a critical public depends, then, not just on the film 'text' or genre but on existing conditions of everyday life, that is, the cultural knowledges that audiences bring to occasions of experiencing film. Lesley Stern frames her analysis of kung fu films' role in shaping public life in Zimbabwe through the questions: 'How do movies move?' How can we understand the 'after life' of movies? Her interest is less in the global circulation of kung fu films than on 'the fertility of encounter generated in "local" places'.[48] Such an analysis demands understanding how films circulate and articulate with social spaces outside of the cinema: it is in the 'space between history and imaginative possibility as well as in geographical space that the relation unfolds'.[49] In Bulawayo (the second largest city of Zimbabwe), the acrobatic skill and energy of the filmic bodies in kung fu films, Stern argues, moved from the screen through the people who watched them, to produce sensations of movement and affective engagement and catharsis, as well as imaginative projections of different modes of being and forms of psychic and social engagement. These fantasies have had great appeal within a context of struggle against first a colonial and then an oppressive post-colonial state, the latter effectively evacuating a functioning public sphere. In Bulawayo, the martial arts of the kung fu films (literally) resonated as an aesthetics and a form of disciplined work on self that seems to offer a means to overcome personal and social adversity. The Amakhosi theatre company incorporated this kung fu training into its process of doing community theatre. Already acquainted with kung fu through movies, 'people came in droves'[50] when the company offered training in kung fu, first in the contained yards of members' homes, then in a small office downtown and then twice a week in an open public square. The community theatre company invited those who came to their kung fu training sessions to take part in public discussions as well, and Amakhosi is now an influential grassroots cultural institution that plays an important role nationally promoting discussion around critical issues of politics, health, women's rights and urban and rural development.[51] Subjected to state surveillance, intimidation, harassment, arrest and detention, in 2008 Cont Mhlanga, the founder of Amakhosi, won the *Freedom to Create* Prize for 'practising protest theatre and challenging state ideologies in Zimbabwe for over 25 years'.[52] Kung fu films were an unlikely but non-trivial part of this process and they were impactful because they resonated with conditions and social meanings in the context.

Thus when the film scholars and film-makers polled by Kirwin Cox identified films that had had some local 'influence' this may be no small thing. And perhaps Gaines is too quick to oppose this local influence to cataclysmic change. And yet to frame documentary film as a circulating discourse without paying close attention to the ways that experiences beyond the film, as well as the concrete site of viewing, affect whether and how it circulates seems to miss important elements of the process. We more fully consider this issue through a close study of *Fix: The Story of an Addicted City*, a film that arguably moved off the screen into the polling booths of the City of Vancouver and into political spaces in other urban contexts. As a circulating discourse that gathered a public, the spaces of the cinema and the city beyond are critical to this process of circulation and reception. As for telling this story, there is no livelier narrator than the director, Nettie Wild.

Gathering a Public: Fix: The Story of an Addicted City *(2002)*

I[53] was told by somebody that there was a meeting that was happening in the bowels of St Paul's hospital. I walked into the room and there was a phenomenal electricity that I had felt in other parts of the world where there's major social change going down. I had just finished making *A Place Called Chiapas* [1998] about the Zapatistas in Chiapas, Mexico. I'd felt it there. I'd felt it up north with people who were battling over First Nations' land claims. I felt it in the Philippines [filming *A Rustling of Leaves: Inside the Philippines Revolution*, 1988]. But I'd never really felt it in my own city before.

Eight months later I was [still] shooting and we had 350 hours of footage [documenting the political process of implementing radical drug and health reform]. I realized that I was having the real privilege of filming the birth of a social movement. And that was pretty darn exciting.

And there are all sorts of surprise elements in the footage, not the least Philip Owen. He was the mayor of Vancouver at the time. Mr Straight. But he did something that most politicians never do; he ended up doing what he thought was right – not what was politically expedient or what would allow him to hold on to his job. So he lost it [his job as mayor].

What happens in the movie is that you see him battling to get the city council on side. He's putting forward a *proposed* Framework for Action[54] but there were three points that drove people crazy and one of them was the supervised injection site. While we were making the film there were huge challenges to him from within his own party. Because don't forget, Philip came from the most conservative party, which makes this story even more astounding. I always like to say that what *Fix* showed me was that there's a point in a social movement where a spark is struck and it [snaps fingers] catches fire. But there are many many sparks that happen over the years and they don't catch and the reason they don't catch is because the kindling hasn't been laid. And what I thought I saw was that in the ten years previous to when we were filming the kindling had been laid by a whole bunch of different people.

In the opening scene of *Fix* – the opening *vérité* scene – you get into the van and you're taking off to a demonstration, and Dean Wilson [President of VANDU, Vancouver Area Network of Drug Users] has to stop because he has to get his methadone or he's going to fall apart. He jumps out of the van and when he comes back moments later he's not sweating anymore. He's got his act together. And where are they going? They're going to city hall to carry a coffin into the council chambers to confront the council who have rebelled against the mayor and have forced him to stop putting forward any kind of progressive drug policies. So I'm in this van with these really intriguing people – Ann and Dean and a whole bunch of people – and they're talking about being extremely strategic. And they're saying: 'The mayor is not the problem. What we've got to do is back the mayor up.' And I didn't understand. I was new to the subject. And I'm going: 'Here are these extremely radical, street entrenched people, and they're finding a way to support the mayor in all of this?' It was a head twist for me because I was carrying assumptions into it and I was assuming that this guy who I'd seen on the news was just this super straight guy. I was a bit muddled about what his take was. But the drug users weren't. He was truly courageous and he was going forward into something that really spooked him. So we [the camera and members of VANDU] go charging into the chambers and that's when the film meets Philip Owen (Figures 4.3 and 4.4).

Eventually I followed three people: Ann and Dean and Philip. And there was also Bryce Rositch [representing a business association against drug reform]. And then we had our fifth figure: the Sarge – Sergeant

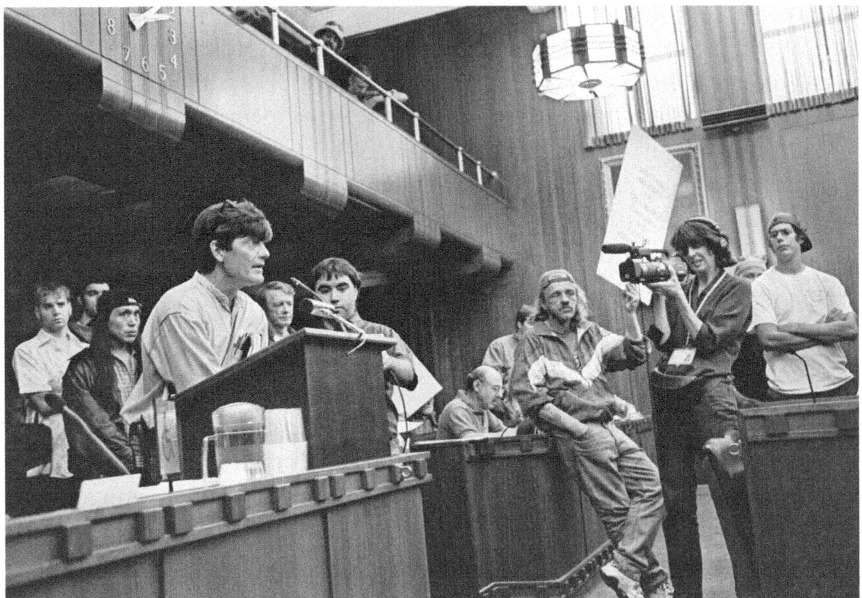

Figure 4.3 Nettie Wild filming Dean at City Council; *Fix: The Story of an Addicted City*. (Photo credit: Elaine Briere.)

Figure 4.4 Mayor Owen managing a public demonstration within Council Chambers, *Fix: The Story of an Addicted City*. (Photo credit: Elaine Briere.)

Lang, who was the cop. And he's not really buying into the line for harm reduction. But he's a wise guy who's been around a long time, and he has this really pragmatic and slightly fed-up attitude.

So those were our five characters. And as this rolled out, the stakes became higher for everybody: the police are in a weird spot [given the illegality of a supervised injection site], the drug users absolutely have to push for this because they're dying [Vancouver had an extraordinarily high drug overdose rate at the time], and Philip is increasingly starting to understand that key members of his party are knifing him in the back because of his progressive stand on creating harm reduction programs for drug users. And then when we were just finishing the editing, we get back to that [snaps fingers] spark. I believe that the spark for Vancouver was the morning that Philip Owen announced that he wasn't going to run for mayor. It was all very polite and all very Canadian [but he was pushed out by a number of members of his own party]. I think it was at that moment Mr. and Mrs. Joe Average picked up the morning paper and went 'Holy shit! This guy is falling on his sword for a bunch of drug users. Maybe I should listen up.' I don't think that Philip's story is any more important than Ann's or Dean's or VANDU's story. They all had their sparks, but this spark of Philip's just hit when finally the kindling was dry enough and there was enough of it.

This was at the beginning of a huge run-up to the election and so we worked really hard to get the film finished. For two reasons: I knew that if we had our film ready we would have a huge audience. And the other part was that I figured this film could really do something. And so we worked like heck to launch that film. And we ran for five weeks at the Granville 7 [a downtown Cineplex] leading up to the election and used the momentum of all that press to get people to come into the cinema. It's at that point that the film was completely stitched into the rhythm of the city. It was so exciting. As an artist and as Jane Citizen, it was fantastic. My job was to get the show biz to kick in, it's about bringing people into a cinema. The theatre is like a village well. Granville 7 said, 'Well, we'll give you an opening week, and then we'll see how the box office goes.' Voom! Went through the roof. And we had talkback sessions at every 7 o'clock show, seven days a week. I would make sure [that there was a panel there]: Ann and Dean were very cooperative, Philip was often there, the Sarge came a lot. We had lots of debate. My job was [to insist] – just like the movie – 'You can't just have everybody on the same side of the road here, because nothing is going to move forward unless we make it very clear that people are welcome no matter what you think. As long as people don't hurt other people in their discussion, you can say anything you want.' I really encouraged people in the audience who were trepidatious about harm reduction to speak about their fears. I was very very clear with the panel respondents that you're in a powerful position up there and you never shut people down.

It just took off. In the movie theatre there's two rules when you do this kind of thing: nothing gets in the way of the next show going up in time, and nobody gets in the way of the popcorn lineup. If you make sure that the house manager sees that you understand that, you can have a great time. There was only a half hour or maybe 45 minutes between shows and I had to get the 7 o'clock audience out and the 9 o'clock audience in, and have a discussion in between. We set it up so that the cinema was self-cleaning. I could say to the cinema managers, 'You don't have to send the cleaners in.' I'd just get everybody in the 7 o'clock show to take all their stuff out so that we could get another five minutes or another seven minutes for discussion. That's how hungry people were for it. I would facilitate the discussion and set up something that really moved. That meant people didn't get to be touchy feely and do all the group grope stuff where they all take forever to introduce themselves and all the rest of it. I would introduce whoever we had on the panel in one sentence and then we'd go straight to questions from the audience. Nobody was given the chance to speechify. I'd make sure the lighting was right, and the microphone was right, and so people could see them when they spoke. It's about community; it's about really respecting, opening up the space, so that what happens after the movie is driven by the audience. And then we would have these extraordinary events.

For me it was really exciting because I felt that we had created a narrative that reflected reality and we were able to get the nuance and make it work as the fabulous high stakes story that it was. It was about a narrative in which there were really high stakes on a very personal level. If you look at the structure of *Fix*, the structure is this: will Dean kick heroin? And will he get the girl [Ann Livingston]? And the second theme is not slight because the biggest thing for somebody who is addicted is whether or not they can be loved. It's very, very hard for somebody to love somebody who's addicted to cocaine and heroin and anything else that is going by.

It's not an activist film. This was me trying to get a bead on that story as best as I can. I was fascinated by the dynamics of people trying to open a supervised injection site. It both makes me smile and makes me really angry when people would accuse me, as they did during the making of *Fix* when we filmed a rally, of staging it! And I'd go, 'Wow, you must think I'm really powerful! There's ten thousand people in the streets.' *Fix* is not me trying to articulate the Framework for Action or anybody else's agenda. With people who introduce me as an activist filmmaker, I'll say, 'No, I want to challenge that because – it's not that I'm against activists or activist filmmakers, I'm just not one of them.' My job as a filmmaker is to do the storytelling. A lot of my stories are around activists. My way of taking them seriously is to really go into the contradictions of what they have to face. And then you get how bloody hard it is. So that's my job. I do find activists really fascinating. They put a lot on the line. It's huge. But I don't think you're doing any service by just trotting out propaganda. A lot of so-called activist films, nobody watches them. They're boring.

All of that changes in distribution. Once the picture's locked and I can go to sleep at night and know that I haven't been coerced or given somebody short shrift because of a political agenda, it's a whole different ball game. Because I want my movie to be seen. Usually what happens at that point is you get on board somebody's train. And in this particular case it was the harm reduction train. The police unions weren't bringing us to town across the country, but the harm reduction people were. This doesn't mean to say we didn't reach out to the police unions. But that's not who was helping us get out there. And so at that point I had become an activist *distributor*.

What happened [in the first instance] was there was the run-up to the election here in Vancouver. [Nettie is quoted in a national magazine as saying: 'It's Canada's first drug election.'[55]] The Mayor's former party abandoned his commitment to drug reform, while the leading opponent's campaign was: 'Vote for me and I'll open a supervised injection site.' And so what happens? The biggest landslide victory in the history of the city [in support for opening the supervised injection site]. [The film] definitely had its role. *McLeans* [magazine] said that there were seven major factors that had influenced this election and *Fix* was one of them. It's interesting if you do the math: we were looking at [audiences of] about three thousand a week, times 5 weeks. So only fifteen thousand had seen the film. But I know that my film ramped up the level of discussion and I think it was a combination of what happened in the theatre on the screen and then what happened in the talkback sessions afterwards. And then, most importantly, how that translated out of the theatre. So it's all those conversations the next morning, at work, in the locker room, and all the rest of it. The film was becoming far bigger than it actually was. It was being referred to so much in the media, and there's a kind of recognition factor. What's happening here is that there's a real place for story and art within the community discourse. So we're rockin' right now. It's just completely taking over: a lot of coverage in the media, huge amount of coverage on television, and radio, and in the press.

And then [after the election] we started to move across the country [to promote harm reduction programs nation-wide]. I toured [the film across Canada] with the Christian Ann, the addict, the mayor and the baby [of Ann and Dean]. We played over 30 cities right across the country. We'd go into a community, and Philip would head straight for the mayor and the chief of police because he knew them. He'd hit town and he'd just start working them, to try and get them to come, or to get councilors to come to the screenings. And the rule was that they'd never be outed at these screenings. If he or she had no idea of how to respond or they were really reactionary, we'd say, 'You can do anything you want, you can hide behind the curtains. We just want you to listen to your community having this discussion.' Ann would start sniffing around for users and try to start organizing them immediately. I'd be dealing with the cinemas. And Dean would be looking to score. We always had our *Fix* crew and then we'd try and match it up with [local people] [In discussion people would always be interested in Vancouver's Downtown Eastside] and we'd go, 'Of course, we're more than happy to respond to questions about Vancouver's Downtown Eastside, but let's always try and tie it back to where we are.' [The issue was very threat-ening]: there were staff within the City of Kelowna [for instance] who got email directives that they were under no circumstances to be seen as public servants at the *Fix* screenings: 'If you're going, you're going on your own time and we really don't want you there.' We were up against forces that were incredibly threatened by this whole rigmarole. And our secret weapon was Philip. You know, myself and Ann and Dean, we were kind of the predictable side, but then you bring in your low flying missile in a three-piece suit.

A couple of moments touring the film were really amazing. One was when we were in Kamloops. We'd been told by the theatre that not many people were going to come and they wouldn't give us more than a couple of nights and they only gave us a 7 o'clock show. And I'd said, 'You're crazy. You don't know what's up in your own town.' But anyway, that's what they would give us. So we came into town, Philip got the RCMP guy to come out, and we're doing all our stuff, and at about 4 o'clock in the afternoon the cinema manager says, 'We're going to have to put on a 9 o'clock show because we're already sold out in advance.' This was a big theatre, it was about a 500-seat theatre. I introduced Philip. When Philip walked down the aisle, the whole theatre rose as one. And Philip knows Kamloops, and he knows how conservative it is, and he knows all the battles that various different people are having. So in Kamloops he had been expecting the worst. The roof went off that building. He answered questions and there was a huge ovation afterwards.

So the next day, we met for breakfast and he looks at me and goes: 'You know, Nettie? In the end, I won, didn't I?' And I said, 'Yeah you big dope, of course you have.' And he said, 'Well, you know words like community and . . . you've taught me the word revolution[56] – it doesn't come easily to me – I find it really hard to even say.' This is what I mean by saying it was a birth of a social movement.

That *Fix* entered into and articulated a public sphere, none of the central protagonists (or media) are in doubt.[57] In Wild's phrasing, it got 'com-pletely stitched into the rhythm of the city'. It became part of a much longer Vancouver-based political process to reshape drug policy in Canada, to fundamentally reframe addiction as a health as opposed to a criminal justice problem. As Wild tells it, the kindling had been set and dried for over a decade and *Fix* was released at a moment when the issue could ignite. The 'text' of the film was no doubt significant to this process of gathering a public. It is a hybrid text with many points of entry and identification: part love story, part graphic battle of one man trying to overcome drug addiction, part awakening of the mayor from middle-class slumber to a knowledgeable passion for the health and well-being of the most marginalised members of the community, part expose of political intrigue within city council, part story of care and community among extremely precarious drug users – one that stretches the intelligibility of who counts as human for a middle-class mainstream viewer. Philip Owen, the low-flying missile in a three-piece suit, and Ann Livingston, a clear-eyed, cynical, take-no-guff from Dean, never-been-addicted advocate for harm reduction – both of these individuals offer points of identification for a wide audience of viewers. As Ann Livingston puts it: 'You can't watch that film and not be altered.'[58]

But the effectiveness of the film is in no way detached from its exhibition: both the actual theatre space and the local contexts in which the film was screened. As Wild presents herself, she is an activist distributor, not an activist film-maker. The material space of the downtown Vancouver Cineplex was itself a barrier that had to be surmounted: at the time it had no facility for digital projection and Wild's video had to be converted to 35mm film at great expense.[59] At the same time, complicating a narrative within film studies of the modern movie multiplex theatre as a consumer space, Wild worked this space and brought it to life as a public space in which a difference of opinion could be presented and debated. Please note that this was a multiplex space, not the neighbourhood theatre beloved by those who envision the cinema as a public sphere. The movie theatre, even the multiplex theatre, then, can be used to get people out for an evening of public discussion – with consequence. Philip Owen tells a story[60] of screening the film in Montreal where the current mayor was unwilling to take a public stand in favour of a supervised injection site, even though the federal government had offered eight million dollars to do so.[61] First reluctant to attend, the Montreal mayor called Owen back: his wife had heard about the film and would like to see it. She wanted to bring her 17-year-old daughter (and her husband) along. Although the mayor attempted to attend anonymously as a private citizen, the media was alerted to his presence and when he left the theatre he 'got scrummed'. To his surprise, his attendance at the film drew favourable media attention, and it was this, in Philip Owen's view, that brought the Montreal mayor in line with the harm-reduction plan (including supervised injection site).[62] Attending the screening of *Fix* in the concrete public space of the theatre was, in other words, consequential. Ann Livingston speaks of the organising generated by the film screenings at the other end of the political spectrum. She would do user organising during the day and invite people along to the film that night, where 'they get to speak to their own local people'. 'As a result of us going across the country with the film, drug user groups started up. Often we would pass the popcorn bag right there and they'd get 800 bucks for local people who wanted to start something. The popcorn bag is a Nettie invention.' It is a smart invention that seems to call up what we want to say about the embodied mobilities of cinema and publics: more than discourse, film can move into the public sphere, but not without traces of the spatiality and materiality of its exhibition practices.

The 'Death of Cinema' and (some of) its Mutations

Miriam Hansen distills debates about the doomed fate of cinema to two claims: first, that the shift from photochemically based images to digital coding has attenuated cinema's relation to reality and, second, that the circulation of digital technology has marginalised theatrical projection and dispersed the viewing of films to various other, often smaller, screens and multi-media platforms. The first she considers to be 'a red herring'.[63] Of the latter she is less certain. Suspicious of the rhetoric of historical breaks, she nonetheless believes that there has been a 'palpable, seismic shift' in cinema's relation to publicness. This goes beyond, she believes, the threat to 'the status of cinema as a space of projection' and 'relates to the transformations of just about everything surrounding the cinema – the amazing reorganization of everyday experience in terms of spatiotemporal coordinates, modes of sensory perception and attention, cognition, affect, and memory, sociability and the circulation of knowledge'. 'Obviously,' she states, 'I am referring to the rise of the Internet' and the ways in which various media and technologies of social networking are combined in mobile devices.[64] Our ambitions in relation to this shift are relatively modest: to consider some of the mutations to cinema that are emerging in the current moment and their relevance to the formation of critical publics and politics.

Cities and Cinemas in Ruins

As Deleuze observed in *The Movement Image* with respect to filmic images of European cities bombed in the Second World War, an urban ruin is also a place of potential; as an 'any-space-whatever' a ruin is wasted, indeterminate and available for something new. It might not be too farfetched to think about this in relation to cinema spaces themselves and the creativity that has emerged in relation to some of them. There is any number of examples.

Consider the cinema ruin noticed by Inass Yassin in 2008: the abandoned Al-Walid cinema in Ramallah, one of the three movie theatres
beloved by Esther Jallad. Purchased by Al-Bakri Stores for demolition
and redevelopment, the building lay in ruins (the redevelopment stalled
by nearby shop owners who, protected by rental contracts, had – at least
temporarily – refused to leave). In May 2008, the caretaker of the building
hesitantly let the artist enter, and her video footage taken through 2008
shows a gutted building strewn with garbage and remnants from its last
days as an exhibition space.[65] The ruin is a living – not a museum but a
living – sedimentation of culture and politics: she found posters of Arab
films from the 1960s, the iconic poster from 2000 of Faris Audeh facing
an Israeli tank holding a stone, a poster of a champion wrestler, another
of Yasser Arafat 'unnoticed which had fallen upside down on the ground',
and 'the green flag of Hamas[66] resting on part of the cut-off building'. On
the walls of the emptied projectionist room are drawings of tools typically
used to repair and ensure the continuity of everyday life: a hammer, pliers,
a wrench and chisel. A 35mm film reel is traced on the wall, with the script
'No God but Allah' inscribed within.[67] As part of an ongoing Projection
project, in 2010 the artist reproduced one of the two posters that she had
found still displayed on the interior walls of the ruin: the publicity poster
for the popular 1969 Egyptian musical *Abi Fawk Ash-Shajarah*. The poster
features the two stars of the film in a romantic embrace.[68] As a limited
edition of 200 copies, these posters were placed in public places throughout Ramallah with a sticker attached announcing that the film would be
screened at the Al-Walid cinema on 12 July 2010 at 8 p.m.; admission
would be free (Figure 4.5). The poster itself elicited divided reactions:
pleasure among those who loved the film – some reported to the artist
that they had viewed it more than fifty times, and opposition from those
for whom a kiss in public is inappropriate (Figure 4.6). On the night of
the promised screening, 80–100 people gathered at the Al-Walid theatre,
not just the expected audience for a 'art event' coming from within the
cultural or intellectual scene, but people from a wider public who had seen
the poster and wanted to see the film. This included a woman in her sixties
wearing jibabi, who waited with her bags from shopping. When asked
why she is there, she replied that she wanted to see *Abi Fawk Eshajarah*
because it reminded her of her youth. Now surrounded by a barrier wall of
twenty-foot corrugated metal fencing, the top of the site further enclosed
by a billowing white tarpaulin, entry was not possible. The songs from the
film emanated from within the ruins. The artist describes the occasion as a
'reversal journey in time' that 'brought people out of their daily context to
the moment of cultural collectiveness from the late 60s', an era that is now

Figure 4.5 Inass Yassin's *Projection*, Poster Appropriation, 2010; the poster on the street. (© Inass Yassin.)

recalled against 'a current political vacuum and the consumerism of an emerging global culture'.[69] The prospective audience had come with their passion for the film and for cinema and their expectation of seeing the film. 'When the songs started, they started to cry.'[70] When the media arrived, the owner of the site became concerned that the experience and the debate instigated by the installation might jeopardise his plans to demolish the building.[71]

The artist has no illusions about the impact of her project; she notes that the project attracted considerable attention among a limited and selective population: academics, intellectuals and the art community. Nonetheless it is worth noting the potency of the cinema as a ruined space as a catalyst for debate. A kiss in public instantiates the strange sociality of the cinema, intermingling public and private, intimacy, politics and commerce. To collectively re-experience the songs of *Abi Fawk Ash-Shajarah* with strangers in the dark, on the street, closed off from what was through the 1950s and 1960s a vibrant site for the transmission and shared reception of Arab-language film and musical culture is to provoke questions and prompt a debate about Palestinian society and the urban restructuring of Ramallah today. The loss of a space in which different ages and languages and classes co-mingled in the past raises questions about the production of urban landscapes as fortified office towers and shopping complexes,

Figure 4.6 Inass Yassin's *Projection*, Poster Appropriation, 2010; the poster.
(© Inass Yassin.)

questions that resonate widely beyond Ramallah. Collective embodied experiences of memories of *Abi Fawk Ash-Shajarah* also raise more particular questions about Palestinian social and political aspirations. The artist reflects:

I'm not sure what the value of my work is in this moment, but we live in a time that reveals every day that we keep losing what we once took for granted. And this process of vanishing spaces, ideas, notions, and values in such a transforming reality exists not only in Ramallah or Palestine but throughout the Arab world.[72] In Ramallah and maybe in the Arab world, the disappearance of cinema houses is not merely manifesting and clarifying the regeneration of the space and the consequences of high-tech entertainment technology; it synchronizes or indicates the emergence of a new social and value system that condemns the cultural and social practice that we lived just yesterday.[73]

In some contexts, new cinema spaces are emerging from the rubble. Writing about the creation of Cinémathèque de Tanger in 2003,[74] for instance, two artists, Bouchra Khalili and Yto Barrada, describe its beginnings within the ruins of failed cinemas in Tangier: 'It all started with the building. Its beauty, its location, its history, the need to restore it. It had to be saved, but for what purpose?'[75] The co-founders wondered if they 'weren't crazy'[76] to open the cinémathèque in the context of cinema closures, the dominance of multiplexes and the proliferation of pirated DVDs. It was at the Casa Barata, the flea market, 'that we fully realized that we were founding a cinémathèque. We were literally picking Super 8 reels, older than we were, off the ground, and dreaming about the treasures they might contain.' These artists had to learn the business of running a cinema in order to

> fill a void and bring a certain kind of magic back into the city . . . to offer Tangier a real center for culture, for creativity, for debate that was lacking in a city of one million inhabitants which has some nice remains, but where there's no theatre, library or concert hall.[77]

> We did not belong to the world of cinema owners, but we were sure that the city needed a beautiful cinema, beautiful films, a cozy café. Today the café is always full, it's a place where young people meet. And the collection of films, anachronistic and elitist as it may at first seem, is a treasure for that very reason.

They run a film club for children aged six to twelve, the Magic Lantern, and have established a second such club at the Metropolis theatre in Beirut.

> These children are our audience for both today and tomorrow, for the future. They'll grow up remembering the films they saw at Cinémathèque and they'll keep coming, because the experience of seeing films in a movie theatre will have been part of their lives from childhood. Because they will have an awareness that cinema has a history, tells stories and accompanies History.[78]

If Cinémathèque de Tanger creates a public sphere in one way in Tangier (and other ways in Tunis, Beirut, Cairo and Ramallah through the Network of Arab Arthouse Screens, co-founded by its creators), the hope is that it will perform in yet another critical way in Barcelona where a satellite cinema was opened in 2011. The hope is that the actual space of the cinema, along with the programme of films, will call attention to an often ignored fact that '75 per cent of the population [of the city] is of immigrant origins, mostly Arab'.[79] What is repressed in Barcelona about immigration and racial diversity might be brought into visibility by the cinema itself.

Alternatively, in Los Angeles, in a city awash with screens and movie houses, David James identifies Cinefamily as one of two exhibition spaces that currently has the largest impact. Housed in the last operating venue dedicated to silent films, the theatre was closed in 1997 for several years, then bought and run as a silent movie venue 'with middling success' and more recently purchased by the current owner in 2007: 'Cinefamily took over the dead space, banished its ghosts, and turned it into carnival.' Paired with unusual programming (the *filmic*) are 'similarly radical innovations in the *cinematic*, the social functions that film sustains'. The Cinefamily's publicly stated goal is to 'foster a spirit of community and a sense of discovery, while reinvigorating the movie-going experience. Like campfires, sporting events and church services, we believe that movies work best as social experiences.' To this end they offer the possibility of unlimited entry for $25 a month, serve coffee on a backyard patio (and turn a blind eye 'to whatever else [audience members] may have smuggled in') and coordinate screenings with musical events and other activities.[80]

In a decidedly non-hipster, seemingly socially conservative mode, the Hollywood theatre in Vancouver has been rented by a pentacostal church. In this, the Hollywood is in no way unique.[81] On Pastors.com, Brandon Cox lists ten reasons to launch a church in a movie theatre; the first speaks to its appeal to a wider public: 'People love walking into theaters. Some cultural barriers between church and non-churchgoer are already out of the way.'[82] Pastor Kasakos also speaks of the power of the cinema to advance the evangelical mission:

> I like to call this 'theo-tainment.' Hundreds of years ago . . . coming to the big city to an epic-sized cathedral with stained glass was a stimulating sight to see and assisted people in mind and heart to focus on the divine. In our modern world, people go to movie theaters to get inspiration and to be taken to new places in their minds. Well, why not use this great technology for God?[83]

Pastor Kasakos' invocation of the cinema as inspirational calls up Vertov's aversion to the mystifying awe invoked by the movie cinema; recall that it was his critique of the 'cinema-church' that led Vertov to create the 'mobile cinema' to show the new 'cine-form' in the original context of its shooting.[84]

Still, the Hollywood is taking shape as a complex social space. Used as a church on Sundays, church members open it to various secular communities at other times. Aware of its not-too-distant past as a more varied performance space (e.g. in November 1959 Doug Hepburn set a world weight-lifting record by curling a 255lbs weight on the stage of the Hollywood theatre), church members tie their hopes for restoration to reinventing the space as a public one, with a base of support coming from across a mash-up of community uses and users.[85] The themed film screenings are periodic – every month or so – and for the most part are the opposite of avant-garde.[86] The funds raised (by donation) from these screenings are used for the restoration of the rented building and shared with other community organisations in the neighbourhood. A year prior to its new life as a church, the building was sold to a local property owner/ developer by the family who built the Hollywood in 1935 and then ran the movie house until 2011. The current owner has no immediate interest in revitalising the theatre or restoring the building itself; in that sense it was a dead space likely being held for demolition and redevelopment. The fact that the Church has rented and reoccupied a building that had been left empty for a year has helped to stabilise the street, if only in the short term. Just as James notes of Cinefamily's effect on its immediate neigh-bourhood (formerly empty storefronts now house bookshops and retail stores), the small business owners close to the Hollywood report that their business has improved. In this sense, restoration of the Hollywood could be slowing rather than speeding up the process of local demolition and redevelopment, as nearby businesses become less economically vulnerable to acquisition. The cinema is simultaneously being reinvented as a prom-isingly incoherent public space.

It is not only that older, often second-run cinemas can be flexible spaces that can be used to foster different forms of sociality; cities tend to have small or large areas of 'interim', 'indeterminate' or 'interstitial' spaces which offer unexpected possibilities for cultural innovation and a range of informal and formal, underground and autonomous activities. Florian Haydn and Robert Temel's *Temporary Urban Spaces* is a manifesto of sorts for the creative possibilities that temporariness offers to those who wish to use urban public space 'in a culturally subversive way'.[87] Temporary or pop-up cinemas are ubiquitous among such temporary urban spaces. As *The Guardian* phrased it in August 2011, 'pop-up cinema is having a moment'.[88] In London alone: Secret Cinema selects locations to more fully immerse audiences in the film: 'We want people to feel like they're stepping into the film' and to re-experience cinema afresh 'like when you went to the movies as child'; Cycle-in Cinema is an ongoing, 'off the grid' pay-what-you-can outdoor cinema powered by audience members on their bikes; Floating Cinema (also ongoing) is a narrow boat turned into a twelve-seat cinema; Films on Fridges projected films from 27 July through to 12 August 2011 amidst discarded refrigerators; Cineroleum was a temporary cinema (summer 2010) in a disused petrol station; Folly for a Flyover was a temporary cinema and café built in summer 2011 under two concrete bridges where they cross the Hackney Cut (a constructed waterway).[89]

All of these projects are or were site-specific and some engage/d directly with ideas of waste, recycling, abandoned or neglected spaces and local histories through their form (and to varying extents film and other programming).[90] Films on Fridges was located on Fish Island in Hackney Wick, at the site of former 'Fridge Mountain' (for a time one of Europe's largest piles of discarded refrigerators). The creator, a spatial planning and urban design graduate student, claims that it speaks

> primarily to the profound transformation in Hackney Wick, Fish Island, and really, the whole of East London. It seeks to resurrect elements of the 'Fridge Mountain' to provide a creative platform for showcasing the past, present, and future histories associated with the local area and allow a space for those varying narratives to co-exist.[91]

To this end, recycled refrigerator doors, obtained from 'the world's largest electronics recycler', were used to frame the screen and construct chairs and tables: 'This was just a brief fun stop in their recycling life-cycle.'[92] Along with this fun, the event was meant to stimulate awareness around local history and environmental issues. The Cineroleum (Figure 4.7) was created by a collective of artists, designers and architects, now named Assemble Studio, and was hand-built from donated and found materials: the screen from a skip found outside the National Theatre and the structure and seats constructed from cheap scrap-board.[93] The abandoned petrol station was found through a search of 'the derelict spaces of London, most of which lie in limbo for a few months before they get turned into flash new flats'.[94] In a collaborative blog entitled *polis* the claim is made: 'This

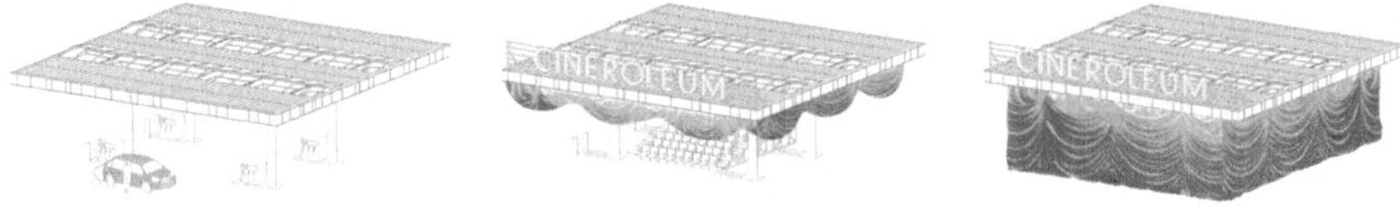

Figure 4.7 Cineroleum. (Courtesy of Assemble Studio.)

project demonstrates the benefits of collective action in the small–scale resilience of the urban fabric.' Recognising that top-down planning will no doubt decide the permanent fate of the site, the blogger goes on to claim that

> this propositional design not only reclaims this valuable city space for the greater public benefit . . . the wider idea of the functioning space also posits an interesting critique of the status quo . . . Perhaps the Cineroleum also tests the reclamation of the city in a post-petroleum landscape . . . It is empowering to consider hundreds of sites re-entering the realm of the possible, to be shaped by a genuine right to the city – the power not only to access the city and its resources but to change them.[95]

The next summer Assemble continued their cinematic interventions in interstitial spaces in London with Folly for a Flyover (Figure 4.8), a temporary multi-use structure built mostly from local recycled materials: the paving stones off-cuts from the London Underground, wooden 'bricks' hand-cut from reclaimed timber from old ferry docks – reddish in hue, they were meant to call up the red brick traditionally used in the area. During the day, the facility was free to the public, 'making the site something of an offbeat community centre'.[96] A café sold locally sourced food, and film events were augmented by other activities such as bug-hotel building workshops, puppet-making and boat tours of the canals. It drew over 20,000 people to a place formerly 'of misdemeanor and anti-social

Figure 4.8 Folly for a Flyover. (Courtesy of Assemble Studio.)

behavior' to which public access had been blocked.[97] Rowan Moore of *The Guardian* wrote of the project:

> It's an endearing-looking object, but more important is the way it brings to life a spot few will have known was there. The place is powerful . . . Usually, it is also desolate and possibly scary, but by putting stuff and events there with a certain wit and spirit, Assemble have revealed its weird beauty. By having daytime events, boat rides and a cheap café, the Folly is also reaching a wider catchment than the largely twentysomething crowd who patronised Cineroleum.[98]

One of the Assemble Studio collective says of the site and the group's intentions: 'This is a dramatic incidental space, one of the largest open spaces near the Olympic Park . . . We're hoping this will unlock the potential of the site, and its proximity to the park, so people are aware of it for the future.'[99]

Mention of the Olympic Park, the main venue for the 2012 summer Olympic and Paralympic Games and a site of controversy and contest (the redevelopment involved evicting some residents and businesses and threatened further redevelopment of the area), raises questions that should be asked about Folly for a Flyover and temporary cinemas in general. The Folly for a Flyover won the Bank of America Merrill Lynch CREATE Art Award 2011, worth £40,000, and was part of the CREATE11 Festival, a Cultural Olympiad-funded summer arts festival.[100] Films on Fridges was not funded by public or private corporate sponsors,[101] but the site and programme of sports-related films were pitched in terms of its location directly across the canal from the Olympic Park: 'Cinema felt like the perfect medium in which to celebrate sport and thus [the creators] came upon the idea of a cinema that would explore the juxtaposition of the old, gritty industrial Hackney and the regeneration of the area in time for the Olympics.'[102] On the crowd funding website that was used to raise funds, the project is billed as 'an event that celebrates the upcoming London 2012 Games'.[103]

Certainly corporate and state funding and a celebratory approach to the Olympics do not disqualify these projects as critical urban and cinematic interventions[104] but they initiate an important conversation about the relationship between pop-up or temporary cinemas, the 'festivalisation' of urban life and neoliberal urbanism. Maeve Connolly has speculated that the proliferation of temporary cinemas as public art 'might well be linked to the fact that [each] appears to offer a localisable form of publicness – potentially generating scenes of social participation that are attractive to commissioners and funders'.[105] Such 'scenes of social participation' are written into the now ubiquitous 'creative city script' associated with and promoted worldwide by Richard Florida. Rather than disruptive or opening urban spaces to 'the realm of the possible', critics argue that this script can be a means of 'freshening up' older urban entrepreneurial narratives, particularly a discourse of interurban competition.[106] (To be a world-class city is to be creative, to be creative is to be a world-class city.) In this sense it furthers or deepens neoliberal urbanism rather than disrupt it. This is a script in which creativity, spectacle and theatricality are highly valued within an illusion of widely accessible public space. Laura Levin and Kim Solga argue with respect to the deployment of creative city discourse in Toronto by business elites, state officials *and* grassroots cultural workers alike that the creative city 'is finally about the spectacle, rather than a performative production, of public space'.[107] Amid all of the laudatory hype, essential questions tend to be ignored: 'which citizens and which practices of urban citizenship, remain outside, even scorned by, the playful frame of civic engagement?'[108] They urge critical arts practitioners to embrace the potential for real difference and conflict rather than presuming and striving for a consensus of community values and experiences. They urge, in other words, a re-engagement with the ideal of the liberal public sphere in which differences in positionality and opinion are critically engaged.

In the end, Connolly adjudicates in favour of the potential of temporary cinemas for exploring publicness. Following her lead, we locate this in two places – again, somewhere between the screen, the place of the cinema, and the world beyond. As event/structures in temporarily unclaimed spaces, they have the potential (albeit of necessity imperfectly realised) to bring diverse audiences to that place. Connolly notes this capacity in relation to the only permanent 'art project' cinema that she considers; it is one that extracts city dwellers living in the city of Mardin in southeastern Turkey, a site of Kurdish–Turkish conflict, from the everyday temporality and territorialisations of their urban lives. Located on the outskirts of the city overlooking the Mesopotamian plain, the hope is that Sun Cinema, an outdoor amphitheatre inaugurated in October 2010, 'might intervene in the social organisation of the city' by allowing Kurdish, Turkish, Syriac and Arab residents a space in which to gather, precisely because it is located at a distance from the public squares of the central city. Deterritorialised and temporary cinemas on disused sites might function the same way. Second, temporary structure/event environments are by definition liminal places that emerge out of and engage in a kind of serious play. As Dening has put it, 'Playfulness is a scandal . . . Being playful in the slightest way suggests that things might be otherwise.'[109] Temporary cinemas are doubly so, given the screen as a fantasy space. Connolly argues that rather than being nostalgic evocations of the sociality of past cinema going, temporary cinemas make explicit 'the importance of desire, fantasy and projection' in our ongoing productions of public space and create a time and space to collectively explore processes through which publics are constituted. Folly for a Flyover was, after all, named as a folly: an amusement and a dream, complete with an imagined history as a building trapped under the motorway. It might be thought of as a time–space in which it was possible to imagine a different future for the site. Viewing *Requiem for Detroit* within the atmospherics of this fabulous site,[110] as some did, could provoke a critical stance to the Olympic Park rather than an incorporative embrace. After all, the film suggests that the capitalist economy did not serve Detroit particularly well.

The Internet, Social Media and the Cinema

The fact that temporary cinemas are 'having a moment' is not at odds with the proliferation of digital technologies; it is made possible by it. The ease with which movies can be made to travel through time and space and gather audiences may mean that formal theatrical exhibition is no longer 'the epicenter' of cinema culture, as Ramon Lobato argues, but films are still viewed somewhere and that somewhere often looks and feels like a kind of public viewing. As Lobato puts it, 'international film culture in its actually existing forms is a messy affair'[111] and one aspect of this messiness is a proliferation of different forms of public audiences. Tom Gunning reminds those who predict the death of cinema that theirs is an ahistorical and reductive account; cinema has always taken diverse forms, always in relation to other media and technologies: 'Cinema has never been one thing. It has always been a point of intersection.'[112] If in the early days of cinema it was the X-ray machine that threatened to displace the projection of films (a number of exhibitors exchanged their motion picture projectors for machines that could X-ray audience members, no doubt exposing them to dangerous levels of radiation),[113] the cinema continued to redefine itself in relation to the telephone, the phonograph, radio and television – and now, digital technologies, the Internet and social media. Gunning sees the current moment as both 'a return to aspects of cinema's origins' and a continuation of this dynamic process of exchange between and across media.[114]

What these new technologies mean for the critical possibilities of cinema and politics more generally is an open and hotly debated question. Lobato in our view is rightly critical of those who simplistically celebrate digital democracy as the liberation of film distribution from studio pipelines and hierarchical distribution (which operated within an urban hierarchy of distribution and exhibition, shown first in the core of major urban centres and then moving outward to less central locations) and as a virtue in and of itself. Urban metaphors are uncritically mapped onto new 'online distribution ecologies': distribution networks like iTunes and Netflix, for instance, have been likened by some commentators to gated communities that offer residents exclusivity, order and safety in contrast to more inclusive, seemingly more democratic peer-to-peer, user-driven networks.[115] But, as Lobato argues, the binary is unhelpful if political and market freedoms are conflated, and consumer choice is elevated to political struggle: 'the mantra of openness that is central to a variety of seemingly progressive movements becomes intertwined with a political philosophy based, ironically, in property rights' that is strongly libertarian.[116] Lobato draws inspiration from Jodi Dean's (and others) scepticism about the extent to which a 'deluge of screens and spectacles' and the expansion and intensification of communication networks has translated into anything approximating engaged publics and politics.[117] What Dean terms the 'postpolitical formation of communicative capitalism' is marked by the proliferation of communication and the almost total 'collapse of democratic deliberation and indeed struggle'.[118] Postpolitics, a term coined by Slavoj Žižek,[119] begins from the 'promise of consensus and cooperation'; issues that might previously have been thought to require debate in (the aspiration of) a public sphere are hived off as personal issues or technical matters. Communicative capitalism is animated by the twinned fantasies of an abundance of communication and the capacity for mass participation (for instance by clicking a button on a computer to add one's name to an Internet petition). The latter is misrecognised as political activity; in Žižek's view it is more accurately framed as 'interpassivity'.[120] Dean argues that a movement like MoveOn exemplifies the kind of technology fetishism that she is critiquing and 'confirms [her] account of the foreclosure of the political . . . No one has to remain committed or be bothered by boring meetings . . . Busy people can think they are active – the technology will act for them.'[121]

Despite her strong critique, Dean recognises the potential of the Internet for mass mobilisation, and she acknowledges MoveOn's effectiveness in mobilising over a million people in 130 countries on 16 March 2003 for a candlelight vigil against the Bush Administration's push for a war against Iraq. In this regard, we call attention to another of MoveOn's embodied initiatives: their use of 'movie parties'. Most recently, these have been used to launch local campaigns to ban fracking: on 14 July 2013, approximately 300 movie parties were held across the United

States to watch the documentary, *Gasland Part II*. After the screening, attendees joined director Josh Fox on a conference call to discuss how to stop fracking at their own local level. Images of these parties on the MoveOn website show attendees at local screenings, most obviously in homes, others possibly in community centres, others in theatre-like settings; in some, attendees wear nametags, suggesting a collection of strangers who have come together to watch the film, perhaps meeting for the first time to discuss the possibilities for a local campaign.[122] As Dean contends, 'the political efficacy of networked media depends on its context',[123] and it needs to be remembered that context is also a concrete place.

We return to our central argument: that the potential for film to create a public lies somewhere between the film on the screen and its distribution and exhibition and that the cinema (in its many forms) remains a critical space within these circulatory networks. Noting that 95 per cent of their distribution occurs through online and other social media, Anna Godas, CEO of Dogwoof, a major UK-based distributor of documentary film, is alert to the ways that online distribution works with rather than replaces the public viewing of films. Traditional cinema in her view

> is crucial to the film industry itself. For a film to become known and for us to get the word out about it, we absolutely rely on the publicity that is produced through being launched in the cinema itself. It becomes the occasion for being reviewed and discussed. Otherwise there is no moment in which it becomes public.[124]

In his discussion of the transformation (and diminishment) of the public sphere through the nineteenth and twentieth century, Habermas contrasted the ideal bourgeois public sphere with the notion of publicity, the latter being a one-way transmission of information and opinion rather than a fuller public discussion and debate.[125] Publicity is not yet or quite the same as the public. But Dogwoof's estimate that 95 per cent of its distribution occurs online actually hides a great deal of public viewing. When Dogwoof acquired the film *Black Gold* in 2006 'there was already a campaign for a more ethical practice in the coffee trade, so we set up discussion sessions at a few cinema screenings'. As the film 'took off' they started community screenings, 'which gave us the idea that people could themselves set up their own community non-theatrical screenings. Many of our subsequent documentary films have attracted dedicated communities of people devoted to the campaigns and issues of our films.' Dogwoof now actively promotes pop-up cinema on their website: 'we market audiences rather than products' and 'we realized that we had to think of other venues than Internet sites, which tend to become very internal. We started

[in 2011] with pop-ups and now it is one of our most successful venues.'
Their pricing varies by usage, place and size of group (e.g. they have grad-
uated pricing: least for film societies, educational institutions and student
unions, and increasing as audiences move from small organisations to
trade unions and political parties through to inter/national organisations
or corporations). Along with films, they provide 'suggestions for discussion and strategies to get people involved'. Dogwoof's CEO estimates that
groups are usually about twenty to twenty-five people in size: sometimes
the goals of the discussion 'are more related to events that are made more
eventful with the inclusion of the film screening but more often than not,
it is the film screening that becomes the event itself'. Dogwoof's pop-up
cinemas occur throughout the UK but most take place in London or other
large cities. In some cases, as with Ken Loach's *The Spirit of '45*, pop-up
screenings have been coordinated in time to enable online screened discussions across public viewings in different places – a kind of real-time,
embodied, electronic polis. In her view, 'we have reached a limit when it
comes to Internet spaces (aside from speed or size or shape)' and people
are increasingly disinclined to watch films in small formats: 'seeing things
on an iPhone is now on the way out'. The locus of innovation in her view
resides in modes distribution and places of access and exhibition, as well
as in film itself.

Jonathon Rosenbaum has observed a generational divide between those
who are pessimistic and those who are enthusiastic about the future of
film and the cinema: an older generation sees the death of the form where
a younger one sees innovation and promise. He notes that the pessimists
and optimists tend not to be talking about the same things: the former
about 35mm film and 'the' movie theatre, the latter about DVDs and
digital media available online. Recognising that digital media make more
widely available the kinds of films for which the former are nostalgic
and that this is stimulating the rebirth of cine-clubs worldwide,[126] he
argues that we need to 'redefine what we mean by community in relation to geography'[127] in order to rethink cinema as a medium and space
that has the capacity to create and gather an audience and a public. Like
Rosenbaum, Miriam Hansen hitches her hopes for cinema to those who
are less tied to old forms. She locates contemporary possibilities of cinema
in its original and enduring qualities: experimentation with technology,
curiosity about engaging with the wider impacts of technology and the
capacity to rediscover and reinvent cinema, publicness and the conditions
for serious reflection within this process.[128]

Much has been claimed for the city and cinema as creative, generative places, as zones of unexpected encounters in which new forms

of sociability, new ways of life, and challenging agonistic engagements across social and cultural differences can be cultivated. This is the city and cinema as 'an agitation of thought and practice'.[129] Alongside this ideal of citiness are our actual often brutal and brutalising cities: increasingly surveilled and securitised, socially polarised, riven by deep social, economic and political disparities. Rather than depleting the former vision, the latter calls up its urgency.

The contemporary moment has been framed by Lauren Berlant as one of impasse in which new idioms of politics and public attachment are needed. In her view existing practices of politics and attachment function as a mode of 'cruel optimism' because they are in effect obstacles to rather than a means towards fulfilling the wants and desires that bring forth that political engagement or attachment. Writing from the context of the United States and France, she argues that we feel optimistic about what liberal democracy might offer but its continual failure to deliver results in chronic forms of social and economic abandonment and blame, including self-blame. We need, she argues, to detach 'from the life-destructive forms of the normative political world' and to pay close attention to art (and other) forms and practices that provide 'atmospheres and spaces in which movement happens through persons' often as 'a space of abeyance', 'a habituation without edges, a soft impasse'.[130] We have argued that the cinema can work formally as this kind of space of abeyance, a temporary suspension from everyday life, in which new relations can come into being. It might create a time-space to 'slow things down and to gather things up, to find things out and to wonder and ponder. "What is going on."'[131] Not just as a fantasy/screen but as an actual concrete space. Not just as a space to gather information but as a space of fantasy, imagination, affect, and bodily reverberation and resonance. Not just as a space of individual reflection but as a space of sociality and discussion.

We have introduced films and spaces that do this in very different ways. The film *Fix* situates the viewer in a mimetic relation to oppositional political action aimed at breaking and remaking the law, redefining the boundary between citizen and criminal, and establishing new claims to health and wellbeing for some of the most marginal urban residents. The talkbacks then brought diverse audiences together to practice for a short while the kind of sociality and agonistic politics experienced while watching the film. These talkbacks articulated the audiences with 'kindling that had been laid' throughout the city by many people over many years. The Folly for a Flyover worked in an entirely different, less overtly political way. Occupying a wasted space as a folly, it was an extravagant waste of time and resources, with no objective beyond coming together to create a temporary accessible fantasy space for an undefined gathering of people. Non-productive play is no small thing in an economic 'powerhouse' like London.[132] Particularly in the context of a stigmatised site, such play can suggest all kinds of possibilities for different urban futures. But it would be unfortunate to miss the opportunity that this place afforded to be fascinated *twice over* – by both the situation and the screen. This is simply to say that the film programming mattered and matters, a simple point no doubt, but one that is too easily overlooked within the hyperbole of the performative creative city. It is, in the end, in the relationship and doubledness – of space and screen – of material and fantasy – that we locate the critical potential of cinema.

Epilogue

As we conclude our work on this book, the documentary film is being hailed as the new celebrity of the film festival circuit and even mainstream cinema. The question of the documentary's importance and political potential is now discussed not just by film theorists but by viewers of film at large. In the 2013 Venice Film Festival, Gianfranco Rosi's *Sacro Gra* received the top prize, the Golden Lion, much to the surprise of film critics. *Sacro Gra*, the first documentary to be granted this recognition, presents encounters with people who live, work or otherwise spend time in the vicinity of the ring road around Rome (Grande Raccordo Anulare). Out of 200 hours of film stock of interviews and location shots, the film has been edited to give an apparent random and quirky view of life on the edges of an already chaotic metropolis. The renowned Italian film-maker Bernardo Bertolucci, head of the festival jury and himself the focus of another documentary shown at the festival, declared that no film matched 'the poetic strength of this documentary', and indeed that documentaries as a category had been the most affecting of the films shown at the festival that year. But there has been considerable debate about the political stakes of such an open-ended film. Commentary ranged from: 'there isn't much in the way of an overarching concern'[1] and expressions of ambivalence about its neutrality,[2] to appreciation of the film's 'compassionate view of life lived on the margins'[3] and the fact that 'without trying to push a political agenda, [the film] taps into the everyday lives of society's fringe dwellers'.[4] Evidently the debate is about not only whether or not the film offers a critical perspective, but what constitutes a critical perspective. The claim that *Sacro Gra* leaves 'a lot of room to interpret what is shown on the screen and to make value judgements' has been regarded as both positive and negative.[5] The critique of the film's lack of politics frequently focuses on its interest in personal stories at the expense of dealing with the specificities of urban space and the physical and social conditions of the ring road. For us, this confirms not only the persistence of arguments about the effectiveness of film, but the ways the conjunction of film and urban space is intricately connected to these arguments. And, of course, Bertolucci is not the only one to evoke the category of documentary while simultaneously revealing the increasing erosion of distinctions between documentary and fiction film.

With the porous boundaries between fiction and the 'real', are the requirements of what constitutes a critically engaged film also changing? Another documentary shown in the Venice Festival, Ettore Scola's *How Strange to be called Federico* (*Che stranno chiamarsi Federico!*, 2013) suggests otherwise and underlines our argument that the debates discussed in this book both endure and take shape differently in different contexts. Initially, this film seems more of a personal tribute from one film-maker to another than a documentary with political aims. Yet it turns out to address one of the recurrent demands about what makes a film political, namely shooting on location. A black-and-white narrative sequence that reconstructs the post-war years shared by Scola and Fellini is followed by a strikingly different sequence that mixes colour with black-and-white film and location shooting with set reconstructions; in contrast to the initial narrative that draws on the appearance of neorealism, the second part presents a hallucinatory drive around Rome's periphery taken at night by the two friends, apparently to deal with Fellini's recurrent insomnia during the 1960s. Evoking Fellini's use of artificiality and excess through the studio set, the film proposes Fellini's preference for working in the studios of Cinecittà as a strategy for challenging the expectations of the 'real' established by neorealism. But it seems to go even further, revealing the sound stage around the edges of the scenes, and intersecting film shot on location with the projection of locations onto back-screens. The film screen emerges as in between actual urban space and cinematic virtual space, and Cinecittà as a site for thinking about how place is imagined in film. As if to underscore the close relation between embodied life and the anarchic stagings of Fellini's films, Scola draws on newsreel footage shot during the three days after Fellini's death in which his body was on show in Cinecittà's famous Studio 5. Scola's film reminds us that artificiality might be more 'real' than naturalism and might be where imaginative and even critical possibilities of film lie.

Claire Simon's *Gare du Nord*, another mixture of the real and the fictive in the 2013 festival circuit, is filmed entirely in the Paris train station and effectively deploys many of the visual and acoustic devices of the traditional documentary. But it is the fictive characters, all of which for different narrative reasons seek to interview people about daily life in the station, who activate the unpredictability of this space and show it to be both constant and transient. Through the interweaving of movements and discussions between fictive characters and actual people, the film seems to suggest that there is little difference between enacting in urban life and enacting in the film. *Gare du Nord*, which has been praised for being 'at once poetic, political, realist and romantic',[6] recalls Vertov's *Man with a Movie Camera* by proposing that shooting on location can be about unleashing the potential of the fictive in the location itself, as well as about capturing something about the materiality of things through the filmic process.

We have argued that claims about the political potential of film are not unchanging, coherent or conclusive, but are always contested and always located within specific political and social contingencies. Moreover, they have become, through the passage of time, located within film's own histories, which have shaped and reshaped the viewer's expectations to the point that something that seemed innovative and effective at one time (such as shooting on location) can later seem conventional and normalising. Innovation at the level of the technology of film did not prove to be 'naturally' politically and socially innovative as was once argued. Walter Benjamin, for instance, argued that film's properties of reproduction and mobility would prove crucial to its political possibilities. But in the long run the technology of film revealed political potential not through its autonomous development but through its engagement with urban space, in effect with the challenge of dealing with actual spaces with actual people.

We conceive of the arguments pursued in this book as part of this ongoing discussion. Our contribution to these debates is first to reveal that certain kinds of claims have persisted, and that these have resurfaced from time to time, altered yet recognisable, apparently aware of the past yet seeking a different future. Film itself, it seems, cannot be contained or defined by revolutionary manifestoes or even the most carefully thought through theory. This is why Lars von Trier's *Five Obstructions*, with its focus on the process of film-making, is particularly effective in making one think about how film works in relation to film-making itself, with repeated demonstrations of how the struggle with a principle can become the ground on which to define a new opening and new possibilities. While we have traced these arguments in separate chapters and think that it is useful to consider what is at stake in the different claims, we do not think that these themes – location, time, memory, relation of screen to urban space – operate apart from each other. On the contrary, we had trouble trying to keep them separate for the purposes of the discussion, just as we had trouble deciding which film to use in relation to each claim. Indeed, most of the films under discussion in any particular chapter could have been used in other chapters and served those arguments equally well.

The films we have chosen to discuss are not comprehensive in any way. We make no claims to historical or geographical coverage. Other choices could have been made, and we hope our discussions will generate consideration of other films in relation to the arguments presented here. But our choices were not haphazard. We have engaged films that claim, implicitly or explicitly, political effectiveness. Moreover, they all have been surrounded by debates that address not only the film but the film's relation to urban space. First and foremost, we selected films that we had found to be good to think within the context of teaching about film and urban space. As the writing project progressed, new films appeared that offered a more current take on a key issue or, like *The Exiles*, emerged from our selected filmic archive over time. We are trying to address film and urban space within a broad geographical and temporal spectrum but we also do not wish to conceal that we are situated in particular places, starting with the city of Vancouver. Few cities can claim the level of entanglement with film as can Vancouver, and this intricate relation proved productive as we initiated and developed this project. We also have a bias for other cities (London, Paris, Rome) because we happen to know them particularly well. The idea that we could write with the same sense of place from everywhere seems disingenuous and runs against our argument, but we also hope that others will be able to bring out specificities that we could not, and thus take up, develop, and push further our discussions.

We started from the idea that there have been recurrent claims about what makes a film political. These claims have been articulated explicitly in manifestoes and implicitly in film writings and discussion. But we soon realised that the rules are not as important as the ideas that emerged from trying to address them. Indeed the inability to comply with a list of demands is as recurrent as the list itself. Along with introducing the written debates we have given film its due by suggesting that a film can propose issues of criticality even if they were not entirely conceived by those who made the film. This is in keeping with the more significant role now granted to the viewer, and the idea that the viewer might find things in a film not foreseen initially but lying as a potential within it. We are saying something beyond this as well. We are not simply shifting the agency of meaning-making from the creators of a film to the audience; in line with Siegfried Kracauer and others, we have argued for the potential of what remains in film, often undigested and unrecognised. Both the urban and materiality of film have been central protagonists in our arguments about this potential. The persistent fascination with the long take, for instance, is tied up with the possibility that something unexpected will emerge on the street, unwittingly captured in film and often unrecognised at the time. Only years after, did the radicality become apparent of the crowd scene at Gilmore Field recorded in *The Atomic City*; we have theorised this within the literature on the enduring liveliness of the archive. The potential of the film archive can require time to emerge, and thus the history of film requires time, even at a time when its technological experimentation seems to have come to an end.

The histories of critical thinking on film seem all the more evident now that analogue film is being displaced by digital technologies. The resistance to this ending is everywhere, even in the attempts to return to film, to teach analogue film-making as something distinctive from digital. There is a tendency to assume that film presents a more serious endeavour, especially in relation to political claims. Michael Haneke is often said to be interested in the relation of film and television but his work is an attempt to argue against the effects of television and for the ethical potential of cinema. Others continue to argue for the relevance of film when film's time seems to be in the past. There is a sense of the importance of the continuing mixing and juxtaposing of visual technologies in order to gain insight about one from the other. Laura Mulvey has proposed very convincing arguments for how we now see things that could not be seen before, and these further extend an already rich set of debates.

We hope that the discussions that we open up remain within the spirit of sharing ideas that initially developed in our seminar on film and urban space, which we taught together at the University of British Columbia between 1999 and 2004. It was teaching together and discussions with students that proved the inception of this book. We had already written on the relation between virtual space and urban forms,[7] and were thus led to think about film and urban space at a time when this key intersection was just beginning to gain scholarly attention. But it was our engagement with our students that made it important to pursue this book, even when we were no longer in the same place and no longer teaching the course together. Students encountered years later would speak of their continued thinking about the course and its concerns, and not just in relation to film. We had the experience, for instance, of going to the graduating show of one of our visual artist students. Sitting on the floor in the corner of the gallery within the darkness of his illuminated show, we found him reading one of the articles assigned in our course long after the course had finished; the reading had become newly and differently meaningful to his art practice away from the course and in relation to his own work. We have argued that discussion of film is a means and a time and space in which to think about the world. This was Deleuze's approach to film, one that has been very productive but also has caused much confusion and resentment in film studies. Deleuze's conception of film, not as fixed representation but as mobile and changing in time, with the potential to trigger unexpected thinking, has proved controversial. We do not think that a serious consideration of film in and of itself and conceiving film as a time/space to think about the world are so separate. Our project is both about film and its effects but also about how dealing with film and urban space can become a productive way to think about the world at large.

We have argued for the importance of the relation of film and urban space at a time when visual technologies seem to be detaching us from physical exchanges. Digital technology not only disrupts any fixed relationship between what is viewed on the screen and the place portrayed; it has fundamentally changed, as discussed in the last chapter, relations of distribution and viewing and therefore relations between film and urban space. We have argued for the importance of holding together film and urban space, as interconnected spaces shared by people who are not already bonded through common beliefs or cultural outlook or generational ties and are aware of each other as different, even at the seemingly mundane level of having different habits while watching a film and hence proving annoying to those in their proximity. We thus resist the idea of the total fragmentation of filmic technologies and experiences, of the inevitable dispersal of the reception of film into the domestic realm or the autonomous space of the individual. We admit to a persistent hope for the cinema itself as a physical space, a space that is both local, in the sense of repeatedly visited and familiar, but also public, unpredictable and sometimes challenging in terms of who will be there and who will sit beside, ahead or behind. Within the space of a week, one of us recently had two very different cinema experiences. At one, a woman sitting directly behind quizzed her companion: 'Are you a movie-talker?' (thankfully, she was not), confirming Miriam Hansen's point that some viewers are bringing their private home-based practices into the cinema to create livelier less circumspect audiences. The other involved attending the annual Queer Film Festival, which manifests as a community celebration and urban party experience. Irritated by the first, charmed by the second, both were profoundly public experiences, each raising questions about what it means to be in public spaces today. Cinemas, we have argued, are places where the norms of and aspirations for public life are being worked out anew.

We are aware of the problems inherent within the question of what makes a film political or ethical. Indeed we have insisted on keeping open this question. After all, the very notion of what is political or how the political works has changed beyond recognition from the early years of film. This would have seemed strange to Dziga Vertov who saw film as an entirely powerful force to change the world, and had no reservations about calling for a particular view of that future. Of course the future could not be fully seen, not even by Vertov, and thus his position was not that different from our own, for which the speed of change seems so intense that it is difficult to see beyond the moment. Still, Vertov was of a culture, time and place where one could propose a vision of the future, while now this imposition of a singular view seems much less tenable. Instead, a return to ethics, both for makers of film and viewers of film, seems more desirable or in keeping with our recognition of other people, of other cultures, and of other worlds. Recent documentaries that argue for a particular issue are now regarded as holding interests as much as politics, and indeed we must acknowledge the extent to which politics has been subsumed by consumerism. We have no illusions that most film produced and viewed today is anything close to politically challenging or engaging. This may well be why ethical behaviour, as film-maker and as film viewer, is what is proposed as the critical goal of film in recent years. But the idea of not imposing one's perspective has not diminished the idea of being self-aware of both one's responsibilities and one's limitations. An ethical approach to film, now placed largely on the shoulders of the viewer, is a very different idea of film's political potential than when film itself was directed to challenge and forge the viewer's perception. Still, as Deleuze and others would argue, it is the making of new possibilities through critical thinking that is important, and perhaps what ultimately creates the preconditions for a political outlook and active political engagement. What is fundamental is a willingness and a capacity to enter into debate in which positions are not predetermined by identity and the outcome is genuinely uncertain. In discussions with students, it was the idea of thinking with film that seemed the most radical, the idea most likely to become productive and generate ideas beyond the course and any specific film. For us it is a critical perspective that defines the terrain of the political and the ethical, that is, the ability to think something through and question assumptions, especially one's own, and to engage and debate with others.

Notes

Introduction

1. In 2011 it was announced that he would repeat this method with Martin Scorcese. The speculation is that this will be an even more fascinating film: 'Leth was an entertaining subject to be tortured last time, but Scorsese is a character who could out-eccentric Von Trier if given the chance', Phil Brown, Collider. http://collider.com/lars-von-trier-martin-scorsese-the-five-obstructions/ (accessed 19 August 2013).
2. On the emergence of critical theory, see John Forester, *Critical Theory and Public Life* (Cambridge, MA: MIT Press, 1987); Andrew Bowie, *From Romanticism to Critical Theory: The Philosophy of Berman Literary Theory* (London: Routledge, 1997); Frederic J. Schwartz, *Blind Spots: Critical Theory and the History of Art in Twentieth-century Germany* (New Haven: Yale University Press, 2005).
3. Walter Benjamin, 'The work of art in the age of mechanical reproduction', in Hannah Arendt (ed.), *Illuminations: Essays and Reflections* (New York: Shocken Books, 1968), p. 218.
4. Siegfried Kracauer, *Theory of Film: The Redemption of Physical Reality* (Princeton: Princeton University Press, [1960], 1997), pp. 46–8.
5. Margarita Tupitsyn, 'Being-in-production: the constructive code', in Margarita Tupitsyn (ed.), *Rodchenko and Popova. Defining Constructivism*, exhibition catalogue, Tate Modern (London: Tate Publishing, 2009), pp. 21–2.
6. On documentary as a political form, see Jack C. Ellis and Betsy A. McLane, *A New History of Documentary Film* (New York: Continuum International Publishing Group Inc, 2005); Graham Roberts, *Forward Soviet!: History and Non-fiction Film in the USSR* (New York: St. Martin's Press, 1999).
7. Flachra Gibbons 'Censors cast shadow over Venice', *The Guardian*, 1 September 2003, http://www.theguardian.com/world/2003/sep/01/filmnews.filmcensorship (accessed 19 August 2013).
8. On current conceptions of ethics, see Todd F. Davis and Kenneth Womack (eds), *Mapping the Ethical Turn: A Reader in Ethics, Culture, and Literary Theory* (Charlottesville: University of Virginia Press, 2001).
9. For a discussion of some of the ethical issues surrounding this recent form of documentary film, see Jane M. Gaines and Michael Renov (eds),

Collecting Visible Evidence (Minneapolis: University of Minnesota Press, 1999).

10. Jennifer L. Borda, 'Documentary dialectics or dogmatism?: Farenhype 9/11, Celsius 41.11, and the new politics of documentary film', in Thomas W. Benson and Brian J. Snee (eds), *The Rhetoric of the New Political Documentary* (Carbondale: Southern Illinois University Press, 2008), pp. 54–77; J. Scott Oberacker, 'The reel deal: Michael Moore, political documentary and the discourse of celebrity', *Celebrity Studies*, 1 (2010), pp. 170–88.

11. Lauren Berlant, 'The subject of true feeling: pain, privacy, and politics', in Austin Sarat and Thomas R. Kearns (eds), *Cultural Pluralism, Identity Politics, and the Law* (Ann Arbor: University of Michigan, 1999), pp. 49–84; Lauren Berlant, 'The epistemology of state emotion', in Austin Sarat (ed.), *Dissent in Dangerous Times* (Ann Arbor: University of Michigan, 2005), pp. 46–78; Geraldine Pratt, *Families Apart: Migrant Mothers and the Conflicts of Labor and Love* (Minneapolis: University of Minnesota Press, 2012).

12. James Donald, *Imagining the Modern City* (Minneapolis: University of Minnesota Press, 1999), p. 77; Frances Guerin, *A Culture of Light: Cinema and Technology in 1920s Germany* (Minneapolis: University of Minnesota Press, 2005), p. 170.

13. Kracauer, *Theory of Film*, p. 52; see also Anthony Vidler, *Warped Space: Art, Architecture, and Anxiety in Modern Culture* (Cambridge, MA: MIT Press, 2001), pp. 111–13.

14. Vidler, *Warped Space*, pp. 111–22.

15. Robert S. C. Gordon, *Bicycle Thieves* (Basingstoke: Palgrave Macmillan for BFI, 2008), pp. 9–11.

16. Karen Lury and Doreen Massey, 'Making connections', *Screen*, 40:3 (1999), pp. 229–38, p. 229.

17. For instance, Ranjani Mazumdar reads the organisation of public and private space in Bombay-based films to chart the evolving moral discourse on women in Indian urban spaces: *Bombay Cinema: An Archive of the City* (Minneapolis: University of Minnesota Press, 2007). For analyses in other contexts, see Stuart Aitken and Leo Zonn (eds), *Place, Power, Situation and Spectacle* (Lanham: Rowman and Littlefield, 1994); Stephen Barber, *Projected Cities: Cinema and Urban Space* (London: Reaktion, 2002); David B. Clarke (ed.), *The Cinematic City* (London: Routledge, 1997); Tim Cresswell and Deborah Dixon (eds), *Engaging Film: Geographies of Mobility and Identity* (Lanham: Rowman and Littlefield, 2002); Richard Koeck and Les Roberts, *The City and the Moving Image: Urban Projections* (New York: Palgrave Macmillan, 2010); Harry Kuoshu, *Metro Movies: Cinematic Urbanism in Post-Mao China* (Carbondale: Southern Illinois University Press, 2011); Myrto Konstantarakos (ed.), *Spaces in European Cinema* (Bristol: Intellect, 2000); Ewa Mazierska and Laura Rascaroli, *From Moscow to Madrid: Postmodern Cities, European Cinema* (London: I. B. Tauris,

2003); Barbara Mennel, *Cities and Cinema* (New York: Routledge, 2008); Francois Penz and Andong Lu (eds), *Urban Cinematics: Understanding Urban Phenomena through the Moving Image* (Bristol: Intellect, 2011); Mark Shiel and Tony Fitzmaurice (eds), *Cinema and the City: Film and Urban Societies in a Global Context* (Oxford: Blackwell, 2001).

18. Aurora Wallace, for instance, argues that Toronto, in order to secure Hollywood-based foreign-location filming activity, has literally and explicitly remade itself to look more like Manhattan: 'When the set becomes permanent: the spatial reconfiguration of Hollywood North', in John David Rhodes and Elena Gorfinkel (eds), *Taking Place: Location and the Moving Image* (Minneapolis: University of Minnesota Press, 2011), pp. 157–80.

19. See for example Michael J. Shapiro, *The Time of the City: Politics, Philosophy and Genre* (London: Routledge, 2010).

20. Guerin, *A Culture of Light*, pp. 169–70.

21. Clarke, *The Cinematic City*, p. 10

22. Aitken and Zonn, *Place, Power, Situation and Spectacle*, p. 4.

23. Generalising about the ways that geographers have engaged with film, Doel and Clarke note that 'So, while much has been written about the geography *of* film and the geography *in* film, the geography of film qua film remains largely unexplored': Marcus Doel and David Clarke, 'Afterimage', *Environment and Planning D: Society and Space*, 25 (2007), pp. 890–910, p. 894.

24. Lury and Massey, 'Making connections'.

25. Ibid. p. 231.

26. The materiality of the cinema is being explored in other interesting ways as well. For instance, Nadia Bozak has examined the energetic and resource throughputs required to create films – that is the ecological footprint associated with film-making: *The Cinematic Footprint: Lights, Camera and Natural Resources* (New Brunswick, NJ: Rutgers University Press, 2011).

27. Yomi Braester, *Painting the City Red: Chinese Cinema and the Urban Context* (Durham: Duke University Press, 2010), p. 13

28. Ibid. p. 13. See also David Clarke, 'Introduction: previewing the cinematic city', in Clarke, *The Cinematic City*; James Hay, 'Piecing together what remains of the cinematic city', in Clarke, *The Cinematic City*, pp. 209–29; Rhodes and Gorfinkel, *Taking Place*; Cresswell and Dixon, *Engaging Film*.

29. Hay, 'Piecing together', p. 214

30. David Clarke, '*The City of the Future* revisited or, the lost world of Patrick Keiller' *Transactions of the Institute of British Geographers*, 32:1 (2007), pp. 29–45, p. 29. The reference is to Walter Benjamin, 'The work of art in the age of mechanical reproduction', in Hannah Arendt (ed.), *Illuminations: Essays and Reflections* (New York: Schocken Books, 1968), p. 236.

31. Donald, *Imagining the Modern City*, p. 92.

32. Yomi Braester and James Tweedie (eds), *Cinema at the City's Edge: Film and Urban Networks in East Asia* (Hong Kong: Hong Kong University Press, 2010).

33. Jean Mitry, *The Aesthetics and Psychology of the Cinema*, trans. Christopher King, (London: Athlone Press, 1998), pp. 99–100; Sidney Gottlieb (ed.), *Roberto Rossellini's* Rome, Open City (Cambridge, Cambridge University Press: 2004), pp. 34–9.

34. Mary Ann Doane, *The Emergence of Cinematic Time. Modernity, Contingency, the Archive* (Cambridge, MA: Harvard University Press, 2002).

35. Gilles Deleuze, *Cinema 1. The Movement-Image*, trans. H. Tomlison and B. Habberjam (Minneapolis: University of Minnesota Press, 1996), pp. 12–28; see Angelo Restivo, 'Into the breach. Between the movement-image and the time-image', in Gregory Flaxman (ed.), *The Brain is the Screen. Deleuze and the Philosophy of Cinema* (Minneapolis: University of Minnesota Press, 2000), pp. 171–92.

36. Michel de Certeau, *The Writing of History*, trans. Tom Conley (Chicago: University of Chicago Press, 1998), pp. 69–86.

37. Vijay Mishra, *Bollywood Cinema: Temples of Desire* (London: Routledge, 2001).

38. T. J. Clark, Serge Guilbaut and Anne Wagner, 'Representation, suspicions, and critical transparency: an interview with Jeff Wall', *Parachute*, 59 (1990), pp. 4–10; Alex Vasudevan, '"The photographer of modern life": Jeff Wall's photographic materialism', *Cultural Geographies*, 14:4 (2007), pp. 563–88.

39. The precarity of these small cinemas is something we return to in Chapter 4: since first drafting this chapter, the Ridge and Hollywood Cinemas have closed and the Park and Fifth Avenue Cinemas have become part of the Cineplex 'family'.

Chapter 1

1. Siegfried Kracauer, *Theory of Film: The Redemption of Physical Reality*, introduction by Miriam Bratu Hansen (Princeton: Princeton University Press, 1997), p. 285.

2. Robert G. Maier, *Location Scouting and Management Handbook. Television. Film. Still Photography* (Boston: Focal Press, 1994), p. 7.

3. On the city film, see James Donald, *Imagining the Modern City* (Minneapolis: University of Minnesota Press, 1999), pp. 63–92; Vlada Petrić, *Constructivism in Film. The Man with the Movie Camera. A Cinematic Analysis* (Cambridge: Cambridge University Press, 1987), pp. 79–80.

4. The second example would include places and cultures unfamiliar to Europeans, which through ethnographic studies were deemed to be closer to nature and to the real; for example, *Nanook of the North*, which keeps to an ethnographic tradition of 'the real'.

5. Kracauer, *Theory of Film*, p. 72.

6. On the changing relation of the actual and the virtual see Gilles Deleuze, *Cinema 2. The Time Image*, trans. H. Tomlinson and R. Galeta (London: Athlone Press, 1989), pp. 68–97.

7. John David Rhodes and Elena Gorfinkel (eds), *Taking Place. Location and the Moving Image* (Minneapolis: University of Minnesota Press, 2011), pp. vii–xxix.

8. Frances Guerin, *A Culture of Light. Cinema and Technology in 1920s Germany* (Minneapolis: University of Minnesota Press, 2005), pp. 69–70.

9. Halliwell's Film and Video Guide, see http://www.tcm.com/tcmdb/title/4096/Roman-Holiday/articles.html.

10. On film as archive, see Laura Mulvey, *Death at 24x a Second. Stillness and the Moving Image* (London: Reaktion Books, 2006), pp. 7–13.

11. Ara Ostell, 'The last place on earth? Allegories of deplacialization in Dennis Hopper's *The Last Movie*', in Rhodes and Gorfinkel, *Taking Place*, pp. 182–7.

12. Maier, *Location Scouting*, p. 7.

13. Ostell, 'The last place on earth?', p. 187.

14. Aurora Wallace, 'When the set becomes permanent: the spatial reconfiguration of Hollywood North', in Rhodes and Gorfinkel, *Taking Place*, p. 165.

15. J. Stevenson, *Lars Von Trier* (London: British Film Institute, 2002), pp. 103–16; R. Kelly, *The Name of this Book is Dogme95* (London: Faber and Faber, 2000).

16. Kracauer, *Theory of Film*, pp. 72, 303.

17. Kracauer's book was published in 1960 but it is generally agreed that it was written over the course of twenty years. Miriam Hansen, 'Introduction', in Kracauer, *Theory of Film*, p. viii.

18. On Kracauer and the street, see Anthony Vidler, *Warped Space. Art, Architecture and Anxiety in Modern Culture* (Cambridge, MA: MIT Press, 2001), pp. 110–13; Giuliana Bruno, 'Motion and emotion: film and the urban fabric', in Andrew Webber and Emma Wilson (eds), *Cities in Transition. The Moving Image and the Modern Metropolis* (London: Wallflower Press, 2008), pp. 15–6; Rhodes and Gorfinkel, *Taking Place*, p. vii.

19. Kracauer, *Theory of Film*, p. 303.

20. Ibid. p. 285.

21. Ibid. pp. 163–72.

22. Ibid. pp. 286–96.

23. Ibid. p. 297.

24. Ibid. p. 302.

25. Ibid. pp. 299–300.

26. Ibid. pp. 304–8.

27. Ibid. pp. 305–6.

28. Ibid. p. 306.

29. On *Man with a Movie Camera*, see Graham Roberts, *The Man with the Movie Camera* (London: I. B. Tauris, 2000); Yuri Tsivian, *Lines of Resistance. Dziga Vertov and the Twenties* (Bloomington: Indiana University Press, 2005), pp. 318–48; Malcolm Turvey, 'Can the camera see? Mimesis in *Man with a Movie Camera*', *October*, 89 (Summer 1999), pp. 25–50; John

Johnston, 'Machinic vision', *Critical Inquiry*, 26:1 (Autumn 1999), pp. 27–48.

30. Petrić, *Constructivism in Film*, pp. 1–5; Roberts, *The Man with the Movie Camera*, p. 18; on debates within Russia about the Kinoki see Jean Mitry, *The Aesthetics and Psychology of the Cinema*, trans. Christopher King (London: Athlone Press, 1998), pp. 99–100; Roberts, *The Man with the Movie Camera*, p. 18.

31. Tsivian, *Lines of Resistance*, pp. 323–7; this is Vertov's first film to do away with inter-titles.

32. Ibid. p. 324.

33. Roberts, *The Man with the Movie Camera*, pp. 5–41.

34. Ibid. pp. 11, 23; Yuri Tsivian, 'Man with a Movie Camera – Lines of Resistance: Dziga Vertov and the Twenties', in Ted Perry (ed.), *Masterpieces of Modernist Cinema* (Bloomington: Indiana University Press, 2006), p. 100.

35. On Vertov's position within contemporary avant garde, see Petrić, *Constructivism in Film*, pp. 2–13;

36. Tsivian, 'Man with a Movie Camera', pp. 91–3.

37. Roberts, *The Man with the Movie Camera*, p. 7.

38. Jeremy Hicks, *Dziga Vertov. Defining Documentary Film* (London: I. B. Tauris, 2007), pp. 22–4; Dziga Vertov, *Kino-Eye. The Writings of Dziga Vertov*, intro. Annette Michelson, trans. K. O'Brien (London: Pluto Press, 1984), p. 18; Petrić, *Constructivism in Film*, pp. 2–13.

39. Hicks, *Dziga Vertov*, p. 25.

40. Marko Daniel, 'The man with the movie camera. Speed of vision, speed of truth?', see http://www.25hrs.org/vertov.htm.

41. Petrić, *Constructivism in Film*, pp. 70–81, especially p. 72.

42. Gilles Deleuze, *Cinema 1. The Movement Image*, trans. H. Tomlinson and B. Habberjm (Minneapolis: University of Minnesota Press, 1986), p. 40.

43. Roberts, *The Man with the Movie Camera*, pp. x, 92.

44. Ibid. pp. 92–3; Tsivian, 'Man with a Movie Camera', pp. 104–8; Petrić, *Constructivism in Film*, p. 90, argues for a political interpretation of the splitting image of the Bolshoi Theatre.

45. On theories of montage, especially the differences between Vertov and Eisenstein, see Deleuze, *Cinema 1*, pp. 29–55.

46. Donald, *Imagining the Modern City*, pp. 63–92; Roberts, *The Man with the Movie Camera*, pp. 92–3.

47. Kracauer, *Theory of Film*, pp. 46–8.

48. On the uncredited cameraman, see Roberts, *The Man with the Movie Camera*, p. ix.

49. On the Kino-Eye see Simon Cook, '"Our eyes, spinning like propellers": wheel of life, curve of velocities, and Dziga Vertov's "Theory of the Interval"', *October*, 121 (Summer 2007), pp. 79–81; Turvey, 'Can the camera see?', pp. 25–50.

50. Turvey, 'Can the camera see?', p. 32.

51. Roberts, *The Man with the Movie Camera*, p. x.

52. On *Rome, Open City*, see Christopher Wagstaff, *Italian Neorealist Cinema. An Aesthetic Approach* (Toronto: University of Toronto Free Press, 2007), pp. 94–184; David Forgacs, *Rome Open City* (London: BFI, 2000); Sidney Gottlieb (ed.), *Roberto Rossellini's Rome, Open City* (Cambridge: Cambridge University Press, 2004).

53. Wagstaff, *Italian Neorealist Cinema*, pp. 35–7, 94–5.

54. On neorealism and its legacies, see Millicent Marcus, *Italian Film in the Light of Neorealism* (Princeton: Princeton University Press, 1987); Peter Bondanella, *Italian Cinema: From Neorealism to the Present* (London: Continuum, 2001); Wagstaff, *Italian Neorealist Cinema*, pp. 37–40; Laura Ruberto, and Kristi Wilson, *Italian Neorealism and Global Cinema* (Detroit: Wayne State University, 2007); Saverio Giovacchini and Robert Sklar, *Global Neorealism: The Transnational History of A Film Style* (Jackson: University Press of Mississippi, 2011).

55. Wagstaff, *Italian Neorealist Cinema*, pp. 20–1.

56. Peter Bondanella, 'The making of Roma città aperta: the legacy of fascism and the birth of neorealism', in Sidney Gottlieb (ed.), *Roberto Rossellini's Rome Open City* (Cambridge: Cambridge University Press, 2004), p. 60.

57. Bondanella, 'The making of Roma città aperta', pp. 47–61, and especially p. 60.

58. Wagstaff, *Italian Neorealist Cinema*, pp. 20–1.

59. Forgacs, *Rome Open City*, p. 22.

60. Gottlieb, *Roberto Rossellini*, p. 39.

61. Angelo Restivo, *The Cinema of Economic Miracles: Visuality and Modernization in the Italian Art Film* (Duke University Press, 2002), pp. 25–7; Vincent F. Rocchio, *Cinema of Anxiety. A Psychoanalysis of Italian Neorealism* (Austin: University of Texas Press, 1999).

62. Siegfried Kracauer, *From Caligari to Hitler. A Psychological History of the German Film* (Princeton: Princeton University Press, 2004), p. 165.

63. Kracauer, *Theory of Film*, p. 250.

64. Ibid. pp. 252–4.

65. Wagstaff, *Italian Neorealist Cinema*, pp. 94–5; on a broader critique of Rossellini, see David Forgacs, 'Rosellini and the critics', in David Forgacs, Sarah Lutton and Geoffrey Howell-Smith (eds), *Roberto Rosellini. Magician of the Real* (London: British Film Institute Publishing, 2000), pp. 1–6.

66. Christopher Wagstaff, 'Rossellini and Neorealism' in *Roberto Rosellini. Magician of the Real*, p. 42.

67. Kracauer, *Theory of Film*, pp. 57–8.

68. André Bazin, *What is Cinema?* vol. 2, trans. H. Grey (Berkeley: University of California Press, 2005), pp. 47–53.

69. Deleuze, *Cinema 2*, pp. 1–13.

70. On the use of maps to define Rome, see Marcus, *Italian Film*, pp. 46–7.

71. Forgacs, *Rome Open City*, p. 43.

72. Wagstaff, *Italian Neorealist Cinema*, p. 100.

73. Ibid. pp. 98–108; Forgacs, *Rome Open City*, p. 26.

74. On ruins in neorealism, see Jaimey Fisher, 'On the ruins of masculinity: the figure of the child in Italian Neorealism and the German rubble-film', in Ruberto and Wilson, *Italian Neorealism and Global Cinema*, pp. 25–53.

75. On this massacre and its political context see Alessandro Portelli, *The Order Has Been Carried Out: History, Memory, and Meaning of a Nazi Massacre in Rome* (New York: Macmillan, 2003); Richard Raiber, *Anatomy of Perjury: Field Marshal Albert Kesselring, Via Rasella, and the GINNY mission* (Newark: University of Delaware Press, 2008); Wagstaff, *Italian Neorealist Cinema*, p. 157.

76. On *Moebius*, see Jens Andermann, New Argentine Cinema (London: I. B. Tauris, 2011), pp. 64–7.

77. Paul H. Lewis, *Guerrillas and Generals: The Dirty War in Argentina* (Westport: Praeger, 2001).

78. The Universidad del Cine is a private national university founded in 1991 by film director Manuel Antin.

79. Everett Hamner, 'Remembering the disappeared: science fiction film in post dictatorship Argentina', *Science Fiction Studies*, 39:1 (March 2012), pp. 60–8; on the political documentary in Argentina, see Carlos Echevarría, 'Documentaries and politics in post-dictatorship Argentina', in *Social Identities: Journal for the Study of Race, Nation and Culture*, Special Issue: Political Documentary Cinema in Latin America, 19:3-4 (2013), pp. 324–39.

80. On the facilities and techniques used for the film, see the website of Universidad del Cine of Buenos Aires, http://www.ucine.edu.ar/.

81. On topological space, see Anna Secor, '2012 Urban Geography Plenary Lecture – Topological city,' *Urban Geography*, 34:4 (2013), pp. 430–44.

Chapter 2

1. Mary Ann Doane, *The Emergence of Cinematic Time. Modernity, Contingency, the Archive* (Cambridge, MA: Harvard University Press, 2002), pp. 30–1.

2. Gilles Deleuze, *Cinema 2. The Time Machine*, trans. H. Tomlinson and R. Galera (London: Athlone Press, 1989), pp. 43, 130.

3. Ibid. p. xii.

4. Laura Mulvey, *Death 24x a Second. Stillness and the Moving Image* (London: Reaktion, 2006), pp. 7–10.

5. On this debate see Doane, *The Emergence of Cinematic Time*, pp. 62–4, 93–107 On the difference between photography and film, see Gilles Deleuze, *Cinema 1. The Movement Image*, trans. H. Tomlinson and B. Habberjm (Minneapolis: University of Minnesota Press, 1986), p. 24.

6. Deleuze, *Cinema 2*, p. 23.

7. Mulvey, *Death 24x a Second*, pp. 1–3.

8. Henri Bergson, *Creative Evolution*, translated by Arthur Mitchell (New

York: Henry Holt, 1926), p. 308. On Bergson and time, see Doane, *The Emergence of Cinematic Time*, pp. 172–5.

9. Doane, *The Emergence of Cinematic Time*, p. 178.
10. Kevin Brownlow, 'Silent Films: What was the right Speed?', *Sight and Sound*, 49:3 (Summer 1980), pp. 164–7.
11. Doane, *The Emergence of Cinematic Time*, p. 172.
12. Ibid. p. 184.
13. Siegfried Kracauer, *Theory of Film: The Redemption of Physical Reality*, introduction by Miriam Bratu Hansen (Princeton: Princeton University Press, 1997), pp. 50–2; Deleuze, *Cinema 1*, pp. 24–32.
14. On Walter Benjamin and montage, see Anthony Vidler, 'Metropolitan montage: the city as film', in *Warped Space. Art, Architecture, and Anxiety in Modern Culture* (Cambridge, MA: MIT Press, 2001), pp. 111–22.
15. Deleuze, *Cinema 1*, p. 39.
16. Malcolm Turvey, 'Can the camera see? Mimesis in *Man with a Movie Camera*', *October*, 89 (Summer 1999), p. 32.
17. Deleuze, *Cinema 1*, p. 40.
18. Ibid. pp. 40–1.
19. On the camera as human body, see Turvey, 'Can the camera see?', pp. 25–35.
20. Deleuze, *Cinema 2*, p. 271.
21. Doane, *The Emergence of Cinematic Time*, pp. 184–5.
22. Ibid. p. 179.
23. Mulvey, *Death 24x a Second*, pp. 12–13.
24. Ibid. pp. 13–15.
25. Deleuze, *Cinema 2*, p. 40; on montage, see pp. 29–55.
26. Doane, *The Emergence of Cinematic Time*, p. 174.
27. On neorealism and its political debates, see André Bazin, *What is Cinema?* vol. 2, trans. H. Grey (Berkeley: University of California Press, 2005), pp. 16–40; Millicent Marcus, *Italian Film in the Light of Neorealism* (Princeton: Princeton University Press, 1987); Peter Bondanella, *Italian Cinema: From Neorealism to the Present* (London: Continuum, 2001); Christopher Wagstaff, *Italian Neorealist Cinema. An Aesthetic Approach* (Toronto: University of Toronto Free Press, 2007), pp. 37–40.
28. Bazin, *What is Cinema?*, pp. 65–6.
29. Doane, *The Emergence of Cinematic Time*, pp. 172–3.
30. Ibid. p. 185.
31. Ibid. pp. 175–80, on Deleuze's fraught relation to Bergson.
32. Deleuze, *Cinema 1*, p. 212.
33. Deleuze, *Cinema 2*, p. 5.
34. Ibid. p. 279.
35. For a discussion of Deleuze's idea of time and the false, see Michael J. Shapiro, *The Time of the City: Politics, Philosophy and Genre* (London: Routledge, 2010), p. 31.

36. The film was released in Rome and other Italian cities on 22 December 1948; on *Bicycle Thieves* see André Bazin, *Bazin and Italian Neorealism*, ed. Bert Cardullo (New York: Continuum, 2011), pp. 61–73; Robert S. C. Gordon, *Bicycle Thieves* (Basingstoke: Palgrave Macmillan for BFI, 2008); Wagstaff, *Italian Neorealist Cinema*, pp. 291–401; Vincent F. Rocchio, *Cinema of Anxiety: A Psychoanalysis of Italian Neorealism* (Austin: University of Texas, 1999), pp. 53–78.
37. Bazin, *What is cinema?*, pp. 54–5.
38. Ibid. p. 59.
39. Ibid. pp. 51, 58.
40. Deleuze, *Cinema 1*, p. 212.
41. Rocchio, *Cinema of Anxiety*, pp. 53–78.
42. Gordon, *Bicycle Thieves*, p. 8.
43. Quoted in John Francis Lane, *The Movie*, 23; see http://www.filmsociety. wellington.net.nz/db/screeningdetail.php?id=232.
44. Kracauer, *Theory of Film*, pp. 245–61.
45. Ibid. p. 254.
46. Henri Lefebvre, *Critique of Everyday Life*, vol. 1 (London: Verso, 2008), and *Everyday Life in the Modern World* (Piscataway: Transaction Publishers, 1984).
47. Michel de Certeau, *The Practice of Everyday Life*, trans. Steven Rendall (Berkeley: University of California Press, 1984), p. xvii.
48. Ibid. p. xi.
49. Ibid. p. xxi, see also pp. 34–9.
50. Ibid. p. xxiv.
51. Ibid. p. xviii.
52. Ibid. p. 108.
53. Ibid. pp. 117–18.
54. Ibid. pp. 25–6.
55. Gordon, *Bicycle Thieves*, p. 13.
56. Ibid. p. 14.
57. Antonio Vitti, *Giuseppe de Santis and the Postwar Italian Cinema* (Toronto: University of Toronto Press, 2000); de Santis' 1949 *Bitter Rice* was a huge international success but was also decried in Italy both by the left for its anti-socialist Hollywood values and by the Vatican for its overt sexuality (Vatican censors placed the film on a list of forbidden works). Ironically, the director conceived the film as a critique of the influence of Hollywood film in manipulating its audience by creating unfulfilable desires.
58. The bridge was dedicated to the Duke of Aosta who was Emanuele Filiberto di Savoia.
59. Built 1939–42 by architect Vincenzo Fasolo.
60. Bazin, *What is cinema?*, p. 51.
61. Deleuze, *Cinema 2*, p. 3.
62. Pasolini ends his first film *Accatone* (1961) with the protagonist stealing a

motorbike that causes his death, and this is only one of many Italian films that draw on *Bicycle Thieves* to speak about Italian film. Satyajit Ray is one of many film-makers that claimed to have been inspired by seeing the film. In Robert Altman's *The Player* (1992), the film is the symbolic counterpart to the usual Hollywood production. More recently, Iranian film has taken up the legacy of *Bicycle Thieves* and relocated it in the everyday life of contemporary Tehran; the celebrated *Children of Heaven* (1999) is about a boy who loses his sister's shoes and the search that ensues. China's *Beijing Bicycle* (2004) and the recently released *Wadjda*, the first film shot in Saudi Arabia and the first to be directed by a woman (Haifaa Al-Mansour), deal with the bicycle within everyday urban life. When the British film magazine *Sight & Sound* held its first international poll of film-makers and critics in 1952, it was voted the greatest film of all time. By 1962, it was down to a tie for sixth, and then it dropped off the list.

63. On *Cleo from 5 to 7*, see Alison Smith, *Agnes Varda* (Manchester: Manchester University Press, 1997), pp. 96–102; Valerie Orpen, *Cleo de 5 a 7* (London: I. B. Tauris, 2007); Barbara Mennel, *Cities and Cinema* (London: Routledge, 2008), pp. 72–6.

64. Mennel, *Cities and Cinema*, p. 72, considers Varda's film as an alternative to the gendering of the city in the films of the Nouvelle Vague; on the French New Wave, see Richard Neupert, *A History of the French New Wave Cinema* (Madison: University of Wisconsin Press, 2007), Peter Graham and Ginette Vincendeau, *The French New Wave: Critical Landmarks* (London: British Film Institute, 2009).

65. Orpen, *Cleo de 5 a 7*, p. 10.

66. Ibid. p. 22.

67. Ibid. p. 9.

68. Ibid. p. 29.

69. On myths of modern Paris, see David Harvey, *Paris, Capital of Modernity* (London: Routledge, 2003), pp. 23–8.

70. On the Haussmannisation of Paris, see Harvey, *Paris*, pp. 1–13.

71. Ibid. pp. 25–8.

72. Janice Mouton, 'From Feminine masquerade to flaneuse: Agnes Varda's Cleo in the city', *Cinema Journal*, 40:2 (2001), pp. 3–16. See also Mennel, *Cities and Cinema*, p. 73.

73. On the tradition of the *flâneur*, see Keith Tester (ed.), *The Flâneur* (London: Routledge, 1994), especially pp. 1–21.

74. Benjamin's writings on the *flâneur* are his 1935 sketch for The Arcades Project, 'Paris – Capital of the Nineteenth Century' and two studies of Baudelaire written in 1938; see Rob Shields, 'Fancy footwork. Walter Benjamin's notes on *flânerie*', in Tester, *The Flâneur*, pp. 61–80.

75. The idea of the *flâneur* was revived in the 1970s and took on the more elite position of Baudelaire's dandy and a critical perspective in relation to consumer culture and urban spectacle. The most influential account is T. J.

Clark, *The Painter of Modern Life. Paris in the Art of Manet and his Followers* (Princeton, Princeton University Press, 1999); Tester, *The Flâneur*, p. 18.

76. Guy Debord, 'Theory of the Dérive,' Situationist International Online: http://www.cddc.vt.edu/sionline/si/theory.html.

77. Tom McDonough, 'Situationist space', in Tom McDonough (ed.), *Guy Debord and the Situationist International. Texts and documents* (Cambridge, MA: MIT Press, 2002), pp. 241–64; Marcus Greil, 'The long walk of the Situationist International', also in *Guy Debord and the Situationist International*, p. 4.

78. McDonough, 'Situationist space', pp. 243–5; Simon Sadler, *The Situationist City* (Cambridge, MA: MIT Press, 1998), pp. 77–8.

79. Mennel, *Cities and Cinema*, pp. 73–5.

80. Orpen, *Cleo de 5 a 7*, p. 26.

81. Ibid. p. 10.

82. Ibid. p. 10.

83. Mennel, *Cities and Cinema*, p. 75.

84. On *The Circle*, see Hamid Reza Sadr, *Iranian cinema. A Political History* (London: I. B. Tauris, 2006), pp. 268–9; Shahla Mirbakhtyar, *Iranian Cinema and the Islamic Revolution* (Jefferson: McFarland and Co., 2006), p. 3; Hamid Dabashi, *Masters and Masterpieces of Iranian Cinema* (Washington, DC: Mage Publishers, 2007), pp. 394–404.

85. Sadr, *Iranian cinema*, p. 268.

86. Dabashi, *Masters and Masterpieces*, p. 400.

87. On Panahi's films, see Dabashi, *Masters and Masterpieces*, pp. 394–404; Panahi is usually considered to be in the third phase of Iranian film-making, the first being 1969 to 1979 (Islamic Revolution), and the second from 1984 to 1997; the third was facilitated by the 1997 election of moderate president Mohammad Khatami; see Mirbakhtyar, *Iranian Cinema*, p. 3.

88. Dabashi, *Masters and Masterpieces*, pp. 417–20.

89. Hamid Dabashi, 'The tragic endings of Iranian Cinema', *Aljazeera*, 21 March 2013.

90. On the representation of women in recent Iranian films, see Sadr, *Iranian Cinema*, pp. 258–67; also on women and cinema, pp. 272–8.

91. Negar Mottahedeh, *Displaced Allegories: Post-Revolutionary Iranian Cinema* (Durham: Duke University Press, 2008), p. 2.

92. Ibid. pp. 2–11.

93. Dabashi, *Masters and Masterpieces*, pp. 400–4.

94. Mohsen Mohammadzadeh, 'Deleuze, Urban Transformation and the role of history in urban projects in the historical cities. (Case Study: The Historical core of Tehran)', see http://www.academia.edu/705515/DELEUZE_URBAN_TRANSFORMATION_AND_THE_ROLE_OF_HISTORY_IN_URBAN_PROJECTS_IN_THE_HISTORICAL_CITIES._CASE_STUDY_THE_HISTORICAL_CORE_OF_TEHRAN.

95. Ibid. 8 (unpaginated).

96. Dabashi, *Masters and Masterpieces*, p. 396.
97. Ibid. pp. 394–5.

Chapter 3

1. Pierre Nora 'Between memory and history: Les Lieux de Mémoire', trans. Marc Roudebush, *Representations*, 26 (1989), pp. 7–24.
2. Ibid. p. 13.
3. Ibid. p. 17.
4. Ibid. p. 17.
5. On this tradition, see Frances A. Yates, *The Art of Memory* (Chicago: University of Chicago Press, 1966); Lina Bolzoni, *The Gallery of Memory* (Toronto: University of Toronto Press, 2001).
6. Patrick Joyce, 'The politics of the liberal archive', *History of the Human Sciences*, 12:2 (1999), pp. 35–49.
7. There is a vast literature on the colonial and disciplinary archive, as instantiated through government archives, libraries, museums and exhibitions; the cinema is critical to some of these accounts. Hodeir draws the links between the architecture of the mid to late nineteenth-century exhibition space and the film set, arguing that exhibitions produced a kind of cinematographic effect in the way spectators were moved through them: Catherine Hodeir, 'Decentering the gaze at French colonial exhibitions', in Paul S. Landau and D. Kaspin (eds), *Images and Empires: Visuality in Colonial and Postcolonial Africa* (Berkeley: University of California Press, 2002), pp. 233–52. David Campbell and Marcus Power trace a short history of cinema as an apparatus of the colonial state and an instrument of colonial conquest in Africa, as well as a medium put to use by anti-colonial movements: 'The scopic regime of "Africa"', in Fraser MacDonald, Klaus Dodds and Rachel Hughes (eds), *Observant States: Geopolitics and Visual Culture* (London: I. B. Tauris, 2010), pp. 167–98.
8. Ann Laura Stoler, *Along the Archival Grain: Archival Anxieties and Colonial Common Sense* (Princeton: Princeton University Press, 2009), p. 20.
9. Mike Featherstone and Couze Venn, 'Problematizing global knowledge and the new encyclopaedia project: an introduction', *Theory Culture and Society*, 23 (2006), pp. 1–20.
10. Thomas Osborne, 'The ordinariness of the archive', *History of the Human Sciences*, 12:2 (1999), pp. 51–64.
11. Quoted in Thomas Osborne, 'Tales of Hoffman', *History of the Human Sciences*, 11 (1998), pp. 115–24, p. 118.
12. Joyce, 'The politics of the liberal archive', p. 47; see also Patrick Joyce, *The Rule of Freedom: Liberalism and the Modern City* (London: Verso, 2003).
13. Henri Lefebvre, *The Production of Space*, trans. Donald Nicholson-Smith (Oxford: Blackwell, 1991).
14. Writing of the excessive monumentalising of Berlin, Karen Till notes that

'the spectres of the past are felt in the contemporary city when groups or individuals intentionally or unexpectedly evoke ghosts such as when they plan another "new" Berlin, identify artefacts and ruins as culturally significant, "discover" and mark formerly deserted landscapes as historic, claim a national heritage and dig for past cities, establish museums and memorials, or visit places of memory through tours.' Karen Till, *New Berlin: Memory, Politics, Place* (Minneapolis: University of Minnesota Press, 2005), p. 6.

15. Maurice Halbwachs argued that such disruptions brought a more intense awareness of one's environment and the social bonds within it. When something is altered, however insignificant – for instance a shop is closed or a building is torn down, we often feel this intensely, both because social change is marked and made concrete and because everyday routines are disturbed. The awareness of something lost is the moment at which the memory is formed. Because memory is formed in shared space through everyday routinised embodied experiences, urban space and its everyday movements become powerful means of forming collective memory. Maurice Halbwachs, *On Collective Memory*, trans. and ed. Lewis S. Coser (Chicago: University of Chicago Press, 1992).

16. There is a much broader interest in the archive, geography and film, for instance in relation to colonialism. For our purposes, we are restricting our attention to the city and film. For a discussion of cinema and colonialism, see Campbell and Power, 'The scopic regime of "Africa".'

17. Charlotte Brunsdon, 'Introduction: screen Londons', *Journal of British Cinema and Television*, 6:2 (2009), pp. 165–72. Patrick Keiller attributes this interest in part to Tom Gunning's work on the cinema of attractions: 'Since Gunning's essay was published in 1986, the cinema of attractions has emerged from underground.' He notes that artists such as Tacita Dean and Steve McQueen have been influenced by this style of film-making. As well, given his interest in cities and landscapes photographed by cameras, 'it was only a matter of time before I became involved with early cinema.' Patrick Keiller, 'Motion pictures', *The Guardian*, 21 May 2005, available at http://www.guardian.co.uk/film/2005/may/21/2 (last accessed 13 August 2013). The reference to Gunning's essay is Tom Gunning, 'The cinema of attractions: early film, the spectator, and the avant-garde', *Wide Angle*, 8 (1986), pp. 63–70.

18. Keiller, 'Motion pictures'. A more recent example of the use of archival film for the purpose of critical reflection is Christian Marclay's *The Clock* (2010), discussed in Chapter 3.

19. David Clarke, '*The City of the Future* revisited, or the lost world of Patrick Keiller', *Transactions of the Institute of British Geographers*, 32:1 (2007), pp. 29–45.

20. Ibid. p. 35.

21. Giorgio Agamben, 'Difference and repetition: on Guy Debord's films', in Tom McDonough (ed.), *Guy Debord and the Situationists International*

(Cambridge, MA: MIT Press, 2002), p. 318, quoted in Clarke, '*The City of the Future*', p. 40.

22. Madison Brookshire, 'Los Angeles in theory and practice: Thom Andersen's *Los Angeles Plays Itself*', *Bright Lights Film Journal*, 68 (2010), p. 1, available at http://www.brightlightsfilm.com/68/68LAplaysitself.php (last accessed 13 August 2013).

23. Norman Klein, *History of Forgetting: Los Angeles and the Erasure of Memory* (London: Verso, 2008), p. 250.

24. Ibid. p. 249. On film noir and urban space see Edward Dimendberg, *Film Noir and the Spaces of Modernity* (Cambridge, MA: Harvard University Press, 2004); Wheeler Winston Dixon, *Film Noir and the Cinema of Paranoia* (New Brunswick, NJ: Rutgers University Press, 2009); Matthew Farish, 'Cities in shade: urban geography and the uses of Noir', *Environment and Planning D: Society and Space*, 23:1 (2005), pp. 95–118; Kelly Oliver and Benigno Trigo, *Noir Anxiety* (Minneapolis: University of Minnesota Press, 2002); Mark Osteen, *Nightmare Alley: Film Noir and the American Dream* (Baltimore: Johns Hopkins University Press, 2013).

25. Klein, *History of Forgetting*, p. 97.

26. Ibid. p. 1.

27. Steven Erie, *Beyond Chinatown: The Metropolitan Water District, Growth and the Environment in Southern California* (Stanford: Stanford University Press, 2006).

28. Paul Arthur, '*Los Angeles Plays Itself*', *Film Comment*, (July/August 2004), pp. 72–3.

29. Richard Lippe, '*Los Angeles Plays Itself*', *Cineaction*, 63 (2004), p. 61.

30. Nick James, '*Los Angeles Plays Itself*', *Sight and Sound*, 15:2 (2005), p. 60.

31. Osborne, 'The ordinariness of the archive', p. 54.

32. Mary Ann Doane, *The Emergence of Cinematic Time: Modernity, Contingency, the Archive* (Cambridge, MA: Harvard University Press, 2002).

33. David James, *The Most Typical Avant-Garde: History and Geographies of Minor Cinemas in Los Angeles* (Berkeley: University of California Press, 2005).

34. Doane, *The Emergence of Cinematic Time*, p. 226.

35. In *Wiping the Warpaint off the Lens: Native American Film and Video* (Minneapolis: University of Minnesota Press, 2001), Beverly Singer traces an early history of marginalisation of Native American actors in Hollywood and their efforts to organise in response to this. In 1936, for instance, the Indian Actors Association's attempt to gain membership to the Screen Actors Guild was unsuccessful because the majority of its members were film extras in non-speaking roles. In 1940, a group of Native American actors led by Thunder Cloud filed a petition with the Bureau of Indian Affairs in Washington, DC for federal recognition as a tribe of 'Indians who worked in films'. The petition was rejected by the Bureau.

36. This itself has become a point of controversy. Years after the film was made,

the cinematographer made a joke about money wasted and the proportion of the production budget spent on alcohol and this was then taken up and reported as reality in a review of the film. Dennis Doros of Milestone disputes the claim on the basis of contracts in the files that indicate that most of the budget was used to pay the cast and lab bills. The actual sums paid to cast members as wages are difficult to decipher because Mackenzie was helping cast members with informal 'loans' until at least 1964; contract documentation indicates that cast members were paid from $1000 to $2500 for their participation in the film. Personal communication with Dennis Doros, 18 September 2013.

37. We thank Jessica Hallenbeck for this point. For further critiques of these representations see *Imagining Indians*, film, directed by Victor Masayesva Jr. USA: Victor Masayesva Jr, 1992; Singer, *Wiping the Warpaint*. For a long tradition of conceiving of the urban as a non-Native space, see Jean Barman, 'Erasing indigenous indigeneity in Vancouver', *BC Studies*, 115 (2007), pp. 3–30; Nicholas Blomley, *Unsettling the City: Urban Land and the Politics of Property* (London: Routledge, 2004); Penelope Edmonds, 'Unpacking settler colonialism's urban strategies: indigenous peoples in Victoria, British Columbia, and the transition to a settler-colonial city', *Urban History Review*, 38 (2010); Victoria Freeman, 'Toronto has no history! Indigeneity, settler colonialism, and historical memory in Canada's largest city', *Urban History Review*, 38:2 (2010), pp. 21–35; Renisa Mawani, 'Legal geographies of Aboriginal segregation: the making and unmaking of the Songhees Reserve', in Carolyn Strange and Alison Bashford (eds), *Isolation: Places and Practices of Exclusion* (London: Routledge, 2003), pp. 173–90; Coll Thrush, *Native Seattle: Histories from the Crossing Over Place* (Seattle: University of Washington Press, 2007).

38. Dolores Hayden, *Power of Place: Urban Landscapes as Public History* (Cambridge, MA: MIT Press, 1995), p. 105. Los Angeles continues to this day to have the largest urban concentration of Native Americans in the United States; Laura Pulido, Laura Barraclough and Wendy Cheng, *A People's Guide to Los Angeles* (Berkeley: University of California Press, 2012).

39. Laura Sachiko Fujikawa, 'Domestic containment: Japanese Americans, Native Americans, and the cultural politics of relocation', unpublished PhD dissertation, University of Southern California, 2011, p. 155.

40. Ibid. p. 158.

41. Ibid. p. 192.

42. For a very different exercise in reinserting Native Americans into the history and present day of Los Angeles, see Pulido, Barraclough and Cheng, *A People's Guide to Los Angeles*. This is an alternative guidebook that disrupts conventional representations of Los Angeles by identifying and celebrating the 'ghosts' of landscapes, peoples and popular struggles that haunt present-day Los Angeles. One of seven thematic tours identified in the guidebook is 'The First Peoples' tour, which begins very close to Bunker Hill.

43. With the release of the DVD in 2008, Douglas Miles, artist and founder of Apache Skateboards and a member of the San Carlos tribe where several of *The Exiles*' cast came from, saw the film and contacted Dennis Doros and Amy Heller of Milestone Film & Video. Finding that Doros and Heller had looked unsuccessfully for two years to find members of the cast, he began the search, speaking to individuals on the reservation until he found a relative of Yvonne (Personal communication with Dennis Doros, 18 September 2013.) Yvonne agreed to do an interview for 'Tell Me More' on National Public Radio. Matthew Fleischer, of *LA Weekly* then published a story that gave an interested audience further details of her life ('*Exiles* on Main Street: searching for the ghosts of Bunker Hill's Native American past resuscitated: 1961 documentary recalls stark lives of L.A.'s urban Indian', *LA Weekly*, 14 August 2008). He states that Yvonne had never seen the film in which she starred. Fujikawa recounts some of Yvonne's personal story in her 2011 dissertation, outlining in detail the death of Yvonne's baby, which was borne during the course of shooting the film, when she returned to the reserve soon after the film was completed. (The baby's death is attributed to the poor quality of the water supply there.) Yvonne subsequently returned to Los Angeles and was later employed in the aerospace industry. Fujikawa reads 'Yvonne's personal history and her experiences of loss' as reflecting 'the long legacy of the United States' relationship with Native Americans within spaces of unequal development, opportunities and access to basic needs. Combined with the social and historical context of the time period, a close reading of Yvonne and her "on-screen husband" Homer Nish as they narrate their lives and negotiate the urban landscape allows the viewer to witness how the politics of Indian-ness, race, gender, and class play out in the 1950's Los Angeles landscape' ('Domestic containment', p. 161). Archives thus have produced new archives and are being deployed to construct and circulate a counter-memory of Los Angeles.

44. Chris Healy, *Forgetting Aborigines* (Sydney: University of New South Wales Press, 2008).

45. Svetlana Boym, *The Future of Nostalgia* (New York: Basic Books, 2001), p. xiv.

46. Through the early eighteenth century it was one of the only legal ways to be granted leave from a number of European armies; after the French Minister of War ordered suppression of leave for convalescence in 1793, for instance, nostalgia was exempted; John J. Su, *Ethics and Nostalgia in the Contemporary Novel* (Cambridge: Cambridge University Press, 2005), p. 4. Nostalgia survived as a medical diagnosis in Israel into the early twentieth century; Boym, *The Future of Nostalgia*, p. 16.

47. Sean Scanlan, 'Introduction: Nostalgia', *Iowa Journal of Cultural Studies*, 5 (2005), p. 46, quoted in Alastair Bonnett and Catherine Alexander, 'Mobile nostalgias: connecting visions of the urban past, present and future amongst

ex-residents', *Transactions of the Institute of British Geographers*, 38:3 (2012), p. 392.

48. Matthew Hannah, 'Biopower, life and left politics', *Antipode*, 43:4 (2011), p. 1034.

49. Boym, *The Future of Nostalgia*, p. 346.

50. Peter Fritzsche, 'How nostalgia narrates modernity', in Peter Fritzsche and Alon Confino (eds), *The Work of Memory: New Directions in the Study of German Society and Culture* (Champaign: University of Illinois Press, 2002), pp. 62–85, quoted in Alastair Bonnett, 'The dilemmas of radical nostalgia in British psychogeography', *Theory, Culture and Society*, 26:1 (2009), p. 48.

51. Rey Chow, 'A souvenir of love', in Esther C. M. Yau (ed.), *At Full Speed: Hong Kong Cinema in a Borderless World* (Minneapolis: University of Minnesota Press, 2001), p. 211.

52. Edward S. Casey, 'The world of nostalgia', *Man and World*, 20:4 (1987), p. 379.

53. Hannah, 'Biopower, life and left politics', p. 1052.

54. Yvonne Roberts, 'The Spirit of '45: where did it go?', *The Guardian*, 2 March 2013, available at http://www.guardian.co.uk/film/2013/mar/02/spirit-45-ken-loach-nhs-history (last accessed 13 August 2013).

55. What this might mean is however an open question. As Casey notes, there has been a tendency over time to internalise nostalgia and to 'deliteralise' place, that is, to read it as a purely temporal and psychological phenomenon. Whereas nostalgia was first thought to be a longing for a specific place there has been a tendency over time to think of home or place as metaphorical. Casey is attempting to mediate between these two extremes and retrieve a place-based understanding of nostalgia. Casey, 'The world of nostalgia'.

56. Ibid. p. 377.

57. Chow, 'A souvenir of love', p. 215.

58. See also Su, *Ethics and Nostalgia*; Paolo Maganoli, 'Critical nostalgia in the art of Joachim Koester', *Oxford Art Journal*, 34:1 (2011), pp. 97–121.

59. On colonial nostalgia in films of the 1990s, see also Campbell and Power, 'The scopic regime of "Africa"'.

60. Fredric Jameson, *Postmodernism or, the Cultural Logic of Late Capitalism* (Durham: Duke University Press, 1991), p. xvii.

61. Chow, 'A souvenir of love', p. 224.

62. Jean Ma, *Melancholy Drift, Marking Time in Chinese Cinema* (Hong Kong: Hong Kong University Press, 2010), p. 12.

63. Stephen Teo, *Wong Kar-wai* (London: British Film Institute, 2005).

64. There is a vast literature on nostalgia and the work of Wong Kar-wai. Tony Rayns coined the term 'poet of time' in a 1995 review to describe his work. 'Few other directors,' wrote Tony Rayns ('Poet of time', *Sight and Sound*, 5:9 (1995), pp. 10–16), 'have ever imbued their movies with such a metaphysical sense of time at work: dilating, stretching, lurching, dragging, speeding by.' For critical appraisals of nostalgia and time in the work of

Wong Kar-wai, see Ackbar Abbas, 'The New Hong Kong Cinema and the *Deja Disparu*', *Discourse*, 16:3 (1994), pp. 65–77; Rey Chow 'Nostalgia of the New Wave: structure in Wong Kar-wai's *Happy Together*', *Camera Obscura*, 42 (1999), pp. 31–50; Chow, 'A souvenir of love'; Ma, *Melancholy Drift*; Sam Rohdie, 'Wong Kar-wei, l'auteur', *Iris*, 28 (1999), pp. 107–21; Teo, *Wong Kar-wai*.

65. The term 'mobile nostalgia' has been coined by Alastair Bonnett and Catherine Alexander to counter the tendency within the literature on nostalgia to adjudicate between good and bad nostalgias. They argue that these tendencies are woven together; Bonnett and Alexander, 'Mobile nostalgias'.

66. Zhen Zhang (ed.), *The Urban Generation: Chinese Cinema and Society at the Turn of the Twenty-first Century* (Durham: Duke University Press, 2007). See also Yingjin Zhang, *Cinema, Space, and Polylocality in a Globalizing China* (Honolulu: University of Hawaii Press, 2010); Shu-chin Wu, 'Time, history, and memory in Jia Zhangke's *24 City*', *Film Criticism*, 36:1 (2011), pp. 3–23.

67. Zhen Zhang, 'Bearing witness: Chinese urban cinema in the "era of trans-formation"', in Zhang, *The Urban Generation*, pp. 4–5. See also Pernin for consideration of the importance of urban space to these film-makers: Judith Pernin, 'Filming space/mapping reality in Chinese Independent Documentary Films', *China Perspectives*, 1 (2010), pp. 23–37.

68. Jason McGrath, 'The independent cinema of Jia Zhangke: from postsocialist realism to a transnational aesthetic', in Zhang, *The Urban Generation*, pp. 81–114.

69. Martha Nochimson, 'Passion for documentation: interview with Jia Zhangke', *New Review of Film and Television Studies*, 7:4 (2009), pp. 412–13.

70. A 7 February 2012 entry on a blog on Chinese urban development notes that the new development, designed by the American architecture firm, Callison, 'is unremarkable in that it follows the same pattern of brand-new development being followed in countless other Chinese cities without breaking any new ground'. Available at http://www.chinaurbandevelopment.com/?p=1559 (last accessed 13 August 2013).

71. Zhangke Jia, 'What remains is silence', trans. Sebastian Veg, *China Perspectives*, 81 (2010), pp. 55–6.

72. Sebastian Veg, 'Building a public consciousness: a conversation with Jia Zhangke', *China Perspectives*, 81 (2010), p. 63. For a close reading of the significance of the blending of documentary and fiction in *24 City* for creating a tension between fictive time and historical time in ways that challenge official history and linear time, see Wu, 'Time, history and memory'.

73. Nochimson, 'Passion for documentation', p. 413.

74. Wu, 'Time, history and memory', pp. 12–15.

75. Jia, 'What remains is silence', p. 54.

76. Pheng Cheah, 'Entering the world from an oblique angle: on Jia Zhangke as

an organic intellectual', in Neelam Srivatava and Francesca Rashmi (eds), *The Postcolonial Gramsci* (London: Routledge, 2012), p. 151.

77. McGrath, 'The independent cinema', p. 99.

78. Joe Morgenstern, '*24 City*: a film by Jia Zhang-Ke, director of *Still Life*', *The Wall Street Journal*, 5 June 2009.

79. Boym, *The Future of Nostalgia*, p. 346.

80. McGrath, 'The independent cinema', p. 100.

81. Jia, 'What remains is silence', p. 55. There are six factory-gate scenes in the film but, as Wu ('Time, history and memory') discusses in detail, rather than representing the repetitiveness of factory time, they mark socio-economic and urban transformation.

82. Jia on the long take: 'I like their distinct discursive appeal: people's natural attitude, in perfect space and time, and the sense of time they convey. But in addition to all of these aesthetic reasons, I think long takes have a distinctly democratic quality: they don't cut off characters but observe them; they contain a latent respect for characters.' (Veg, 'Building a public consciousness', p. 64.)

83. Laura Marks, *The Skin of the Film: Intercultural Cinema, Embodiment, and the Senses* (Durham: Duke University Press, 2000).

84. Veg, 'Building a public consciousness', p. 64.

85. Chris Berry, 'Getting real: Chinese documentary, Chinese postsocialism', in Zhang, *The Urban Generation*, pp. 124–5.

86. Vinicius Navarro, 'Nonfiction performance from portrait films to the Internet', *Cinema Journal*, 51:3 (2012), p. 139.

87. McGrath, 'The independent cinema', p. 100. See also Wu, 'Time, history and memory' for a discussion of the long take, portraits and empty space in *24 City*.

88. While working on his earlier film, *Xiao Wu* (*Pickpocket*), Jia told his sound engineer to leave in as much authentic random noise as possible. As the story goes, she quit because she was concerned that the film would harm her professional reputation. Evan Osnos, 'The long shot', *The New Yorker*, 8 May 2009, pp. 88–95.

89. Dudley Andrew, 'Interview with Jia Zhang-Ke', *Film Quarterly*, 62:4 (2009), p. 80.

90. Cheah, 'Entering the world', p. 137.

91. Ibid. p. 161.

92. Ibid. p. 161.

93. Gilles Deleuze, *Cinema 2. The Time Image*, trans. Hugh Tomlinson and Barbara Habberjam (London: Athlone Press, 1989), p. 54.

94. On Haneke's critical approach to the image, and especially the filmic image, see Peter Brunette, *Michael Haneke* (Urbana: University of Illinois Press, 2010), pp. 113–30; Catherine Wheatley, *Michael Haneke's Cinema. The Ethic of the Image* (New York: Berghahn Books, 2009), pp. 1–37.

95. On *Caché*, see Wheatley, *Michael Haneke's Cinema*, pp. 153–87; Max

Silverman, 'The violence of the cut: Michael Haneke's *Caché* and cultural memory', *French Cultural Studies*, 21:1 (2010), pp. 57–65; Ara Osterweil, 'Caché', *Film Quarterly*, 59:4 (2006), pp. 35–9.

96. See for instance, Martin Jay's *Downcast Eyes: The Denigration of Vision in Twentieth-Century French Thought* (Berkeley: University of California Press, 1994); Neil Christian Pages, 'What's hidden in *Caché*, *Modern Austrian Studies*, 43:1 (2011), pp. 1–24; Tomasz Dobrogoszcz, 'The hidden gaze of the other in Michael Haneke's *Hidden*', *Text Matters – A Journal of Literature, Theory and Culture*, 1:1 (2010), pp. 226–38.

97. On this essay, see Steven Best and Douglas Kellner, *Postmodern Theory. Critical Interrogations* (New York: Guilford Press, 1991), pp. 45–8.

98. Jacques Derrida, *Archive Fever. A Freudian Impression*, trans. Eric Prenowitz (Chicago: University of Chicago Press, 1996), p. 11.

99. Herman Rapaport, 'Archive trauma', *Diacritics*, 28:4 (1998), p. 69. On the process of negation and disavowal, see Julia Kristeva, *Black Sun. Depression and Melancholia*, trans. Leon S. Roudiez (New York: Columbia University Press, 1989), pp. 43–7.

100. Susan Van Zyl, 'The other and other others: post-colonialism, psycho-analysis and the South African question', *American Imago*, 55:1 (1998), pp. 77–100.

101. Hal Foster, 'An archival impulse', *October*, 110 (2004), pp. 3–22.

102. Roger Luckhurst, *The Trauma Question* (London: Routledge, 2008), pp. 1–15.

103. Rapaport, 'Archive trauma', p. 76.

104. Interview with Michael Haneke in *The Michael Haneke Collection*, Artificial Eye DVD (2006).

105. On this incident, which remained hidden until relatively recently and was much discussed after the film, see Jean-Paul Brunet, 'Police violence in Paris, October 1961: historical sources, methods and conclusions', *The Historical Journal*, 51:1 (2008), pp. 195–204; Jim House and Neil MacMaster, *Paris 1961: Algerians, State Terror, and Memory* (Oxford: Oxford University Press, 2006).

106. Derrida, *Archive Fever*, pp. 83–91.

107. Ibid. pp. 33–44.

108. Oliver C. Speck, 'Thinking the event: the virtual in Michael Haneke's films', in Ben McCann and David Sorfa (eds), *Cinema of Michael Haneke* (New York: Columbia University Press, 2011), p. 59.

109. Derrida, *Archive Fever*, pp. 16–17.

110. Ibid. pp. 97–101.

111. Speck, 'Thinking the event', p. 61.

112. Derrida, *Archive Fever*, p. 19.

113. On *Caché* and surveillance, see Thomas Y. Levin, 'Five tapes, four halls, two dreams. Vicissitudes of surveillant narration in Michael Haneke's *Caché*', in Roy Grundmann (ed.), *A Companion to Michael Haneke* (Oxford:

Wiley-Blackwell, 2010), pp. 75–90; Jennifer Burris, 'Surveillance and the indifferent gaze in Michael Haneke's *Caché* (2005)', *Studies in French Cinema*, 11:2 (2011), pp. 151–63.

114. *Caché* is the first of Haneke's films shot in digital rather than analogue film, but critics have noted the director continues to use analogue film in later projects.

115. On street surveillance, see David Lyon, *The Electronic Eye: The Rise of Surveillance Society* (Minneapolis: University of Minnesota Press, 1994); David Lyon, Aaron Doyle and Randy Lippert (eds), *Eyes Everywhere: The Global Growth of Camera Surveillance* (London: Routledge, 2011).

116. Osterweil, 'Caché', p. 8.

117. Nikolas Rose, *Powers of Freedom. Reframing Political Thought* (Cambridge: Cambridge University Press, 1999), p. 243.

118. Paulo Vaz and Fernanda Bruno, 'Types of self-surveillance: from abnormality to individuals "at risk"', *Surveillance and Society*, 1:3 (2003), pp. 272–91.

119. John Rajchman, 'Foucault's art of seeing', *October*, 44 (1988), pp. 89–117.

120. Paul Gilroy, 'Shooting crabs in a barrel', *Screen*, 48:2 (2007), pp. 233–5.

121. There are many discussions of this scene, see Ricardo Domizio, 'Digital cinema and the "schizophrenic" image: the case of Michael Haneke's *Hidden*', in Ben McCann and David Sorfa (eds), *Cinema of Michael Haneke* (New York: Columbia University Press, 2011), pp. 242–3; Levin, 'Five tapes, four halls', pp. 76–7.

122. Derrida, *Archive Fever*, p. 36.

123. Osterweil, 'Caché', p. 9.

Chapter 4

1. For details, see http://www.urbanrepublic.ca/drive.htm (accessed 14 August 2013).

2. For the blog, see http://dearvideomatica.livejournal.com/ and for more details, see http://www.film.ubc.ca/film_studies/videomatica_collection.shtml (accessed 14 August 2013)

3. See https://vimeo.com/60331356 (accessed 14 August 2013).

4. See http://churchatthehollywood.ca/love/ (accessed 14 August 2013).

5. Laura Marks, 'Immersed in a single channel: experimental media from theatre to gallery', *Millennium Film Journal*, 55 (2012), pp. 14–23.

6. In this Laura Marks (ibid.) is also exceptional insofar as she argues that the appropriateness of the viewing context (immersive theatre experience as compared to distracted art gallery viewing) depends on the film on view.

7. Ramon Lobato, *Shadow Economies of Cinema: Mapping Informal Film Distribution* (London: Palgrave Macmillan, 2012), p. 2, original emphasis.

8. Judith Mayne, *Cinema and Spectatorship* (London: Routledge, 1993), p. 165.

9. For a review of concepts of the public, see Michael Warner, *Publics and Counterpublics* (New York: Zone Books, 2002). Warner writes of the idea as

a 'kind of engine of translatability, putting down new roots wherever it goes' (p. 11) but nonetheless it retains the basic association with civil society, collectivity and critical discourse.

10. Miriam Hansen, *Babel and Babylon: Spectatorship in American Silent Film* (Cambridge, MA: Harvard University Press, 1991).

11. Ibid. p. 108.

12. Ibid. p. 112.

13. Ibid. p. 93.

14. Roy Rosenzweig, *Eight Hours for What We Will: Workers and Leisure in an Industrial City, 1870–1920* (Cambridge: Cambridge University Press, 1983), pp. 201, 217.

15. Hansen, *Babel and Babylon*, p. 117. See also Kathy Peiss, *Cheap Amusements: Working Women and Leisure in Turn-of-the-Century New York* (Philadelphia: Temple University Press, 1986).

16. Hansen, *Babel and Babylon*, p. 105.

17. Anne Friedberg, *The Virtual Window: From Alberti to Microsoft* (Cambridge, MA: MIT Press, 2006).

18. Ibid. p. 167.

19. Margarita Tupitsyn, 'Being-in-production: the constructive code', in Margarita Tupitsyn (ed.), *Rodchenko and Popova. Defining Constructivism*, exhibition catalogue, Tate Modern (London: Tate Publishing, 2009), p. 22.

20. Friedberg, *The Virtual Window*, pp. 170, 169 (original emphasis).

21. Roland Barthes, 'Leaving the movie theatre', trans. Richard Howard, reprinted in Philip Lobate (ed.), *The Art of the Personal Essay: An Anthology from the Classical Era to the Present* (New York, First Anchor Books, 1995), pp. 418–22, 419.

22. See Philip Rosen (ed.). *Narrative, Apparatus, Ideology: A Film Theory Reader* (New York: Columbia University Press, 1986).

23. Barthes, 'Leaving', p. 421.

24. Friedberg, *The Virtual Window*, p. 166.

25. Ibid. p. 166.

26. See http://www.heritagevancouver.org/topten/topten2012.html (accessed 14 August 2013).

27. With the grant from the Heritage Foundation came the donation of Benjamin Moore paint. The Heritage Foundation excavated the original paint chips from under many coats of paint on the exterior of the theatre. Not finding these heritage colours amongst their existing colour stock, Benjamin Moore recreated them. These will be marketed as Hollywood Cream and Hollywood Red.

28. For the segregation of the African American cinema-goer, see Eric Olund, 'Cinema's milieux: governing the picture show in the United States during the Progressive Era', *Journal of Historical Geography*, 38 (2012), pp. 57–68; Jacqueline Stewart, 'Negroes laughing at themselves? Black spectatorship and the performance of urban modernity', *Critical Inquiry*, 29:4 (2003),

pp. 650–77. In an entirely different context, during the colonial period in Nigeria, cinema exhibition practices in Kano were racially stratified by the pricing of the seats: two nights of the week were reserved for Europeans and Arabs and two nights for Africans: Brian Larkin, 'Theatres of the profane: cinema and colonial urbanism', *Visual Anthropology Review*, 14:2 (1998), pp. 46–62. Considering the issue of gender inclusivity, in certain contexts, cinemas have not been the accessible places for women described by Hansen: e.g. after the introduction of shari'a law in 2001 in Nigeria women were prohibited until separate seating could be built. Through the 1990s, Larkin argues that most women who attended the cinema in Kano were sex workers: Brian Larkin, *Signal and Noise: Media, Infrastructure, and Urban Culture in Nigeria* (Durham: Duke University Press, 2008).

29. Raja Shehadeh, *Occupation Diaries* (London: Profile Books, 2012), pp. 152, 153. For a history of the three cinemas in Ramallah see also Inass Yassin, 'Projection: three cinemas in Ramallah & Al-Bireh', *Jerusalem Quarterly*, 42:3 (2010), pp. 49–60.

30. Shehadeh, *Occupation Diaries*, p. 155.

31. Ibid. pp. 156–7.

32. Azar Nafisi, *Reading Lolita in Tehran: A Memoir in Books* (New York: Random House, 2004), p. 206. By 1988 cinemas had been volatile sites for years in Iran. When Ayatollah Khomeini returned in 1979, demonstrators attacked cinemas, along with bars that sold alcohol, and banks. The cinemas were attacked because censorship had been very lax under the Shah's regime and films showing sex and violence were common. Within nine months of the Shah's departure, 125 cinemas were burnt down or closed and most were never reopened: Nadar Homayoun (dir.), *Iran a Cinematographic Revolution* (2006).

33. There is a large, fascinating and varied literature that distinguishes the immersed mode of viewing in the cinema with distracted viewership in other contexts and it would trivialise the various theoretical claims to suggest that distraction works the same way in the home, for instance, as in an art gallery. With respect to the latter, Laura Marks ('Immersed in a single channel') questions current arguments in favour of the criticality that comes from watching single channel artist videos in the distracting space of the art gallery. She argues persuasively that critics of cinematic immersion come close to equating immersion with passivity and miss the rich social environments that such viewers bring to their experience of watching. That is, immersed viewing is not an asocial blindly absorptive activity. In her view, distracted viewing prompts a stronger cognitive (and less fully affective) response; the viewer stays just long enough to get an 'idea' of the film. It results, she argues, in 'cognitive consumerism where the artwork is reduced to a set of ideas to be mastered'.

34. Anne Friedberg, *Window Shopping: Cinema and the Postmodern* (Berkeley: University of California Press, 1993). On the other hand, Miriam Hansen

('Early cinema, late cinema: permutaitons of public sphere', *Screen*, 34:3 (1993), pp. 197–8) has noted the potential for home viewing practices to return to the cinema in unexpected ways, for instance, in the form of an unruly audience undisciplined by middle-class viewing conventions, that is, viewing with concentration in silence. The viewing of cult films is also often anything but uneventful. See for instance, Ernest Mathijs, 'Bad reputations: the reception of trash cinema', *Screen*, 46:4 (2005), pp. 451–72.

35. Barbara Klinger, *Beyond the Multiplex: Cinema, New Technologies, and the Home* (Berkeley: University of California Press, 2006). A twist on this narrative is Amit Rai's *Untimely Bollywood: Globalization and India's New Media Assemblage* (Durham: Duke University Press, 2009). Rai argues that 'an era of cinema exhibition is coming to the end of its particular duration'. Developing a Deleuzian-inspired analysis of media assemblages, he argues that 'preindividual ecologies of sensations' 'resonate at points where body and population meet' (p. 3). They are, in other words, neither individual nor social in any conventional sense. This is, he argues, 'a qualitatively different kind of solicitation of the body's essential creativity' (p. 14), which 'does not have an essential politics, it is always and everywhere political' (p. 115). There is no disputing the significance of the assemblages of sound–image–sensation circulating in and through and across exhibition spaces, advertising, blogs, ring tones, interactive games, and other media; in this sense, we offer an abbreviated account of film experience that relies on more conventional and bounded understandings of place, the social and politics.

36. Warner, *Publics and Counterpublics*, p. 62.

37. Hannah Arendt, *The Human Condition*, p. 57.

38. Warner, *Publics and Counterpublics*, p. 113.

39. Ibid. p. 66.

40. Ibid. p. 77.

41. Jane Gaines, 'Political mimesis', in Jane Gaines and Michael Renov (eds), *Collecting Visible Evidence* (Minneapolis: University of Minnesota Press, 1999), p. 85.

42. Ibid. p. 85.

43. Ibid. p. 85.

44. See, for example, Gaines and Renov (eds), *Collecting Visible Evidence* ; Chris Berry, Lu Xinyu and Lisa Rofel (eds), *The New Chinese Documentary Film Movement: For the Record* (Hong Kong: Hong Kong University Press, 2010). The reasons for this blurring of genres and move to a 'witnessing' rather than objective or realist stance differ depending on context. Within Anglo-American contexts, the debates around the so-called crisis of representation have been decisive. In China new perspectives on documentary are taking shape in response to a past history of social realism.

45. Gaines, 'Political mimesis', p. 89.

46. Vivian Sobchack, 'Toward a phenomenology of nonfictional film expe-

rience', in Jane M. Gaines and Michael Renov (eds), *Collecting Visible Evidence* (Minneapolis: University of Minnesota Press, 1999), p. 244.

47. Personal interview, 1 August 2013.

48. Lesley Stern, 'How movies move (between Hong Kong and Bulawayo, between screen and stage)', in Natasa Durovicová and Kathleen Newman (eds), *World Cinemas, Transnational Perspectives* (New York: Routledge, 2010), pp. 186–216,189; see also S. V. Srinivas for the take-up of kung fu films in South India. He makes a similar point: in order to understand how these films are taken up it is necessary to understand how they merge into existing experiences, affective structures, commitments and belief systems: 'Hong Kong action film in the India B Circuit', *Inter-Asia Cultural Studies*, 4:1 (2003), pp. 40–62.

49. Stern, 'How movies move', p. 190.

50. Ibid. p. 210.

51. K. C. Chinyowa, 'Emerging paradigms for applied drama and theatre practice in African contexts', *Research in Drama Education: The Journal of Applied Theatre and Performance*, 14:3 (2009), pp. 329–46.

52. For details, see http://www.freedomtocreate.com/cont-mhlanga.

53. The following is extracted from an interview with Nettie Wild, 20 June 2012.

54. This was a fundamentally new drug policy based on models from Europe, for which Vancouver momentarily earned the aphorism,Vansterdam. This strategy was squarely at odds with the US war on drugs.

55. Nettie Wild quoted in Liam Lacey, 'It's a Wild road show: Nettie Wild's documentary *Fix: The Addicted City* is touring the country to promote the issue of safe-injection sites', *The Globe and Mail*, 16 October 2003, p. R4. Surveys conducted after the election tend to confirm this view: the election had a very high voter turnout and one in four voters indicated that drug addiction in the Downtown Eastside was the most important issue to them personally, far outpacing the nearest competitor issue (education and social services at 11 per cent). Political scientists, Cutler and Matthews, argue that municipal elections in North America are not typically issue focused and that the electorate tends to be ill informed about the issues, making the electorate's concern in 2002 about this one issue very unusual. Fred Cutler and J. Scott Matthews, 'The Challenge of municipal voting: Vancouver 2002', *Canadian Journal of Political Science*, 38:2 (2005), pp. 359–82.

56. This theme of revolution was taken up by the media as well. See Ken MacQueen, 'Needles, love and revolution', *Macleans*, 115:46 (2002), p. 120.

57. Ann Livingston: 'Of course it had an effect. Of course it did.' She tells a story of being on a ferry from Vancouver to Bowen Island with Dean: 'This guy came out of his car and said, "You know, I'm a police officer and I recognize you guys from the film. I just want to say that I really respect the work that you are doing and I had no idea. I was completely opposed until

I understood."' See also, Will Gudrun, 'Timely *Fix* clear and compelling: *Fix: The Story of an Addicted City* at Granville Seven', *Vancouver Courier*, 27 October 2002; Lacey, 'It's a Wild road show'; MacQueen, 'Needles, love and revolution'.

58. Personal interview, 22 July 2013.

59. Itself a good story. After first seeing the film at a private screening Philip Owen, 'sits down next to me. He says, "What's your plan with this film?" I said, "Well, I think we've got to get it to the cinemas, but we've shot it on video so we've got to get it to 35mm, and Telefilm Canada [the funding agency], for whatever reasons, has decided not to give us the money to do that." "How much does that cost?" I said, "It'll cost eighty grand just to get it onto celluloid." And he goes, "Why can't you show it on video?" And I said, "Well, because I really think we should be in the cinemas with it [and at that point there were no facilities to screen video there]. This is destined for television, but there's work that can be done with this film. I just have a nose for it." And he goes, "Eighty thousand . . . How about if we raise you a hundred thousand in one night?" I met with his son [a stockbroker who took on the responsibility for fund-raising] and he said, "I know the guy who owns the Vogue and we'll do a screening and a benefit. Are you in?" And so here's me, Miss Lefty Schmefty; I thought about it for about a nanosecond and said, "Yeah, I'm in." Because I wanted my movie in the cinema. The fund-raiser at the Vogue was a hundred dollars a seat. The screening was billed as a benefit, a kind of goodbye to Philip. That's how it was billed. And everybody who was anybody in the city in terms of the movement was there. And we had so many media. I don't think there was one media outlet that wasn't there for that opening. Because it was about far more than the film. But what we had to do in that moment was capitalize on that and get the money to get into 35 millimeter. And then open three days later in the Granville 7 and use that momentum of all that press to get people to come into the cinemas.'

60. Philip Owen tells the story thus: 'Tremblay was elected mayor of Montreal. We were having a Big City Mayor's Conference in Vancouver and he'd been mayor for about three or four months and his office said that he couldn't come because he's a new mayor and he's just too busy. So I phoned him and I just said "I'd like to show you something that we're working on. Because you were offered 8 million dollars [by the federal government] to open a supervised injection site and we've got one running and I'd like to show it to you and show you the Downtown Eastside and explain this to you, because it's going to be on the national scene and I think with Montreal being such an important city in the country and vital in the life of Canada you should at least be aware of it.' And he came. [They toured the Downtown Eastside.] So I suddenly had him on side . . . [Later] we got to Montreal with *Fix*: Nettie and I and Dean and Ann Livingston and a couple of others. I phoned Mayor Tremblay and I said we're going to be showing *Fix* in Montreal and

I was wondering if you would consider coming to see it. [He said] "I don't know. It's such a controversial issue." And I said: "This is the theatre and I'm sure you could get in and out if you want to do it anonymously and quietly. Just show up by yourself and I'll make arrangements for someone to meet you at the door or I'll be at the door and if we can find out roughly the time you're coming we'll get you properly seated and so on." Well, he called me back, he said "I've just talked to my wife and she wants to go and we have a 17-year-old daughter. Can I bring my wife and my daughter?" And so he didn't tell any of the media. He came in, sat down and saw the film. And he was there for the questions and answers. And his daughter actually asked a question. So I was walking out with them, and the word went out from the theatre that the mayor was inside watching this movie and he got scrummed. I've never seen so much media. There was 'lights, action, camera', film, guys clicking pictures. I said "Where did this come from?" He says, "I don't know. [I guess] somebody recognized me and phoned the media." And so, he had to be interviewed. He left and I left the next day and we didn't see each other for [some time] before we ran into each other in the lobby [of a hotel in Ottawa]. And I said, "So what happened after that big scrum you were in after seeing *Fix*?" He said, "You know Philip. It was the best thing I ever did. I got such good media out of that. I got scrummed and I just want to thank you for giving me the opportunity to be there. My wife enjoyed it. My daughter really enjoyed it. And my family are on-side." And he said, "I got such favourable media. I was tagged as a guy that's for drug policy reform." He didn't open the supervised injection site. [He failed to get council approval, in Owen's view because of the recent metropolitan amalgamation that brought more conservative suburban areas into council.] But he got that reputation. He got that reputation. He wasn't as pushy as I'd like him to be. But he certainly got that tag and he accepted that tag. And he liked that tag. And that was because of *Fix*. He was suddenly going to be on-side with this issue.' (Personal interview, 26 July 2013.) Hardly principled, the film screening nevertheless had the desired effect.

61. In 2003, eight million dollars were offered by the federal government to Vancouver, Toronto and Montreal to set up harm reduction programmes. Only Vancouver took up the opportunity to open a supervised injection site, and it remains the only such facility in North America. The political winds in Ottawa have subsequently cooled to supervised injection sites (which require an exemption from federal drug laws). The current conservative federal government favours tougher drug laws and a law enforcement approach and has tried exceedingly hard to close down the Vancouver supervised injection site. In 2008, the Conservative government sought to deny further exemptions to the programme, initiating a series of lower court decisions and appeals that culminated in a landmark Supreme Court ruling on 30 September 2011 in favour of maintaining the supervised injection facility. As we write, harm reduction activists in a number of Canadian

cities are racing against the clock (and the passage of C-65, which would add new requirements to applications for exemptions from federal drug laws: see http://globalnews.ca/news/734875/canadas-next-supervised-injection-site-ottawa/) to open further supervised injection sites. (Accessed 14 August 2013.)

62. Personal interview, 26 July 2013.

63. The idea that film has a special affinity to the world is in her view 'useful only as part of a larger discussion on referentiality'. Miriam Hansen, 'Max Ophuls and instant messaging: reframing cinema and publicness', in Gertrud Koch, Volker Pantenburg and Simon Rohtöhler (eds), *Screen Dynamics: Mapping the Borders of Cinema* (Vienna: Synema – Gesellshaft für Film und Medien, 2012), pp. 22–9, 22.

64. Ibid. pp. 22–3.

65. We thank Inass Yassin for sharing this video material with us.

66. Inass Yassin notes that although the green flag looks like the Saudi Arabia flag, it has been associated with the politicised Islamist movement in Palestine and specifically Hamas, which reached the Palestinian Parliament for the first time in 2006. Personal communication, 13 October 2013.

67. Yassin, 'Projection', p. 52.

68. The 'kiss count' of this film – apparently fifty-nine in all – 'was the content of popular chat' (Yassin, 'Projection', p. 58).

69. Personal communication with artist, 30 September 2013.

70. Personal interview with artist, 14 August 2013.

71. It had not been easy to finalise permission to demolish the more than fifty-year-old theatre because of the efforts of the Riwaq Institute, which has the mission to protect, rehabilitate and promote architectural and cultural heritage in Palestine. (The Institute won the Aga Khan Award for Architecture for the Revitalisation of Birzeit Historic Centre in 2013.)

72. The censorship bureau of the Federation of Egyptian Radio and Television banned the film early in 2012 in the course of its systematic review of Egyptian films made in the last fifty years. This is because it contains what the Bureau considers to be inappropriate acts, such as kissing. While Islam Abdul Hamid, a supervisor of the talent committee of the Muslim Brotherhood, considers this to be a 'positive step', Jihad Mahboub of the production department at Egyptian television notes the systematic eradication of historical documentation of Egyptian life in the 1960s and 1970s. Waleed Abu al-Kair, 'Egyptian TV begins censoring scores of movies', *Al-Shorfa*, 16 April 2012, see http://al-shorfa.com/en_GB/articles/meii/features/main/2012/04/16/feature-01 (accessed 30 September 2013).

73. Personal communication with artist, 30 September 2013.

74. We thank Laura Marks for our introduction to Cinémathèque de Tanger through O. Berrada and Y. Barrada (eds), *Album Cinémathèque de Tanger* (Barcelona: La Virreina Centre de la Imatge, 2012), p. 17.

75. Yto Barrada and Bouchra Khalili in conversation with Omar Berrada,

'Cinémathèque de Tanger frequently asked questions', in *Album Cinémathèque de Tanger*, p. 33.

76. Ibid. p. 35.

77. Ibid. p. 38.

78. Ibid. p. 36.

79. Carles Guerra, 'Film burns', in Berrada and Barrada, *Album Cinémathèque de Tanger*, p. 19.

80. David E. James, 'L.A.'s Hipster Cinema', *Film Quarterly*, 63:1 (2009), pp. 56–67, 62.

81. The EMD cinema in Walthamstow, East London was purchased by the UCKG, a Brazilian evangelical church, in 2003 with plans to create a miniplex cinema: six screens with a total of 690 seats, a training centre, children's area, bookshop, café and two flats. The theatre has been vacant for a decade because planning permission has thus far been denied: see http://www.bbc.co.uk/news/uk-england-london-22673870 (accessed 14 August 2013). The Connexus community evangelical church of Barrie Ontario meet in different theatres of the Galaxy Cinemas: see http://www.connexuscommunity.com/im-new/barrie-campus/directions/ (accessed 14 August 2013). The evangelical EastLake Community Church in Virginia has met at the WestLake Cinema since 29 May 2011. The Pastor is quoted as saying: 'We believe that we have to be creative and relevant in our approach to proclaiming the greatest message in the world. Jesus Christ can change your life. The Cinema allows us to do these things.' See http://www.bedfordbulletin.com/content/cinema-church-eastlake-community-church-opens-new-venue-westlake (accessed 14 August 2013). Members of the Sky Cinema church in Hong Kong appreciate the capacity to bring 'church alive on the big screen'. See http://skycitychurch.com/cinema-church-launching-october-6-2012. And so on.

82. Number seven is: 'No political issues. Right now, we're praying for other church plants located in schools whose meeting space is now under possible threat because of church-state issues.' See http://pastors.com/10-reasons-to-launch-a-church-in-a-movie-theater/ (accessed 14 August 2013).

83. Quoted by Ariana Moon who writes in the Unification News ('Movie theater churches report their successes', see http://unificationnews.com/article/movie_theater_churches_report_their_successes (accessed 14 August 2013).

84. Margarita Tupitsyn, 'Being-in-production: the constructive code', in Margarita Tupitsyn (ed.), *Rodchenko and Popova. Defining Constructivism*, exhibition catalogue, Tate Modern (London: Tate Publishing, 2009), p. 22.

85. Over the past year a number of other organisations have used the space for secular public events: a night of music by local musicians was co-sponsored by Kitsilano Neighbourhood House; the 24 Hour Theatre Under the Gun Festival was sponsored by Pacific Theatre; and a Community Transit Forum was sponsored by the University of British Columbia Alma Mater Society.

86. In December 2012 there were multiple screenings of *It's a Wonderful Life*; in January and February a series of screenings of films focused on heritage films about Vancouver (which filled the 500 seat capacity); in April *Lawrence of Arabia* was screened; and *My Big Fat Greek Wedding* was shown during the local Greek Days street festival in June. In August there was a weekend's worth of screenings of *Back to the Future* along with dress-up contest and music focused around a1950s theme.

87. Florian Haydn and Robert Temel (eds), *Temporary Urban Spaces: Concepts for the Use of City Space*. (Basel: Birkhäuser, 2006), p. 20.

88. 'Pop-up cinemas: top 10 tips for creating your own', film blog *The Guardian*, see http://www.guardian.co.uk/film/flimblog/2011/aug/22/pop-up-cinemas-top-tips.

89. See James, 'L.A.'s Hipster Cinema' for a similarly dizzying array of temporary cinemas in Los Angeles. Responding to what she terms 'the cinematic turn' evident in contemporary art over the last two decades, Maeve Connolly reviews five functioning cinemas created as art projects between 2006 and 2010, four of which are temporary. 'Temporality, Sociality, Publicness: Cinema as Art Project', *Afterall*, 29 (2012), see http://www.afterall.org/journal/issue.29/temporality-sociality-publicness-cinema-as-art-project (accessed 14 August 2013).

90. The programming associated with The Floating Cinema is closely associated with the specificity of its site. In 2013 The Floating Cinema commissioned a variety of new work, including an animation project involving a collaboration between artists, a scientist, a sound artist and three community groups in East London to create a film, using animation and archive footage, about microscopic creatures that dwell in the waterways of East London as well as the broader history of the waterways. A film on the River Lea was also commissioned. A third commission involved selecting twelve 'extra-ordinary' East Londoners to tell their stories about East London.

91. 'Films on Fridges: cool cinema on Fish Island', *Hackney Citizen*, 1 August 2011, see http://hackneycitizen.co.uk/2011/08/01/films-on-fridges-fish-island-hackney-wick/ (accessed 14 August 2013).

92. Ibid.

93. The Cineroleum was an improvisation on the movie palace and was meant to call up the sociality of the neighbourhood cinema. The five-week programme was an eclectic mix of classics and independent shorts that drew roughly two thousand visitors. See http://eme3.org/?p=2974 (accessed 9 August 2013).

94. Anna Trench, 'Cineroleum: cinema in a petrol station', *Telegraph*, 30 August 2010, see http://www.telegraph.co.uk/culture/film/film-blog/7971999/Cineroleum-cinema-in-a-petro-station.html.

95. 'The Cineroleum: an urban takeover', see http://www.thepolisblog.org/2010/09/cineroleum-urban-takeover.html (accessed 14 August 2013).

96. Sarah Birch, 'Folly for a Flyover charms Hackney', *Hackney Citizen*, 11 July 2011, see http://hackneycitizen.co.uk/201107/11/folly-for-a-fly over-charms-hackney/.

97. See http://eme3.org/?p=2974 (accessed 9 August 2013).

98. Rowan Moore, 'Silence; Folly for a Flyover; 2004 Indian Ocean Tsunami Memorial – review, *The Observer/The Guardian*, 10 July 2011, see http://www.theguardian.com/artanddesign/2011/jul/10/folly-for-flyover-assem ble-silence.

99. 'Folly for a Flyover: pop-up architecture', see http://www.ideastap.com/ ideasmag/all-articles/folly-for-a-flyover (accessed 14 August 2013).

100. Cineroleum had a smaller budget of £14,000 and was funded by a small £2500 grant from Ideas Tap (an arts network and funding body) and reliant on sponsorship from various sources (Tyvek, National Theatre). It won the Ideastap Group Innovator Award, was number 1 in *The Observer*'s 'Top Ten Architectural Moments of 2010', and has been exhibited at Maison D'Architecture and Pavillon D'Arsenal in Paris (http://www.eme3. org/?p=2974; accessed 9 August 2013).

101. The creators relied on a 'crowd funding' website, Kickstart, designed to attract funding for creative projects. (Fifty-one backers pledged a total of $7050 within 30 days. These certainly were not large corporate sponsors: the majority gave less than $50.)

102. 'Sarfraz Mansoor Films on Fridges: from cold mountain to cool cinema', film blog, *The Guardian*, 1 August 2011, see http://www.theguardian.com/ film/filmblog/2011/aug/01/films-on-fridges-cinema-recycling (accessed 14 August 2013).

103. See www.kickstarter.com/projects/11976329/films-on-fringes/posts/891 04 (accessed 14 August 2013).

104. Indeed, Folly for a Flyover can make a number of claims for its criticality: Assemble Practice worked closely with a number of community groups such as The Discover Center, Hackney Marshes User Group, Building Exploratory and The Hackney Podcast and a range of other arts cultural groups. The construction process involved over 200 volunteers which was meant to create 'a tangible sense of local ownership' prior to opening. See http://eme3.org/?p=2974 (accessed 9 August 2013).

105. Connolly, 'Temporality, sociality, publicness', p. 8.

106. Jamie Peck, 'Struggling with the creative class', *International Journal of Urban and Regional Research*, 24:4 (2005), pp. 740–70; Peck, 'The cult of urban creativity', in R. Keil and R. Mahon (eds), *Leviathon Undone?* (Toronto: University of British Columbia Press, 2009); Peck, 'Recreative city: Amsterdam, vehicular ideas and the adaptive spaces of creative policy', *International Journal of Urban and Regional Research*, 36:3 (2012), pp. 462–85.

107. Laura Levin and Kim Solga 'Building utopia: performance and fantasy of urban renewal in contemporary Toronto', *TDR: The Drama Review*, 53:3 (2009), pp. 37–53, 39.

108. Ibid. p. 44.

109. Greg Dening, *Performances* (Chicago; University of Chicago Press, 1996).

110. The filmic programme was curated by the Barbican Art Gallery and included: a screening of early and classic fairy tales; *The Adventures of Prince Achmed* (1926); *Baron Munchausen* (1988); a selection of shorts on motorways; *The Beast from 20,000 Fathoms* (1953); *Requiem for Detroit* (2010); *Tron* (1982); *Trip to the Moon and Other Shorts* (1902); *Flash Gordon* (1980); *Toy Story* (1995); *Akira* (1988); *Space Odessey* (1968) and *Wizard of Oz* (1939).

111. Lobato, *Shadow Economies*, p. 1

112. Tom Gunning, 'Moving away from the index: cinema and the impression of reality', in Koch, Pantenburg and Rothöhler (eds), *Screen Dynamics*, pp. 42–60.

113. Ibid. p. 47.

114. Ibid. p. 48.

115. Virginia Heffernan, 'The death of the open web', *New York Times Magazine*, 17 May 2010, p. 16. Cited in Lobato, *Shadow Economies*, p. 98.

116. Ibid. p. 115.

117. Jodi Dean, 'Communicative capitalism, circulation and the foreclosure of politics', in Megan Boler, *Digital Media and Democracy: Tactics in Hard Times* (Cambridge, MA: MIT Press, 2008), pp. 101–21.

118. Ibid. p. 103.

119. Slavoj Žižek, *The Ticklish Subject* (London: Verso, 1999), p. 198. Quoted in Dean, 'Communicative capitalism', p. 105.

120. Slavoj Žižek, *The Plague of Fantasies* (London: Verso, 1997), p. 21. Quoted in Dean, 'Communicative capitalism', p. 109.

121. Dean, 'Communicative capitalism', pp. 118–19.

122. See http://front.moveon.org/moveon-members-launch-local-campaigns-to-ban-fracking-host-300-gasland-ii-screening-events/ (accessed 14 August 2013). MoveOn has been staging movie parties for some time, for instance around *Uncovered* (2004), *Out-Foxed* (2004), *Wal-Mart* (2005) and *Iraq for Sale* (2006).

123. Dean, 'Communicative capitalism', p. 103.

124. Personal interview, 1 August 2013.

125. Jürgen Habermas, *The Structural Transformation of the Public Sphere: An Inquiry into a Category of Bourgeois Society*, trans. Thomas Burger (Cambridge, MA: MIT Press, 1989).

126. On the significance of cineclubs to the flourishing production of film-making in China, see Seio Nakajima, 'Watching documentary: critical public discourses and contemporary urban Chinese film clubs', in Berry, Xinyu and Rofel, *The New Chinese Documentary Film Movement*, pp. 117–34.

127. Jonathon Rosenbaum, 'End or beginning: the new cinephilia', in Koch, Pantenburg and Rohtöhler, *Screen Dynamics*, pp. 30–41, 39. Rosenbaum

discusses his fantasy of the return of the cine-club and gives some compelling examples.

128. Hansen, 'Max Orphuls'.
129. Ash Amin and Nigel Thrift, *Cities: Reimaging the Urban* (Cambridge: Polity, 2002), p. 177.
130. Lauren Berlant, *Cruel Optimism* (Durham: Duke University Press, 2011), pp. 229–30.
131. Lauren Berlant, 'Thinking about feeling historical', *Emotion, Space and Society*, 1:1 (2008), pp. 4–9, 5.
132. For a discussion of the political significance of performative nonproductivity, see Miranda Joseph, 'The performance of production and consumption', *Social Text*, 54 (1998), pp. 25–61; Peggy Phelan, *Unmarked: The Politics of Performance* (London: Routledge, 1993).

Epilogue

1. Oliver Lyttleton, *The Playlist*, September 2013.
2. Jay Weissberg, *Variety*, September 2013.
3. Lee Marshall, *Screen International*, September 2013.
4. Deborah Young, 'Sacro GRA, Tales from Rome's Ring Road', in *The Hollywood Reporter*, September 2013.
5. Ibid.
6. Jonathan Romney, *BFI London Film Festival*, 9–20 October 2013 (London: BFI, 2013), p. 81.
7. R. M. San Juan and G. Pratt, 'Virtual cities: film and the urban mapping of virtual space', *Screen*, 43:3 (2002), pp. 250–70; G. Pratt and R. M. San Juan 'In search of the horizon: Utopia in the *The Truman Show* and *The Matrix*', in Loretta Lees (ed.), *Emancipatory Cities* (London: Sage, 2004), pp. 192–206.

Bibliography

Abbas, Ackbar, 'The New Hong Kong Cinema and the *Deja Disparu*', *Discourse*, 16:3 (1994), pp. 65–77.

Agamben, Giorgio, 'Difference and repetition: on Guy Debord's films', in Tom McDonough (ed.), *Guy Debord and the Situationists International* (Cambridge, MA: MIT Press, 2002), pp. 313–19.

Aitken, Stuart and Leo Zonn (eds), *Place Power, Situation and Spectacle: A Geography of Film* (Lanham: Rowman and Littlefield, 1994).

Amin, Ash and Nigel Thrift, *Cities: Reimaging the Urban* (Cambridge: Polity, 2002).

Andermann, Jens, *New Argentine Cinema* (London: I. B. Tauris, 2011).

Andrew, Dudley, 'Interview with Jia Zhang-Ke', *Film Quarterly*, 62:4 (2009), pp. 80–3.

Arendt, Hannah, *The Human Condition* (Chicago: University of Chicago Press, 1958).

Arthur, Paul, '*Los Angeles Plays Itself*', *Film Comment*, July/August (2004), pp. 72–3.

Barber, Stephen, *Projected Cities: Cinema and Urban Space* (London: Reaktion, 2002).

Barman, Jean, 'Erasing indigenous indigeneity in Vancouver', *BC Studies*, 115 (2007), pp. 3–30.

Barthes, Roland, 'Leaving the movie theatre', trans. Richard Howard, reprinted in Philip Lobate (ed.), *The Art of the Personal Essay: An Anthology from the Classical Era to the Present* (New York: First Anchor Books, 1995), pp. 418–22.

Bazin, André, *What is Cinema?* vol. 2, trans. H. Grey (Berkeley: University of California Press, 2005).

Bazin, André, *Bazin and Italian Neorealism*, ed. Bert Cardullo (New York: Continuum, 2011), pp. 61–73.

Benjamin, Walter, 'The work of art in the age of mechanical reproduction', in Hannah Arendt (ed.), *Illuminations: Essays and Reflections* (New York: Shocken Books, 1968), pp. 217–52.

Bergson, Henri, *Creative Evolution*, trans. Arthur Mitchell (New York: Henry Holt, 1926).

Berlant, Lauren, 'The subject of true feeling: pain, privacy, and politics', in Austin Sarat and Thomas R. Kearns (eds), *Cultural Pluralism, Identity Politics, and the Law* (Ann Arbor: University of Michigan, 1999), pp. 49–84.

Berlant, Lauren, 'The epistemology of state emotion', in Austin Sarat (ed.), *Dissent in Dangerous Times* (Ann Arbor: University of Michigan, 2005), pp. 46–78.

Berlant, Lauren, 'Thinking about feeling historical', *Emotion, Space and Society*, 1 (2008), pp. 4–9.

Berlant, Lauren, *Cruel Optimism* (Durham: Duke University Press, 2011).

Bernini, Emilio, 'Politics and the documentary film in Argentina during the 1960s', *Journal of Latin American Cultural Studies: Travesia*, 13:2 (2004), pp. 155–70.

Berrada, Omar and Yto Barrada (eds), *Album Cinémathèque de Tanger* (Barcelona: La Virreina Centre de la Imatge, 2012).

Berry, Chris, 'Getting real: Chinese documentary, Chinese postsocialism', in Zhen Zhang (ed.), *The Urban Generation: Chinese Cinema and Society at the Turn of the Twenty-first Century* (Durham: Duke University Press, 2007), pp. 115–36.

Berry, Chris, Lu Xinyu and Lisa Rofel (eds), *The New Chinese Documentary Film Movement: For the Record* (Hong Kong: Hong Kong University Press, 2010).

Best, Steven and Douglas Kellner, *Postmodern Theory. Critical Interrogations* (New York: Guilford Press, 1991).

Birch, Sarah, 'Folly for a Flyover charms Hackney', *Hackney Citizen*, 11 July 2011, http://hackneycitizen.co.uk/201107/11/folly-for-a-flyover-charms-hackney/ (last accessed 13 August 2013).

Blomley, Nicholas, *Unsettling the City: Urban Land and the Politics of Property* (London: Routledge, 2004).

Bolzoni, Lina, *The Gallery of Memory* (Toronto: University of Toronto Press, 2001).

Bondanella, Peter, *Italian Cinema: From Neorealism to the Present* (London: Continuum, 2001).

Bonnett, Alastair, 'The dilemmas of radical nostalgia in British psychogeography', *Theory, Culture and Society*, 26:1 (2009), pp. 45–70.

Bonnett, Alastair and Catherine Alexander, 'Mobile nostalgias: connecting visions of the urban past, present and future amongst ex-residents', *Transactions of the Institute of British Geographers*, 38:3 (2012), pp. 391–402.

Borda, Jennifer L., 'Documentary dialectics or dogmatism?: Farenhype 9/11, Celsius 41.11, and the new politics of documentary film', in Thomas W. Benson and Brian J. Snee (eds), *The Rhetoric of the New Political Documentary* (Carbondale: Southern Illinois University Press, 2008), pp. 54–77.

Bowie, Andrew, *From Romanticism to Critical Theory: the Philosophy of Berman Literary Theory* (London: Routledge, 1997).

Boym, Svetlana, *The Future of Nostalgia* (New York: Basic Books, 2001).

Bozak, Nadia, *The Cinematic Footprint: Lights, Camera and Natural Resources* (New Brunswick, NJ: Rutgers University Press, 2011).

Braester, Yomi, *Painting the City Red: Chinese Cinema and the Urban Context* (Durham: Duke University Press, 2010).

Braester, Yomi and James Tweedie (eds), *Cinema at the City's Edge: Film and Urban Networks in East Asia* (Hong Kong: Hong Kong University Press, 2010).

Brookshire, Madison, 'Los Angeles in theory and practice: Thom Andersen's *Los Angeles Plays Itself*', *Bright Lights Film Journal*, 68 (2010), http://www.brightlightsfilm.com/68/68LAplaysitself.php (last accessed 13 August 2013).

Brown, Phil, 'Lars Von Trier to remake *The Five Obstructions* with Martin Scorcese', Collider.Com, 2011, http://collider.com/lars-von-trier-martin-scorsese-the-five-obstructions/ (accessed 19 August 2013).

Brownlow, Kevin, 'Silent Films: What was the right Speed?', *Sight and Sound*, 49:3 (Summer 1980), pp. 164–7.

Brunet, Jean-Paul, 'Police violence in Paris, October 1961: historical sources, methods and conclusions', *The Historical Journal*, 51:1 (2008), pp. 195–204.

Brunette, Peter, *Michael Haneke* (Urbana: University of Illinois Press, 2010).

Brunsdon, Charlotte, 'Introduction: screen Londons', *Journal of British Cinema and Television*, 6:2 (2009), pp. 165–72.

Burris, Jennifer, 'Surveillance and the indifferent gaze in Michael Haneke's *Caché* (2005)', *Studies in French Cinema*, 11:2 (2011), pp. 151–63.

Campbell, David and Marcus Power, 'The scopic regime of "Africa"', in Fraser MacDonald, Klaus Dodds and Rachel Hughes (eds), *Observant States: Geopolitics and Visual Culture* (London: I. B. Tauris, 2010).

Casey, Edward S., 'The world of nostalgia', *Man and World*, 20:4 (1987), pp. 361–84.

Cheah, Pheng, 'Entering the world from an oblique angle: on Jia Zhangke as an organic intellectual', in Neelam Srivatava and Francesca Rashmi (eds), *The Postcolonial Gramsci* (London: Routledge, 2012), pp. 137–64.

Chinyowa, Kennedy C., 'Emerging paradigms for applied drama and theatre practice in African contexts', *Research in Drama Education: The Journal of Applied Theatre and Performance*, 14:3 (2009), pp. 329–46.

Chow, Rey, 'Nostalgia of the New Wave: structure in Wong Kar-wai's *Happy Together*', *Camera Obscura*, 42 (1999), pp. 31–50.

Chow, Rey, 'A souvenir of love', in Esther C. M. Yau (ed.), *At Full Speed: Hong Kong Cinema in a Borderless World* (Minneapolis: University of Minnesota Press, 2001), pp. 209–30.

Clark, T. J., *The Painter of Modern Life. Paris in the Art of Manet and his Followers* (Princeton: Princeton University Press, 1999).

Clark, T. J., Serge Guilbaut and Anne Wagner, 'Representation, suspicions, and critical transparency: an interiew with Jeff Wall', *Parachute*, 59 (1990), pp. 4–10.

Clarke, David B., *The Cinematic City* (London: Routledge, 1997).

Clarke, David B., 'Introduction: previewing the cinematic city', in David Clarke (ed.), *The Cinematic City* (London: Routledge, 1997), pp. 1–18.

Clarke, David B., '*The City of the Future* revisited, or the lost world of Patrick

Keiller', *Transactions of the Institute of British Geographers*, 32:1 (2007), pp. 29–45.

Connolly, Maeve, 'Temporality, sociality, publicness: cinema as art project', *Afterall*, 29 (2012), http://www.afterall.org/journal/issue.29/temporality-sociality-publicness-cinema-as-art-project (last accessed 13 August 2013).

Cook, Simon, '"Our eyes, spinning like propellers": wheel of life, curve of velocities, and Dziga Vertov's "Theory of the Interval"', *October*, 121 (Summer 2007), pp. 79–81.

Cresswell, Tim and Deborah Dixon (eds), *Engaging Film: Geographies of Mobility and Identity* (Lanham: Rowman and Littlefield, 2002).

Cutler, Fred and J. Scott Matthews, 'The challenge of municipal voting: Vancouver 2002', *Canadian Journal of Political Science*, 38:2 (2005), pp. 359–82.

Dabashi, Hamid, *Masters and Masterpieces of Iranian Cinema* (Washington, DC: Mage Publishers, 2007).

Davis, Todd F. and Kenneth Womack (eds), *Mapping the Ethical Turn: A Reader in Ethics, Culture, and Literary Theory* (Charlottesville: University of Virginia Press, 2001).

Dean, Jodi, 'Communicative capitalism, circulation and the foreclosure of politics', in Megan Boler, *Digital Media and Democracy: Tactics in Hard Times* (Cambridge, MA: MIT Press, 2008), pp. 101–21.

de Certeau, Michel, *The Practice of Everyday Life*, trans. Steven Rendall (Berkeley: University of California Press, 1984).

de Certeau, Michel, *The Writing of History*, trans. Tom Conley (New York: Columbia University Press, 1988).

Deleuze, Gilles, *Cinema 1. The Movement-Image*, trans. Hugh Tomlinson and Barbara Habberjam (Minneapolis: University of Minnesota Press, 1996).

Deleuze, Gilles, *Cinema 2. The Time Image*, trans. Hugh Tomlinson and Robert Galeta (London: Athlone Press, 1989).

Dening, Greg, *Performances* (Chicago: University of Chicago Press, 1996).

Derrida, Jacques, *Archive Fever. A Freudian Impression*, trans. Eric Prenowitz (Chicago: University of Chicago Press, 1996),

Dimendberg, Edward, *Film Noir and the Spaces of Modernity* (Cambridge, MA: Harvard University Press, 2004).

Dixon, Wheeler Winston, *Film Noir and the Cinema of Paranoia* (New Brunswick, NJ: Rutgers University Press, 2009).

Doane, Mary Ann, *The Emergence of Cinematic Time: Modernity, Contingency, the Archive* (Cambridge, MA: Harvard University Press, 2002).

Dobrogoszcz, Tomasz, 'The hidden gaze of the other in Michael Haneke's *Hidden*', *Text Matters – A Journal of Literature, Theory and Culture*, 1:1 (2010), pp. 226–38.

Doel, Marcus and David Clarke, 'Afterimage', *Environment and Planning D: Society and Space*, 25 (2007), pp. 890–910.

Domizio, Ricardo, 'Digital cinema and the "schizophrenic" image: the case of Michael Haneka's *Hidden*', in Ben McCann and David Sorfa (eds), *Cinema of Michael Haneke* (New York: Columbia University Press, 2011), pp. 237–46.

Donald, James, *Imagining the Modern City* (Minneapolis: University of Minnesota Press, 1999).

Edmonds, Penelope, 'Unpacking settler colonialism's urban strategies: indigenous peoples in Victoria, British Columbia, and the transition to a settler-colonial city', *Urban History Review*, 38:2 (2010), pp. 4–20.

Ellis, Jack C. and Betsy A. McLane, *A New History of Documentary Film* (New York: Continuum, 2005).

Eme3, 'The Cineroleum', *EME3*, 24 January 2013, http://eme3.org/?p=2974 (last accessed 13 August 2013).

Erie, Steven, *Beyond Chinatown: The Metropolitan Water District, Growth and the Environment in Southern* (Stanford: Stanford University Press, 2006).

Farish, Matthew, 'Cities in shade: urban geography and the uses of Noir', *Environment and Planning D: Society and Space*, 23:1 (2005), pp. 95–118.

Featherstone, Mike and Couze Venn, 'Problematizing global knowledge and the new encyclopaedia project: an introduction', *Theory Culture and Society*, 23 (2006), pp. 1–20.

Fleischer, Matthew, '*Exiles* on Main Street: searching for the ghosts of Bunker Hill's Native American past resuscitated: 1961 documentary recalls stark lives of L.A.'s urban Indian', *LA Weekly*, 14 August 2008.

Forester, John (ed.), *Critical Theory and Public Life* (Cambridge, MA: MIT Press, 1987).

Forgacs, David, *Rome Open City* (London: BFI Publishing, 2000).

Forgacs, David, Sarah Lutton and Geoffrey Howell-Smith (eds), *Roberto Rosellini. Magician of the Real* (London: BFI Publishing, 2000).

Foster, Hal, 'An archival impulse', *October*, 110 (2004), pp. 3–22.

Freeman, Victoria, 'Toronto has no history! Indigeneity, settler colonialism, and historical memory in Canada's largest city', *Urban History Review*, 38:2 (2010), pp. 21–35.

Friedberg, Anne, *Window Shopping: Cinema and the Postmodern* (Berkeley: University of California Press, 1993).

Friedberg, Anne, *The Virtual Window: From Alberti to Microsoft* (Cambridge, MA: MIT Press, 2006).

Fujikawa, Laura Sachiko, 'Domestic containment: Japanese Americans, Native Americans, and the cultural politics of relocation', unpublished PhD dissertation, University of Southern California, 2011.

Gaines, Jane M. and Michael Renov (eds), *Collecting Visible Evidence* (Minneapolis: University of Minnesota Press, 1999).

Gibbons, Flachra, 'Censors cast shadow over Venice', *The Guardian*, 1 September 2003, http://www.theguardian.com/world/2003/sep/01/filmnews.filmcensorship (accessed 19 August 2013).

Gilroy, Paul, 'Shooting crabs in a barrel', *Screen*, 48:2 (2007), pp. 233–5.

Giovacchini, Saverio and Robert Sklar, *Global Neorealism: The Transnational History of A Film Style* (Jackson: University Press of Mississippi, 2011).

Gordon, Robert S. C., *Bicycle Thieves* (Basingstoke: Palgrave Macmillan for BFI, 2008).

Gottlieb, Sidney (ed.), *Roberto Rossellini's* Rome, Open City (Cambridge: Cambridge University Press, 2004).

Graham, Peter and Ginette Vincendeau, *The French New Wave: Critical Landmarks* (London, British Film Institute, 2009).

Gudrun, Will, 'Timely *Fix* clear and compelling: *Fix: The Story of an Addicted City* at Granville Seven', *Vancouver Courier*, 27 October 2002.

Guerin, Frances, *A Culture of Light: Cinema and Technology in 1920s Germany* (Minneapolis: University of Minnesota Press, 2005).

Gunning, Tom, 'The cinema of attractions: early film, the spectator, and the avant-garde', *Wide Angle*, 8 (1986), pp. 63–70.

Gunning, Tom, 'Moving away from the index: cinema and the impression of reality', in Gertrud Koch, Volker Pantenburg and Simon Rohtöhler (eds), *Screen Dynamics: Mapping the Borders of Cinema* (Vienna: Synema – Gesellshaft für Film und Medien, 2012), pp. 42–60.

Habermas, Jürgen, *The Structural Transformation of the Public Sphere: An Inquiry into a Category of Bourgeois Society*, trans. Thomas Burger (Cambridge, MA: MIT Press, 1989).

Halbwachs, Maurice, *On Collective Memory*, trans. and ed. Lewis S. Coser (Chicago: University of Chicago Press, 1992).

Hamner, Everett, 'Remembering the disappeared: science fiction film in post dictatorship Argentina', *Science Fiction Studies*, 39:1 (March 2012), pp. 60–8.

Hannah, Matthew, 'Biopower, life and left politics', *Antipode*, 43:4 (2011), pp. 1034–55.

Hansen, Miriam, 'Early cinema, late cinematic permutations of the public sphere', *Screen*, 34: 3 (1993), pp. 197–210

Hansen, Miriam, *Babel and Babylon: Spectatorship in American Silent Film* (Cambridge, MA: Harvard University Press, 1991).

Hansen, Miriam, 'Max Ophuls and instant messaging: reframing cinema and publicness', in Gertrud Koch, Volker Pantenburg and Simon Rohtöhler (eds), *Screen Dynamics: Mapping the Borders of Cinema* (Vienna: Synema – Gesellshaft für Film und Medien, 2012).

Harvey, David, *Paris, Capital of Modernity* (London: Routledge, 2003).

Hay, James, 'Piecing together what remains of the cinematic city', in David Clark (ed.), *The Cinematic City* (London: Routledge, 1997), pp. 209–29.

Hayden, Dolores, *Power of Place: Urban Landscapes as Public History* (Cambridge, MA: MIT Press, 1995).

Haydn, Florian and Robert Temel (eds), *Temporary Urban Spaces: Concepts for the Use of City Space* (Basel: Birkhäuser, 2006).

Healy, Chris, *Forgetting Aborigines* (Sydney: University of New South Wales Press, 2008).

Hicks, Jeremy, *Dziga Vertov. Defining Documentary Film* (London: I. B. Tauris, 2007).

House, Jim and Neil MacMaster, *Paris 1961: Algerians, State Terror, and Memory* (Oxford: Oxford University Press, 2006).

James, David E., *The Most Typical Avant-Garde: History and Geographies of Minor Cinemas in Los Angeles* (Berkeley: University of California Press, 2005).

James, David E., 'L.A.'s Hipster Cinema', *Film Quarterly*, 63:1 (2009), pp. 56–67.

James, Nick, '*Los Angeles Plays Itself*', *Sight and Sound*, 15:2 (2005), p. 60.

Jameson, Fredric, *Postmodernism or, the Cultural Logic of Late Capitalism* (Durham: Duke University Press, 1991).

Jay, Martin, *Downcast Eyes: The Denigration of Vision in Twentieth-Century French Thought* (Berkeley: University of California Press, 1994).

Jia, Zhangke, 'What remains is silence', trans. Sebastian Veg, *China Perspectives*, 81 (2010), pp. 54–7.

Johnston, John, 'Machinic vision', *Critical Inquiry*, 26:1 (Autumn 1999), pp. 27–48.

Joseph, Miranda, 'The performance of production and consumption', *Social Text*, 54 (1998), pp. 25–61.

Joyce, Patrick, 'The politics of the liberal archive', *History of the Human Sciences*, 12:2 (1999), pp. 35–49.

Joyce, Patrick, *The Rule of Freedom: Liberalism and the Modern City* (London: Verso, 2003).

Keiller, Patrick, 'Motion pictures', *The Guardian*, 21 May 2005, http://www.guardian.co.uk/film/2005/may/21/2 (last accessed 13 August 2013).

Kelly, R., *The Name of this Book is Dogme95* (London: Faber and Faber, 2000).

Klein, Norman, *History of Forgetting: Los Angeles and the Erasure of Memory* (London: Verso, 2008).

Klinger, Barbara, *Beyond the Multiplex: Cinema, New Technologies, and the Home* (Berkeley: University of California Press, 2006).

Koeck, Richard and Les Roberts (eds), *The City and the Moving Image: Urban Projections* (New York: Palgrave Macmillan, 2010).

Konstantarakos, Myrto (ed.), *Spaces in European Cinema* (Bristol: Intellect, 2000).

Kracauer, Siegfried, *Theory of Film: The Redemption of Physical Reality* (Princeton: Princeton University Press, [1960] 1997).

Kracauer, Siegfried, *From Caligari to Hitler. A Psychological History of the German Film* (Princeton: Princeton University Press, 2004).

Kristeva, Julia, *Black Sun. Depression and Melancholia*, trans. Leon S. Roudiez (New York: Columbia University Press, 1989).

Kuoshu, Harry, *Metro Movies: Cinematic Urbanism in Post-Mao China* (Carbondale: Southern Illinois University Press, 2011).

Lacey, Liam, 'It's a Wild road show: Nettie Wild's documentary *Fix: The Addicted City* is touring the country to promote the issue of safe-injection sites', *The Globe and Mail*, 16 October 2003.

Landau, Paul S. and D. Kaspin (eds), *Images and Empires: Visuality in Colonial and Postcolonial Africa* (Berkeley: University of California Press, 2002).

Larkin, Brian, 'Theatres of the profane: cinema and colonial urbanism', *Visual Anthropology Review*, 14:2 (1998), pp. 46–62.

Larkin, Brian, *Signal and Noise: Media, Infrastructure, and Urban Culture in Nigeria* (Durham: Duke University Press, 2008).

Lefebvre, Henri, *Everyday Life in the Modern World* (Piscataway, Transaction Publishers, 1984).

Lefebvre, Henri, *The Production of Space*, trans. Donald Nicholson-Smith (Oxford: Blackwell, 1991).

Lefebvre, Henri, *Critique of Everyday Life*, vol. 1 (London: Verso, 2008).

Levin, Laura and Kim Solga, 'Building Utopia: performance and fantasy of urban renewal in contemporary Toronto', *The Drama Review*, 53:3 (2009), pp. 37–53.

Levin, Thomas Y., 'Five tapes, four halls, two dreams. Vicissitudes of surveillant narration in Michael Haneke's *Caché*', in Roy Grundmann (ed.), *A Companion to Michael Haneke* (Oxford: Wiley-Blackwell, 2010), pp. 75–90.

Lewis, Paul H., *Guerrillas and Generals: The Dirty War in Argentina* (Westport: Praeger, 2001).

Lippe, Richard, '*Los Angeles Plays Itself*', *Cineaction*, 63 (2004), pp. 59–61.

Lobato, Ramon, *Shadow Economies of Cinema: Mapping Informal Film Distribution* (London: Palgrave Macmillan, 2012).

Luckhurst, Roger, *The Trauma Question* (London: Routledge, 2008).

Lury, Karen and Doreen Massey, 'Making connections', *Screen*, 40:3 (1999), pp. 229–38.

Lyon, David, *The Electronic Eye: The Rise of Surveillance Society* (Minneapolis: University of Minnesota Press, 1994).

Lyon, David, Aaron Doyle and Randy Lippert (eds), *Eyes Everywhere: The Global Growth of Camera Surveillance* (London: Routledge, 2011).

Ma, Jean, *Melancholy Drift, Marking Time in Chinese Cinema* (Hong Kong: Hong Kong University Press, 2010).

MacQueen, Ken, 'Needles, love and revolution', *Macleans*, 115:46 (November 2002), p. 120.

Maganoli, Paolo, 'Critical nostalgia in the art of Joachim Koester', *Oxford Art Journal*, 34:1 (2011), pp. 97–121.

Maier, Robert G., *Location Scouting and Management Handbook. Television. Film. Still Photography* (Boston: Focal Press, 1994), p. 7.

Mansoor, Sarfraz, 'Films on Fridges: from cold mountain to cool cinema', Film Blog, *The Guardian*, 1 August 2011, http://www.theguardian.com/film/filmblog/2011/aug/01/films-on-fridges-cinema-recycling (last accessed 13 August 2013).

Marcus, Millicent, *Italian Film in the Light of Neorealism* (Princeton: Princeton University Press, 1987).

Marks, Laura, *The Skin of the Film: Intercultural Cinema, Embodiment, and the Senses* (Durham: Duke University Press, 2000).

Marks, Laura, 'Immersed in a single channel: experimental media from theatre to gallery', *Millennium Film Journal*, 55 (2012), pp. 14–23.

Mathijs, Ernest, 'Bad reputations: the reception of trash cinema', *Screen*, 46:4 (2005), pp. 451–72.

Mawani, Renisa, 'Legal geographies of Aboriginal segregation: the making and unmaking of the Songhees Reserve', in Carolyn Strange and Alison Bashford (eds), *Isolation: Places and Practices of Exclusion* (London: Routledge, 2003), pp. 173–90.

Mayne, Judith, *Cinema and Spectatorship* (London: Routledge, 1993).

Mazierska, Ewa and Laura Rascaroli, *From Moscow to Madrid: Postmodern Cities, European Cinema* (London: I. B. Tauris, 2003).

Mazumdar, Ranjani, *Bombay Cinema: An Archive of the City* (Minneapolis: University of Minnesota Press, 2007).

McDonough, Tom (ed.), *Guy Debord and the Situationist International. Texts and documents* (Cambridge, MA: MIT Press, 2002).

McGrath, Jason, 'The independent cinema of Jia Zhangke: from postsocialist realism to a transnational aesthetic', in Zhen Zhang (ed.), *The Urban Generation: Chinese cinema and society at the turn of the twenty-first century* (Durham: Duke University Press, 2007), pp. 81–114.

Mennel, Barbara, *Cities and Cinema* (London: Routledge, 2008).

Mirbakhtyar, Shahla, *Iranian Cinema and the Islamic Revolution* (Jefferson: McFarland and Co., 2006).

Mishra, Vijay, *Bollywood Cinema: Temples of Desire* (London: Routledge, 2001).

Mitry, Jean, *The Aesthetics and Psychology of the Cinema*, trans. Christopher King (London: Athlone Press, 1998).

Moon, Ariana, 'Movie theater churches report their successes', *Unification News*, 27 November 2012, http://unificationnews.com/article/movie_theater_churches_report_their_successes (last accessed 13 August 2013).

Moore, Rowan, 'Silence; Folly for a Flyover; 2004 Indian Ocean Tsunami Memorial – review', *The Observer*, 10 July 2011, http://www.theguardian.com/artanddesign/2011/jul/10/folly-for-flyover-assemble-silence (last accessed 13 August 2013).

Morgenstern, Joe, '*24 City*: a film by Jia Zhang-Ke, director of *Still Life*', *The Wall Street Journal*, 5 June 2009.

Mottahedeh, Negar, *Displaced Allegories: Post-Revolutionary Iranian Cinema* (Durham: Duke University Press, 2008).

Mouton, Janice, 'From feminine masquerade to flaneuse: Agnes Varda's Cleo in the city', *Cinema Journal*, 40:2 (2001), pp. 3–16.

Mulvey, Laura, *Death at 24x a Second. Stillness and the Moving Image* (London: Reaktion Books, 2006), pp. 7–13.

Nafisi, Azar, *Reading Lolita in Tehran: A Memoir in Books* (New York: Random House, 2004).

Navarro, Vinicius, 'Nonfiction performance from portrait films to the Internet', *Cinema Journal*, 51:3 (2012), pp. 136–41.

Neupert, Richard, *A History of the French New Wave Cinema* (Madison: University of Wisconsin Press, 2007).

Nochimson, Martha, 'Passion for documentation: interview with Jia Zhangke', *New Review of Film and Television Studies*, 7:4 (2009), pp. 411–19.

Nora, Pierre, 'Between memory and history: Les Lieux de Mémoire', trans. Marc Roudebush, *Representations*, 26 (1989), pp. 7–24.

Oberacker, Scott J., 'The reel deal: Michael Moore, political documentary and the discourse of celebrity', *Celebrity Studies*, 1 (2010), pp. 170–88.

Oliver, Kelly and Benigno Trigo, *Noir Anxiety* (Minneapolis: University of Minnesota Press, 2002).

Olund, Eric, 'Cinema's milieux: governing the picture show in the United States during the Progressive Era', *Journal of Historical Geography*, 38 (2012), pp. 57–68.

Orpen, Valerie, *Cleo de 5 a 7* (London: I. B. Tauris, 2007).

Osborne, Thomas, 'Tales of Hoffman', *History of the Human Sciences*, 11 (1998), pp. 115–24, p. 118.

Osborne, Thomas, 'The ordinariness of the archive', *History of the Human Sciences*, 12:2 (1999), pp. 51–64.

Osnos, Evan, 'The long shot', *The New Yorker*, 8 May 2009, pp. 88–95.

Osteen, Mark, *Nightmare Alley: Film Noir and the American Dream* (Baltimore: Johns Hopkins University Press, 2013).

Osterwell, Ara, 'Caché', *Film Quarterly*, 59:4 (2006), pp. 35–9.

Pages, Neil Christian, 'What's hidden in *Caché*', *Modern Austrian Studies*, 43:1 (2011), pp. 1–24.

Peck, Jamie, 'Struggling with the creative class', *International Journal of Urban and Regional Research*, 24:4 (2005), pp. 740–70.

Peck, Jamie, 'The cult of urban creativity', in Roger Keil and Rianne Mahon (eds), *Leviathan Undone? Towards a political economy of scale* (Toronto: University of British Columbia Press, 2009).

Peck, Jamie, 'Recreative city: Amsterdam, vehicular ideas and the adaptive spaces of creative policy', *International Journal of Urban and Regional Research*, 36:3 (2012), pp. 462–85.

Peiss, Kathy, *Cheap Amusements: Working Women and Leisure in Turn-of-the-Century New York* (Philadelphia: Temple University Press, 1986).

Penz, Francois and Andong Lu (eds), *Urban Cinematics: Understanding Urban Phenomena through the Moving Image* (Bristol: Intellect, 2011).

Pernin, Judith, 'Filming space/mapping reality in Chinese Independent Documentary Films', *China Perspectives*, 1 (2010), pp. 23–37.

Petrić, Vlada, *Constructivism in Film. The Man with the Movie Camera. A Cinematic Analysis* (Cambridge: Cambridge University Press, 1987).

Phelan, Peggy, *Unmarked: The Politics of Performance* (London: Routledge, 1993).

Portelli, Alessandro, *The Order Has Been Carried Out: History, Memory, and Meaning of a Nazi Massacre in Rome* (New York: Macmillan, 2003).

Pratt, Geraldine, *Families Apart: Migrant Mothers and the Conflicts of Labor and Love* (Minneapolis: University of Minnesota Press, 2012).

Pratt, Geraldine and Rose Marie San Juan, 'In search of the horizon: Utopia in the *The Truman Show* and *The Matrix*', in Loretta Lees (ed.), *Emancipatory Cities* (London: Sage, 2004), pp. 192–206.

Pulido, Laura, Laura Barraclough and Wendy Cheng, *A People's Guide to Los Angeles* (Berkeley: University of California Press, 2012).

Rai, Amit, *Untimely Bollywood: Globalization and India's New Media Assemblage* (Durham: Duke University Press, 2009).

Raiber, Richard, *Anatomy of Perjury: Field Marshal Albert Kesselring, Via Rasella, and the GINNY mission* (Newark: University of Delaware Press, 2008).

Rajchman, John, 'Foucault's art of seeing', *October*, 44 (1988), pp. 89–117.

Rapaport, Herman, 'Archive trauma', *Diacritics*, 28:4 (1998), pp. 68–81.

Rayns, Tony, 'Poet of time', *Sight and Sound*, 5:9 (1995), pp. 10–16.

Restivo, Angelo, 'Into the breach: between the movement-image and the time-image', in Gregory Flaxman (ed.), *The Brain is the Screen: Deleuze and the Philosophy of Cinema* (Minneapolis: University of Minnesota Press, 2000), pp. 171–92.

Restivo, Angelo, *The Cinema of Economic Miracles: Visuality and Modernization in the Italian Art Film* (Duke University Press, 2002).

Rhodes, John David and Elena Gorfinkel (eds), *Taking Place: Location and the Moving Image* (Minneapolis: University of Minnesota Press, 2011).

Roberts, Graham, *Forward Soviet!: History and Non-fiction Film in the USSR* (New York: St. Martin's Press, 1999).

Roberts, Graham, *The Man with the Movie Camera* (London: I. B.Tauris, 2000).

Roberts, Yvonne, 'The Spirit of '45: where did it go?', *The Guardian*, 2 March 2013, http://www.guardian.co.uk/film/2013/mar/02/spirit-45-ken-loach-nhs-history (last accessed 13 August 2013).

Rocchio, Vincent F., *Cinema of Anxiety. A Psychoanalysis of Italian Neorealism* (Austin: University of Texas Press, 1999).

Rohdie, Sam, 'Wong Kar-wei, l'auteur', *Iris*, 28 (1999), pp. 107–21.

Rose, Nikolas, *Powers of Freedom. Reframing Political Thought* (Cambridge: Cambridge University Press, 1999).

Rosen, Philip (ed.), *Narrative, Apparatus, Ideology: A Film Theory Reader* (New York: Columbia University Press, 1986).

Rosenzweig, Roy, *Eight Hours for What We Will: Workers and Leisure in an Industrial City, 1870–1920* (Cambridge: Cambridge University Press, 1983).

Ruberto, Laura and Kristi Wilson, *Italian Neorealism and Global Cinema* (Detroit: Wayne State University, 2007).

Sadler, Simon, *The Situationist City* (Cambridge, MA: MIT Press, 1998).

Sadr, Hamid Reza, *Iranian cinema. A Political History* (London: I. B. Tauris, 2006).

San Juan, Rose Marie and Geraldine Pratt, 'Virtual cities: film and the urban mapping of virtual space', *Screen*, 43:3 (2002), pp. 250–70.

Schwartz, Frederic J., *Blind Spots: Critical Theory and the History of Art in Twentieth-Century Germany* (New Haven: Yale University Press, 2005).

Shapiro, Michael J., *The Time of the City: Politics, Philosophy and Genre* (London: Routledge, 2010).

Shehadeh, Raja, *Occupation Diaries* (London: Profile Books, 2012).

Shiel, Mark and Tony Fitzmaurice (eds), *Cinema and the City: Film and Urban Societies in Global Context* (Oxford: Blackwell, 2001).

Silverman, Max, 'The violence of the cut: Michael Haneke's *Caché* and cultural memory', *French Cultural Studies*, 21:1 (2010), pp. 57–65.

Singer, Beverly, *Wiping the Warpaint off the Lens: Native American Film and Video* (Minneapolis: University of Minnesota Press, 2001).

Smith, Alison, *Agnes Varda* (Manchester: Manchester University Press, 1997).

Sobchack, Vivian, 'Toward a phenomenology of nonfictional film experience', in Jane M. Gaines and Michael Renov (eds), *Collecting Visible Evidence* (Minneapolis: University of Minnesota Press, 1999), pp. 241–54.

Speck, Oliver C., 'Thinking the event: the virtual in Michael Haneke's films', in Ben McCann and David Sorfa (eds), *Cinema of Michael Haneke* (New York: Columbia University Press, 2011), pp. 49–64.

Srinivas, S. V., 'Hong Kong action film in the India B Circuit', *Inter-Asia Cultural Studies*, 4:1 (2003), pp. 40–62.

Stern, Lesley, 'How movies move (between Hong Kong and Bulawayo, between screen and stage)', in Natasa Durovicová and Kathleen Newman (eds), *World Cinemas, Transnational Perspectives* (New York: Routledge, 2010), pp. 186–216.

Stevenson, J., *Lars Von Trier* (London: BFI, 2002).

Stewart, Jacqueline, 'Negroes laughing at themselves? Black spectatorship and the performance of urban modernity', *Critical Inquiry*, 29:4 (2003), pp. 650–77.

Stoler, Ann L., *Along the Archival Grain: Archival Anxieties and Colonial Common Sense* (Princeton: Princeton University Press, 2009).

Su, John J., *Ethics and Nostalgia in the Contemporary Novel* (Cambridge: Cambridge University Press, 2005).

Teo, Stephen, *Wong Kar-wai* (London: British Film Institute, 2005).

Tester, Keith (ed.), *The Flâneur* (London: Routledge, 1994).

Thrush, Coll, *Native Seattle: Histories from the Crossing Over Place* (Seattle: University of Washington Press, 2007).

Till, Karen, *New Berlin: Memory, Politics, Place* (Minneapolis: University of Minnesota Press, 2005).

Trench, Anna, 'Cineroleum: cinema in a petrol station', *Telegraph*, 30 August 2010, http://www.telegraph.co.uk/culture/film/film-blog/7971999/Cineroleum-cinema-in-a-petro-station.html (last accessed 13 August 2013).

Tsivian, Yuri, *Lines of Resistance. Dziga Vertov and the Twenties* (Bloomington: Bloomington: Indiana University Press, 2005).

Tsivian, Yuri, 'Man with a Movie Camera – Lines of Resistance: Dziga Vertov and the Twenties', in Ted Perry (ed.), *Masterpieces of Modernist Cinema* (Indiana University Press, 2006), p. 100.

Tsivian, Yuri, 'Turning objects, toppled pictures: give and take between Vertov's films and constructivist art', *October*, 121 (2007), pp. 92–110.

Tupitsyn, Margarita, 'Being-in-production: the constructive code', in Margarita Tupitsyn (ed.), *Rodchenko and Popova. Defining Constructivism*, exhibition catalogue, Tate Modern (London: Tate Publishing, 2009), pp. 13–30.

Turvey, Malcolm, 'Can the camera see? Mimesis in *Man with a Movie Camera*', *October*, 89 (Summer 1999), pp. 25–50.

Van Zyl, Susan, 'The other and other others: post-colonialism, psychoanalysis and the South African question', *American Imago*, 55:1 (1998), pp. 77–100.

Vasudevan, Alex, '"The photographer of modern life": Jeff Wall's photographic materialism', *Cultural Geographies*, 14:4 (2007), pp. 563–88.

Vaz, Paulo and Fernanda Bruno, 'Types of self-surveillance: from abnormality to individuals "at risk"', *Surveillance and Society*, 1:3 (2003), pp. 272–91.

Veg, Sebastian, 'Building a public consciousness: a conversation with Jia Zhangke', *China Perspectives*, 81 (2010), pp. 58–64.

Vertov, Dziga, *Kino-Eye. The Writings of Dziga Vertov*, intro. Annette Michelson, trans. K. O'Brien (London: Pluto Press, 1984).

Vidler, Anthony, *Warped Space: Art, Architecture, and Anxiety in Modern Culture* (Cambridge, MA: MIT Press, 2001).

Vitti, Antonio, *Giuseppe de Santis and the Postwar Italian Cinema* (Toronto: University of Toronto Press, 2000).

Wagstaff, Christopher, *Italian Neorealist Cinema. An Aesthetic Approach* (Toronto: University of Toronto Free Press, 2007).

Wallace, Aurora, 'When the set becomes permanent: the spatial reconfiguration of Hollywood North', in John David Rhodes and Elena Gorfinkel (eds), *Taking Place: Location and the Moving Image* (Minneapolis: University of Minnesota Press, 2011), pp. 157–80.

Warner, Michael, *Publics and Counterpublics* (New York: Zone Books, 2002).

Webber, Andrew and Emma Wilson (eds), *Cities in Transition. The Moving Image and the Modern Metropolis* (London: Wallflower Press, 2008).

Wheatley, Catherine, *Michael Haneke's Cinema. The Ethic of the Image* (New York: Berghahn Books, 2009).

Wu, Shu-chin, 'Time, history, and memory in Jia Zhangke's *24 City*', *Film Criticism*, 36:1 (2011), pp. 3–23.

Yassin, Inass, 'Projection: three cinemas in Ramallah & Al-Bireh', *Jerusalem Quarterly*, 42:3 (2010), pp. 49–60.

Yates, Frances A., *The Art of Memory* (Chicago: University of Chicago Press, 1966).

Zhang, Yingjin, *Cinema, Space, and Polylocality in a Globalizing China* (Honolulu: University of Hawaii Press, 2010).

Zhang, Zhen (ed.), *The Urban Generation: Chinese Cinema and Society at the Turn of the Twenty-first Century* (Durham: Duke University Press, 2007).

Filmography

A Farewell to the Ridge Theatre, film, directed by Curtis Emde. Canada, 2013, https://vimeo.com/60331356 (last accessed 13 August 2013).

A Place Called Chiapas, film, directed by Nettie Wild. Canada: Canada Wild Productions, 1998.

A Rustling of Leaves: Inside the Philippines Revolution, film, directed by Nettie Wild. Canada: Canada Wild Productions, 1988.

Abi Fawk Ash-Shajarah (*My Father's on a Tree*), film, directed by Hussain Karnal. Egypt, 1969.

Black Gold, film, directed by Marc Francis and Nick Francis. UK: Fulcrum Productions and Speak-it Productions, 2006.

Bless Their Little Hearts, film, directed by Billy Woodberry. USA: UCLA Film and Television Archive, 1984.

Bush Mama, film, directed by Haile Gerima. USA, 1975 (released UCLA Film and Television Archive, 1979).

Caché (*Hidden*), film, directed by Michael Haneke. France, Austria, Germany, Italy, USA: France 3 Cinema, Canal + and Bavaria Film, 2005.

Che stranno chiamarsi Federico! (*How Strange to be called Federico*), film, directed by Ettore Scola, Italy: BIM, Istituto Luce, 2013.

Chinatown, film, directed by Roman Polanski. USA: Paramount Pictures, and Penthouse, 1974.

Cleo from 5 to 7, film, directed by Agnès Varda. France, Italy: Ciné Tamaris, and Rome Paris Films, 1961.

Dayereh (The Circle), film, directed by Jafar Panahi. Iran: Artificial Eye, 2000.

Det perfekte menneske (*The Perfect Human*), film, directed by Jørgen Leth. Denmark, 1967.

Double Indemnity, film, directed by Billy Wilder. USA: Paramount Pictures, 1944.

El Norte, film, directed by Gregory Nava. USA/UK: Cinecom International, 1983.

Er shi si cheng ji (24 City), film, directed by Jia Zhangke. China: Bandai Visual Company, Bitters End, China Resources, Office Kitano, Shanghai Film Group, and X Stream Pictures, 2008.

Fix: the Story of an Addicted City, film, directed by Nettie Wild. Canada: Canada Wild Productions, 2002.

Gare du Nord, film, directed by Claire Simon, France: Les Films d'ici, 2013.

Gasland Part II, film, directed by Josh Fox. USA: HBO Documentary Films, 2013.

Imagining Indians, film, directed by Victor Masayesva Jr. USA: Victor Masayesva Jr, 1992.

Iran a Cinematographic Revolution, film, directed by Nadar Homayoun. France: Arte and Avenue B Productions, 2006.

Killer of Sheep, film, directed by Charles Burnett. USA: UCLA Film and Television Archive, 1977 (rereleased Milestone Films, 2007).

L.A. Confidential, film, directed by Curtis Hanson. USA: Warner Bros., 1997.

Ladri di Biciclette (Bicycle Thieves), film, directed by Vittorio De Sica. Italy: Ente Nazionale Industrie Cinematografiche, 1948.

Little Zizou, film, directed by Sooni Taraporevala. India: Jigri Dost Productions, 2008.

Los Angeles Plays Itself, film, directed by Thom Andersen. USA: Thom Andersen Productions, 2003.

Man with a Movie Camera, film, directed by Dziga Vertov. USSR: VUFKU, 1928.

Memento, film, directed by Christopher Nolan. USA: Newmarket Capital Group, Team Todd, I Remember Productions and Summit Entertainment, 2000.

Moebius, film, directed by Gustavo Mosquera and students of Universidad del Cine, Argentina: Universidad del Cine, 1996.

Roma città aperta (Rome, Open City), film, directed by Roberto Rossellini. Italy: Minerva Film Spa, 1945.

Roman Holiday, film, directed by William Wyler. USA: Paramount Pictures, 1953.

Sacro Gra, film, directed by Gianfranco Rosi. Italy: Doc and Films International, 2013.

Sanxia haoren (Still Life), film, directed by Jia Zhangke. China, Hong Kong: X Stream Pictures, and Shanghai Film Studios (in association with), 2006.

Shot on This Day in 1895, film, directed by August and Louis Lumière. France: Lumière, 1895.

The Atomic City, film, directed by Jerry Hopper. USA: Paramount Pictures,1952.

The City of the Future, filmic installation/exhibition, directed by Patrick Keiller. UK: BFI, 2007.

The Exiles, film, directed by Kent MacKenzie. USA: USC Moving Image Archive, UCLA Film & Television Archive, 1961 (restored and rereleased 2008 by Milestone Cinematheque).

The Five Obstructions, film, directed by Lars von Trier and Jorgan Leth.Denmark: Zentropa, 2003.

The Spirit of '45, film, directed by Ken Loach. UK: Fly Film Company and Channel Four Films, 2013.

The World, film, directed by Jia Zhangke. China, Japan, France: Office Kitano, Lumen Films, X Stream Pictures, Bandai Visual Company (in association with), Shanghai Film Group, Xinghui Production (Hong Kong), 2004.

This is not a Film, film, directed by Jafar Panahi. Iran; France: Kanibal Films Distribution, 2011.

Who Framed Roger Rabbit, film, directed by Robert Zemeckis. USA: Touchstone Pictures, Amblin Entertainment, Silver Screen Partners III (in association with), Walt Disney Feature Animation (uncredited), 1988.

Xiao Wu (Pickpocket), film, directed by Jia Zhangke. China, Hong Kong: Hu Tong Communications, and Radiant Advertising Company, 1997.

Zhantai (Platform), film, directed by Jia Zhangke. China, Hong Kong, Japan, France: Artcam International, Bandai Entertainment Inc., Hu Tong Communications, Office Kitano, and T-Mark, 2000.

Websites

'24 City Rises in Southeast Chengdu', *China Urban Development* Blog, http://www.chinaurbandevelopment.com/?p=1559 (last accessed 13 August 2013).

Church at the Hollywood http://churchatthehollywood.ca/love/ (last accessed 13 August 2013).

'Cinema Church: EastLake Community Church opens new venue in WestLake', *Bedford Bulletin*, 26 May 2011, http://www.bedfordbulletin.com/content/cinema-church-eastlake-community-church-opens-new-venue-westlake (last accessed 13 August 2013).

Connexus community evangelical church, http://www.connexuscommunity.com/ (last accessed 13 August 2013).

Dear Videomatica, http://dearvideomatica.livejournal.com/ (last accessed 13 August 2013).

Freedom to Create, http://www.freedomtocreate.com/cont-mhlanga (last accessed 13 August 2013).

Heritage Vancouver Society, http://www.heritagevancouver.org/ (last accessed 13 August 2013).

'Pop-up cinemas: top 10 tips for creating your own', Film Blog, *The Guardian*, 22 August 2011, http://www.guardian.co.uk/film/flimblog/2011/aug/22/pop-up-cinemas-top-tips (last accessed 13 August 2013).

Sky Cinema Church, Hong Kong, http://skycitychurch.com/ (last accessed 13 August 2013).

'The Cineroleum: an urban takeover', The Polis Blog, http://www.thepolisblog.org/2010/09/cineroleum-urban-takeover.html (last accessed 13 August 2013).

Urban Republic, http://www.urbanrepublic.ca/drive.htm (last accessed 13 August 2013).

Videomatica Collection at UBC Film Studies, http://www.film.ubc.ca/film_studies/videomatica_collection.shtml (last accessed 13 August 2013).

Index

Note: illustrations are shown as page numbers in *italics*; the letter n following a page number indicates an endnote

EU Authorised Representative:

Easy Access System Europe Mustamäe tee 50, 10621 Tallinn, Estonia

gpsr.requests@easproject.com

Printed and bound by CPI Group (UK) Ltd, Croydon, CR0 4YY

13/05/2026

02110124-0006